A First Dictionary
of Cultural Literacy

A First Dictionary of
CULTURAL LITERACY

What Our Children Need to Know

Edited by E. D. Hirsch, Jr.

ASSOCIATE EDITORS

William G. Rowland, Jr. & Michael Stanford

HOUGHTON MIFFLIN COMPANY · BOSTON

For Benjamin Lacy Hirsch

Born March 15, 1989

Library of Congress Cataloging-in-Publication Data

A First dictionary of cultural literacy: what our children need to
know / edited by E.D. Hirsch, Jr.; associate editors, William G.
Rowland, Jr., Michael Stanford.
p.   cm.
Bibliography: p.
Includes index.
Summary: Presents an outline of the knowledge that should be
acquired by the end of sixth grade, according to the Cultural Literacy Foundation,
in such categories as literature, religion and philosophy, history, geography,
mathematics, science, and technology.
ISBN 0-395-59901-6
1. United States — Civilization — Dictionaries, Juvenile.
2. Civilization — Dictionaries, Juvenile.   3. English language —
Dictionaries, Juvenile.   [1. Encyclopedias and dictionaries.]
I. Hirsch, E. D. (Eric Donald), 1928- .   II. Rowland, William G., 1953- .
III. Stanford, Michael, 1953- .
E169.1.F538   1989   89-33776
903 — dc20   CIP
AC

Selected descriptions used in the Guide to Further Reading in the back of this
dictionary have appeared previously in *Reference Books for Children's Collections*,
compiled by the Children's Reference Committee, The New York Public Library,
copyright © 1988 by The New York Public Library. These are reprinted by
permission of The Office of Children's Services, The New York Public Library.

Printed in the United States of America
Book design by Robert Overholtzer

D 10 9 8 7 6 5 4 3 2 1

Contents

Maps

Acknowledgments

My special thanks go to Dr. William G. Rowland, Jr., and Dr. Michael Stanford, two brilliant scholars devoted to the cause of cultural literacy for all, whose work on this book was pervaded by an intensity of commitment that went far beyond merely doing a good job. Although they have gone on to university teaching careers while I have stayed behind to rewrite these entries several times during the past year, so much of the first draft of this book was composed by them that I have thought it simple justice as well as an expression of my gratitude to place their names on the title page. My special thanks go also to Andrea Rowland, who composed the first draft of the section on mathematics, and to Giuseppe Trogu, who helped with the design.

I am warmly grateful to Monty Caldwell and Jean Haines, who, together with their principal, Robert F. Levee, and the entire faculty of an elementary school, the C. B. Lamb School of Wrightstown, New Jersey, advised us about the list of entries. I am equally grateful to Phyllis Wilken, who vigorously led an advisory task force of experienced teachers in Champaign-Urbana, Illinois, and who made hard choices with thoughtfulness and decisiveness.

As the book moved on to production, I had the expert help of publisher Jonathan P. Latimer, senior editor Paul Bernabeo, manuscript editor Luise M. Erdmann, designer Robert Overholtzer, art editor Margaret Anne Miles, cartographer Jacques Chazaud, and illustrator Laurel Cook. Thanks are also due the following people for their editorial and production assistance: Borgna Brunner, Jim Craig, Kaethe Ellis, Beth Jaffe, Christopher Leonesio, Patricia McTiernan, Miriam E. Palmerola, and Rebecca Saikia-Wilson.

Above all, I would like to thank the members of the Cultural Literacy Network, not only for improving the sixth-grade list on which this compilation is based, but also for sending heartening messages of support for our attempts to define core knowledge for early schooling. The network, which comprises teachers, principals, and superintendents as well as parents and concerned citizens, now has on its rolls about a thousand members.

To Parents and Teachers

This dictionary outlines the knowledge that, in the opinion of several hundred teachers and parents across the nation, American children should acquire by the end of sixth grade. Of course, children should know many more things as well, depending on their local situation and individual interests, but they should at least share this common core of knowledge with other children across the nation. This compilation has been continually revised over a period of two years on the basis of comments and suggestions from all fifty states and from hundreds of teachers, school administrators, and parents who belong to the Cultural Literacy Network. If you have young children in your care who are not making good progress toward learning most of the information gathered here, they are being cheated, with the best of intentions, by, among other things, wrongheaded theories about the primary importance of teaching skills rather than traditional content — theories that have dominated instruction in American schools in the past few decades.

If that indictment sounds too sweeping, consider what a parent had to say in the following letter that arrived just as I began to write this introduction. (I have received hundreds of such letters since the publication in 1987 of my book *Cultural Literacy*.) The letter eloquently expresses the experience of hundreds of thousands of parents who have felt that something has been going wrong in the schooling of their children.

> For our children, the elementary school years were, with the exception of one teacher, a notable void. This still saddens me, as I suspect from my own experience that there is a luminosity to knowledge acquired in those years that is unique. I visit England twice a year and have a friend there with children the ages of our children. Informal comparisons of homework assignments came out as one might have expected; her children were *learning* things, like the names of rivers and parts of a flower. Ours had reams of ugly, sparsely written upon, very faint ditto sheets. There was very little to be learned from them at all.

The frustrations of our conferences with a majority of our children's elementary school teachers are still surprisingly fresh. We were quickly put on the defensive. The gist of the teachers' arguments was the claim that knowledge changes so rapidly as to be swiftly outmoded. Our knowledge, then, was largely irrelevant to the wonderful new knowledge our children were being taught *how* to acquire. (Baloney! By the time our children finally got to high school, much of the knowledge of their AP [Advanced Placement] courses was the same as or an expansion of the knowledge we had acquired decades before.)

In *Cultural Literacy*, I explained why about eighty percent of the knowledge commonly shared by literate Americans has not changed for more than a hundred years and is not likely to be quickly outmoded. The remaining twenty percent of shared literate knowledge does indeed change year by year, and my colleagues and I have taken account of such changes in this book. But at least eighty percent of what is listed will probably be just as central and valid ten years from now as it is today.

The current emphasis on skills in the primary grades, combined with trivial, incoherent, and watered-down content, has caused American education to decline in absolute terms, as measured by standardized test scores, and also in relative terms, as measured by comparisons with the achievements of children from other countries. In recent comparisons among developed nations, the United States ranks dead last in math, science, and world geography — subjects that are the same everywhere.

Our schools' emphasis on skills rather than knowledge has also had the unintended effect of injuring disadvantaged students more than advantaged ones. Since most so-called skills are really based upon specific knowledge, those who have already received literate knowledge from their homes are better able to understand what teachers and textbooks are saying and are therefore better able to learn new things than are children from nonliterate backgrounds. Consequently, when schools emphasize skills above knowledge, they consistently widen the gap between the haves and have-nots instead of narrowing it. Such schools unwittingly heighten economic and social inequalities instead of helping to overcome them.

This dictionary cannot take the place of good parenting and teaching or of good books, tapes, and videos that convey literate knowledge coherently and vividly. The dictionary can only hope to indicate what should be known by the end of sixth grade and encourage parents, teachers, and students themselves to make sure that such knowledge is effectively taught and learned. My colleagues and I hope that putting such a compilation between the covers of a book will be helpful to those who desire guidance about the specific knowledge that is the true foundation of our children's academic skills. A selection of some books that will help children learn more about the main topics we cover is provided in the back of the dictionary.

The list on which the dictionary entries are based is constantly being revised as comments and criticisms are sent to the Cultural Literacy Foundation. The present compilation reflects the composition of the sixth-grade list as of March 1989. Readers are invited to address their recommendations for improvements, additions, and deletions to the Cultural Literacy Foundation, 2012-B Morton Drive, Charlottesville, Virginia 22901.

E. D. HIRSCH, JR.
Charlottesville, Virginia
March 1989

To Young Readers:
How to Use This Dictionary

This dictionary is divided into twenty-one *sections*, each devoted to what you should know about a subject such as fine arts, mathematics, or world geography by the time you finish sixth grade. You can find out what you still need to learn about a subject by looking through a particular section, and you can find a list of the sections by looking at the *contents* page. You can also look up an item by using the *index* at the back of the book.

Reading a dictionary, however, isn't the best way to gain the knowledge you need. If you discover a subject that you want to learn more about, you should ask the school librarian to suggest a good book about it for your age. For instance, if you want to know more about the stories of the Greek gods and their amazing activities, you could read a book about Greek myths. If you are interested in the people and places of South America, you could read a history of South America or study an atlas. In the back of the dictionary, we list good reference works that will help you learn more about what you need to know.

In the geography sections of the dictionary, you will find maps and special symbols to help you learn where places are in the world. In the history sections, you will find time bars to help you locate events and people in their proper place in time.

Cross-references occur throughout the dictionary and are printed in small capital letters (for example, ABRAHAM LINCOLN, EQUILATERAL TRIANGLE, FOLK SONG). A cross-reference is a related topic that is defined in this dictionary. Usually you will find the cross-reference in the same section. If you don't find it there, turn to the *index* in the back. It lists every entry in the dictionary and gives the page number where it is found.

This dictionary will be useful in giving you a general picture of what you already know and what you still need to learn. Knowledge builds on knowledge. The more you already know about many different things, the easier it will be to learn about new things. If you and your classmates know many things in common, you will find that your classes will be more interesting than before, and you will be better able to understand what your teachers and textbooks are saying. Learning will be faster and much more exciting for everybody.

If you and your teachers have ideas about how to make this dictionary better, we shall pay attention to your advice. Write to me at the Cultural Literacy Foundation, 2021-B Morton Drive, Charlottesville, Virginia 22901.

This dictionary has been written and designed with you in mind. Enjoy making good use of it!

E. D. HIRSCH, JR.

Pronunciation System

Some entries in this dictionary include a pronunciation guide, which shows you how to say a word. More than one pronunciation is given if a word can be pronounced properly in more than one way. The pronunciation guide, which appears in parentheses after the entry term, is easy to use and does not require any special symbols. Hyphens separate syllables, and the syllable that takes primary stress in pronunciation is printed in capital letters. The following key explains how to pronounce the simple combinations of letters that are used in this system.

When the sound appears as	It should be pronounced as in
a	pat
ay	pay, make
air	fare, pear, hair
ah	father, are, guard
b	bib
ch	church, cello
d	deed, filled
e	bet, berry, bury
ee	bee, each, conceit
f	fife, phase, rough
g	gag, ghost
h	hat, who, Gila monster, José
i	bit, spinach, manage
eye	by, bite, aisle, buy
eer	ear, pier, clear, beer, weird, cereal
j	edge, gem, jelly, judge, manage
k	kick, cat, pique, chaos, crack
kw	choir, quart, acquire
l	lad, lull
m	mum, column, paradigm
n	no, sin, sudden
ng	sing, anchor, angle
o	pot, water, honest
oh	no, owe, sew, moan, broach, low
aw	all, flaw, caucus, talk, Utah, broad, bought
oo	book
ooh	boot, Peru
oy	noise, boy
ow	out, house, bough, fowl, hour
p	pop
r	roar, rhythm, wren
s	sauce, cellar

When the sound appears as	It should be pronounced as in
sh	ship, dish, addition, anxious
t	tight, stopped, bought
th	breath
thh	breathe, feather
u	cut, income, does
yoo	purée, your, purify, uranium
yooh	few, beautiful, feud, ukase
uh	about, item, edible, lemon, circus, attention
ur	urge, firm, term, word, heard
v	valve, of, love, Wagner (German)
w	with, one, guano
y	yes, onion, hallelujah
z	zebra, xylem, anxiety, does
zh	garage, pleasure, vision

The letter x presents special problems because it has several possible pronunciations:

z	xylophone (ZEYE-luh-fohn)
ks	box (BOKS), excessive (ik-SES-iv)
gz	exact (ig-ZAKT), exist (ig-ZIST)
gzh	luxury (LUG-zhur-ee), luxurious (lug-ZHOOR-ee-uhs)
ksh	anxious (ANGK-shuhs)

A few foreign words that appear in this dictionary require special sounds not usually found in English. They are:

The sound	As pronounced in	Appears as
ö	schön	eu
āo	São Paulo (sownn-POW-looh)	nn
ü	grün	uu

Proverbs

A proverb is an old, familiar saying that has been handed down over many years. Thus, when we hear a proverb, it is as if we were hearing the advice of our ancestors.

Proverbs often express ideas about how to act in daily life. There are proverbs to fit almost any situation. If a task needs careful attention — such as building a model or sewing with tiny stitches — someone might advise you that "haste makes waste" (that is, don't go too fast or you may ruin your work). In another situation, you might need to hurry. If there is only one day left to sell raffle tickets for the school fair or only two tickets left for a baseball game, the proverb "He who hesitates is lost" makes the most sense.

Many proverbs are as memorable for the way they sound as for the things they say. For instance, the use of rhyme helps us remember "An apple a day keeps the doctor away." So, too, a repeated sound ("pr") helps us remember "Practice what you preach."

Here are some of the most widely used proverbs in English and what they mean.

Actions speak louder than words It is safer to rely on what people do rather than what they say.

All for one and one for all Every member supports the group and the group supports every member. (This saying is used by members of a group when they want to express their loyalty to each other.) The proverb itself comes from the book *The Three Musketeers*, by Alexandre Dumas.

All's well that ends well In any effort, what matters is a good outcome.

apple a day keeps the doctor away, An Apples help to keep us healthy.

April showers bring May flowers Unpleasant things may bring about good things, just as rainy days cause flowers to bloom later on.

Beauty is only skin deep People should be judged not by their appearance but by their inner qualities.

Beggars can't be choosers People who have very little can't be fussy about what they get.

best-laid plans of mice and men oft go awry, The No matter how carefully you plan, something may still go wrong.

1

Better late than never   It is better to do something after it was supposed to be done than not to do it at all.

Better safe than sorry   Be careful before you act, or you may suffer later.

bigger they are, the harder they fall, The   The more powerful and successful people are, the more spectacular is their downfall.

bird in the hand is worth two in the bush, A   What you already have is more dependable than something that you only hope to get.

Birds of a feather flock together   People are attracted to others who are like themselves.

Do unto others as you would have them do unto you   Treat other people with the same kindness that you would like them to show to you. This saying comes from the Bible and is known as the Golden Rule.

Sayings similar to the Golden Rule occur in Confucianism and Buddhism as well as in Judaism and Christianity. ❧

dog is a man's best friend, A   A dog is even more faithful to its owner than human friends.

Don't count your chickens before they hatch   Don't assume that you'll get the things you want before you actually have them.

Don't cry over spilt milk   It doesn't do any good to be unhappy about something that has already happened.

Don't cut off your nose to spite your face   Don't take some action in anger that will hurt you more than it hurts anyone else.

Don't judge a book by its cover   Don't judge the value of a thing simply by its appearance.

Don't lock the stable door after the horse is stolen   After the damage has already been done, it's pointless to take the actions that could have prevented it.

Don't look a gift horse in the mouth   If you get something for nothing, don't complain if it's not exactly what you want. The proverb refers to the practice of deciding how much a horse is worth by looking at its teeth to estimate its age.

Don't put all your eggs in one basket   Don't make all your plans depend on one thing, because that one thing could go wrong and destroy your plans. It's safer to depend on several things; it's better to depend on two friends than just one.

Don't put the cart before the horse   Begin at the beginning; do things in their proper order.

Early to bed and early to rise/Makes a man healthy, wealthy, and wise   This saying was written by Benjamin Franklin in *Poor Richard's Almanack*.

early bird catches the worm, The   To achieve a goal, get an early start.

Every cloud has a silver lining   There is something good in every misfortune.

fool and his money are soon parted, A   Foolish people spend their money as soon as they get it.

friend in need is a friend indeed, A   Someone who helps us when we are in trouble is a real friend.

God helps those who help themselves   Don't expect to get what you want without working hard for it yourself.

grass is always greener on the other side, The   Some people are never satisfied with what they have; they always think that others are more fortunate.

Great oaks from little acorns grow   Great things or people often have humble beginnings.

Half a loaf is better than none   To have something is better than to have nothing at all.

Haste makes waste   If you do something too quickly, it will not turn out well.

He who hesitates is lost   A person who spends too much time thinking about what to do misses the chance to act at all.

He who laughs last laughs best   People may be laughed at when they try to achieve a goal, but when they succeed, they will be able to laugh at those who laughed at them.

Hitch your wagon to a star   Aim high; hope for great things.

> This advice was written by the American poet and essayist Ralph Waldo Emerson. ❧

If at first you don't succeed, try, try again   Never give up.

If wishes were horses, then beggars would ride   If wishing could make things happen, we would all have everything we wanted.

Laugh, and the world laughs with you; weep, and you weep alone   Most people would rather be around happy people than sad ones; so happy people have many friends, and sad people are often alone.

leopard cannot change his spots, The   People cannot change their basic nature, the way they are deep inside.

Let bygones be bygones   Don't hold grudges; let past offenses stay in the past.

Lightning never strikes twice in the same place   Good luck or bad luck never comes to the same person twice in exactly the same way. In the actual world, lightning can strike twice in the same place.

Little strokes fell great oaks   Persistent effort can accomplish great things, just as a person can chop down even the largest tree by staying at the task long enough.

Live and learn   We should learn from our mistakes.

Live and let live   We should live the way we choose and allow others to do the same.

Look before you leap   We should know what we are getting into before we act.

Make hay while the sun shines   When you have a chance to do something, do it; you will not have the chance forever.

Many hands make light work   Large tasks become easier when they are divided among several people.

Mind your p's and q's   Be on your best behavior. This saying is taken from a teacher's warning to keep handwriting neat by not mixing up the lower-case letters p and q.

miss is as good as a mile, A   If you fail at a task, it doesn't matter if you almost succeeded; losing a game by one point is still losing.

Money is the root of all evil   Most wrongdoing occurs because people are greedy for money and the things it will buy. This saying is taken from the NEW TESTAMENT, which says, "For the love of money is the root of all evils" (1 Timothy 6:10).

more the merrier, The   If many people take part in something, it will be more fun than if just a few participate. This saying is often used to welcome people who would like to join in an activity.

Necessity is the mother of invention   When people really need something, they will think of a way to fill the need.

never over till it's over, It's   Until a competition (such as a game or an election) has come to an end, you can never predict the winner. Things can always change at the last minute.

Never put off till tomorrow what you can do today   Don't put off doing the things you have to do.

never too late to mend, It's   It's never too late to change your ways.

Once bitten, twice shy   If you've done something that has made you suffer, you will avoid doing it in the future (just as you would shy away from an animal that had bitten you).

One rotten apple spoils the whole barrel   One bad person can ruin a larger group.

ounce of prevention is worth a pound of cure, An   It's better to make the small effort to plan ahead so that things don't go wrong than to need to do a lot of fixing up afterward. Another proverb that expresses the same idea is "A stitch in time saves nine."

penny saved is a penny earned, A   Money not spent is money in one's pocket.

picture is worth a thousand words, One   A visual image can give people a better sense of something than the written word.

place for everything and everything in its place, A   Things should be kept in order.

Practice makes perfect   Doing something over and over makes one better at it.

Practice what you preach   You yourself should follow the advice you give others.

Procrastination is the thief of time   Putting off doing something makes us lose valuable time. (Procrastination is a "thief" because it "steals" time away from us.)

proof of the pudding is in the eating, The   If you want to find out if something is good, you must try it out yourself.

road to hell is paved with good intentions, The   Good intentions don't matter if wicked actions result. People should be judged by their actions, not their intentions.

Rome wasn't built in a day   It takes a long time to achieve anything worthwhile.

Seeing is believing   This proverb is usually said when you doubt a thing is true, but you will believe it when it is shown to be true.

show must go on, The   People are counting on us to do this, and we must not disappoint them.

This is an old show business saying, meaning that nothing must stop a performance from going on as scheduled. ❧

stitch in time saves nine, A   It's easier to take precautions than to try to fix things after they go wrong (just as, by putting a single stitch in a garment, a person might prevent a tear that would take nine stitches to close). The same idea is expressed in the proverb "An ounce of prevention is worth a pound of cure."

Strike while the iron is hot   You should act on an opportunity as soon as it arises (just as a blacksmith shapes iron by striking it with his hammer when it is red hot).

There's more than one way to skin a cat There are usually several ways to accomplish a particular task.

There's no place like home Home is the best place to be.

Time heals all wounds As time passes, people get over insults, injuries, and hatreds.

Truth is stranger than fiction Sometimes the things that happen in real life are stranger than the things that take place in imaginary stories.

Two heads are better than one Some problems can be solved more easily by two people working together than by one person working alone.

Two wrongs don't make a right A wrongdoing shouldn't be answered by more wrongdoing. For example, if someone hurts you in some way, that doesn't mean that it's right for you to be hurtful in return.

Waste not, want not If we don't waste the things we have, we won't lack ("want") the things we need.

watched pot never boils, A When we impatiently wait for something to happen, it seems to take forever.

Well begun is half done Getting off to a good start on some task means that you've already accomplished a lot.

What will be, will be Some things will happen no matter what we do, so we should accept life as it comes.

> **T**his proverb is heard in Spanish as *Lo que será, será* and in Italian as *Che sarà, sarà.* ✒

When it rains, it pours When bad luck comes, it seems that a lot of bad things happen at once.

When in Rome, do as the Romans do You should adapt yourself to the ways of the people around you.

Where there's a will, there's a way If you really want to do something, you will find a way to accomplish it.

You can lead a horse to water, but you can't make him drink You can give someone an opportunity, but you can't make him take advantage of it.

You can't teach an old dog new tricks A person who has had one way of doing something for a long time won't want to do it any other way.

Idioms

An idiom is a special word or phrase that always appears in a particular form. Many idioms use metaphors or comparisons to make simple ideas more vivid. For instance, to say "You're making a mountain out of a molehill" is a more interesting way of saying, "You're exaggerating." In the same way, "Let's take the bull by the horns" is a more vivid way of saying, "Let's face this problem."

It is important to remember that an idiom always appears in a basic form. No one says, "Make a mountain out of an *ant*hill" or "Take the *cow* by the horns."

A few of the terms we list here are words from foreign languages. Others are common abbreviations or shorter ways of writing words or phrases.

A.D.   *See* A.D. *under "World History to 1600."*

A.M.   A.M. is an abbreviation for the Latin words *ante meridiem*, meaning "before noon." "In the A.M." means "in the morning." *Compare* P.M.

as the crow flies   "As the crow flies" describes the straightest, most direct route between two places. "It takes an hour to drive from Jonestown to Hamilton, though it's only twenty miles as the crow flies."

back to the drawing board   When someone says, "Back to the drawing board," it means that he or she has failed at a task and has to start all over again. "The boat we built sank as soon as we put it in the water, so I guess it's back to the drawing board."

bark is worse than his bite, his   If a person sounds harsh or mean but does not really act that way, we say that "his bark is worse than his bite," alluding to the way some dogs behave. "Although Dad sounded angry when we came in late, I don't think he'll punish us. His bark is worse than his bite."

B.C.   *See* B.C. *under "World History to 1600."*

beat around the bush   When you're talking seriously with someone who keeps changing the subject or won't come to the point, that person is probably "beating around the bush." "I wish you'd stop beating around the bush and tell me what you think of my story."

bee in his bonnet   Someone who has a "bee in his bonnet" is always complaining about one particular thing. "Mr. Turner has a bee in his bonnet about kids who skate on the sidewalk."

birthday suit   When you are "in your birthday suit" you are completely naked (as you were when you were born). "Please close the door while I change into my swimming trunks. I don't want anyone to see me in my birthday suit."

bite the dust   When someone is defeated or killed, he or she is said to "bite the dust." "Our soccer team is still undefeated. Every team we've played this year has bitten the dust."

bite the hand that feeds you   When you attack someone who has been helping or supporting you, you may be said to "bite the hand that feeds you." "When Rita started criticizing her boss, I said, 'Don't bite the hand that feeds you.' "

blow hot and cold   If you're constantly changing your mind about something, you're "blowing hot and cold." "First Mom said I could go to the party; then she said I couldn't. I wish she'd stop blowing hot and cold."

break the ice   When people are shy or tense in a situation and something happens to make them feel more comfortable, it is said to "break the ice." "It really broke the ice when Paul and I found out we both love stamp collecting."

> **B**ecause the ice on rivers would have to be broken to let ships get through in the winter, "to break the ice" means to make things easier for someone. 🐾

bull in a china shop, a   Someone who deals with a situation awkwardly or clumsily is said to be "a bull in a china shop."

bury the hatchet   When you "bury the hatchet," you agree to end a quarrel or fight. "Jerry and Joe have been avoiding each other since their argument, but I saw them together

this morning, so they must have buried the hatchet."

can't hold a candle to   When something "can't hold a candle to" something else, it is not nearly as good. "The other school may have a better football team, but their marching band can't hold a candle to ours."

catch-as-catch-can   In a "catch-as-catch-can" situation, you must make do or get along with what you have. "We don't have enough textbooks for all the students, so it'll be catch-as-catch-can."

chip on one's shoulder, a   Someone who has "a chip on his shoulder" is very touchy. "Joe really has a chip on his shoulder. Whenever I speak to him, he takes it the wrong way." In the past, a young boy would place a wood chip on his shoulder and dare anyone to knock it off as a way of showing how tough he was.

clean bill of health, a   If you are given "a clean bill of health," you have been told you are perfectly healthy. "Margaret just had a checkup, and the doctor gave her a clean bill of health."

cold feet   To have "cold feet" is to change your mind about doing something because it now seems unwise or dangerous. "I was going to compete in the race but got cold feet."

cold shoulder, the   Someone who deliberately avoids you is giving you "the cold shoulder." "At the party Carol tried to talk to Jim, but he gave her the cold shoulder."

crocodile tears   A person who acts sad but does not really mean it is shedding "crocodile tears." (A legend says that crocodiles weep before they eat their victims.) "You're not really sorry for Jean. You're just shedding crocodile tears."

easier said than done   If you are advised to do something that is very difficult, you might say that it's "easier said than done." "The doctor told my father to lose thirty pounds, but that's easier said than done."

eat crow   You "eat crow" when you have to take back something you once said (for example, an assertion about something). "The captain of the other team bragged that he would crush us. After we beat them, he was forced to eat crow."

eat humble pie   When you admit to an embarrassing mistake, you have been forced to "eat humble pie." "After I showed Jim that most of the statements in his paper were wrong, he was forced to eat humble pie."

eat someone out of house and home
Someone who eats a great deal of food may be said to "eat you out of house and home." "Mrs. Goldstein complained that her three teenagers were eating her out of house and home."

eleventh hour   The "eleventh hour" is the latest possible time at which something may be done. "The water bombers arrived at the eleventh hour — just in time to keep the forest fire from spreading to the town."

etc.   Etc. is an abbreviation for the Latin words *et cetera* ("and other things"). It is used to mean "and so on." "Dear Mom, Please remind Paul while I'm at camp to feed all my pets — the fish, the lizards, the gerbils, the worms, etc."

Eureka!   Eureka! is a Greek word that means "I have found it!" "When I finally found the quotation after looking through all those books, I yelled, 'Eureka!'"

feather in your cap, a   "A feather in your cap" is an accomplishment to be proud of. "I'm glad Maria won that science award. It's a real feather in her cap."

few and far between   Things that are "few and far between" are very scarce. "Gas stations are few and far between for the next hundred miles, so don't be too picky about the kind of gas you want."

first come, first served   "First come, first served" means that the people who arrive first will be waited on first. "The ad for the tickets said that it would be first come, first served, so we got in line early."

fish out of water, like a   When you are someplace you feel you don't belong, you may feel "like a fish out of water." "Everyone at the party was so much older than we were, I really felt like a fish out of water."

O ther idioms that refer to fish are "to fish for compliments" and "that's a fishy story" (that is, something that doesn't smell right). &

follow your nose   When you "follow your nose," you're using instinct or common sense. "The job isn't complicated; just follow your nose."

for the birds   Something that is "for the birds" is worthless. "That boring movie was for the birds."

forgive and forget   When you "forgive and forget," you refuse to hold a grudge against someone. "They are still good friends because Barb was willing to forgive and forget."

forty winks   "Forty winks" means a nap or a brief sleep during the day. "I want to grab forty winks. Please wake me up in half an hour."

get a taste of one's own medicine
Someone who treats others badly and then gets treated the same way is "getting a taste of his own medicine." "Mark got a taste of his

own medicine when everyone started playing practical jokes on him."

get up on the wrong side of the bed Someone who seems grouchy for no particular reason is said to have "gotten up on the wrong side of the bed." "Mr. Murphy has been in a bad mood all day. He must have gotten up on the wrong side of the bed this morning."

give the devil his due When you "give the devil his due," you are giving credit to an opponent. "I disagree with everything Henry says, but to give the devil his due, he is a good debater."

go to pot If something "goes to pot," it decays or becomes run-down. "It was sad to see how our old neighborhood had gone to pot."

gracias *Gracias* is the Spanish word meaning "thank you."

hit the nail on the head When you "hit the nail on the head," you have gone straight to the heart of a matter. "Nancy hit the nail on the head when she said that my sister was jealous of my success."

in hot water When you are in deep trouble, you are "in hot water." "When Marjorie failed the math test, she knew she would be in hot water with her folks."

keep your fingers crossed People who hope that nothing will happen to ruin their plans are said to "keep their fingers crossed." "Anna will find out tomorrow whether she was chosen for the school play. In the meantime, she's keeping her fingers crossed."

kill two birds with one stone When you "kill two birds with one stone," you accomplish two goals with one action. "If we can buy gas and have lunch at the next rest stop, we shall kill two birds with one stone."

land of Nod When you go to the "land of Nod," you fall asleep. "The principal's speech was so boring that half the students went to the land of Nod."

last straw, the "The last straw" is also referred to as "the straw that broke the camel's back." It is the last in a series of problems that finally forces you to lose patience. "I've had nothing but trouble since I joined the football team, and now I've sprained my knee! Well, that's the last straw: I quit!"

let the cat out of the bag When you "let the cat out of the bag," you reveal a secret. "We planned a surprise party for José, but someone let the cat out of the bag."

In early America or Europe, a dishonest person might offer to sell someone a pig (a valuable farm animal) in a bag but put a cat in the bag instead. Someone who let the cat out would be revealing the deception.

lock, stock, and barrel "Lock, stock, and barrel" means everything or the whole thing. "The store looks completely different since I shopped there last; they've changed it lock, stock, and barrel." The three items in this idiom are the parts of an old type of rifle.

madame *Madame* is the French word for "Mrs." or "mistress."

mademoiselle *Mademoiselle* is the French word for "miss."

make ends meet When you "make ends meet," you are earning enough money to provide for your basic needs. "Since my father lost his job, we can barely make ends meet."

make a mountain out of a molehill When you "make a mountain out of a molehill," you act as if something is very important when actually it is trivial. "You shouldn't call your sister a thief because she borrowed one of your shirts. You're making a mountain out of a molehill."

merci   *Merci* is the French word for "thank you."

money burning a hole in your pocket   If you have money that you can't wait to spend, you can say that it's "burning a hole in your pocket." "The day I got my allowance, I rushed down to the bookstore with the money burning a hole in my pocket."

monsieur   *Monsieur* is the French word for "Mr."

nose out of joint   When your "nose is out of joint," you're annoyed because someone else is in the limelight or you feel unappreciated. "Bill's nose is out of joint because his brother Tim made the baseball team and he didn't."

old hat   If something is "old hat," it is old-fashioned or out of date. "Mom, those dances are old hat!"

on its last legs   Something that is "on its last legs" is almost worn out. "I wouldn't bother to repair that bicycle; it's on its last legs."

on tenterhooks   Someone who is "on tenterhooks" is nervously awaiting news. "When we heard about the accident, we were on tenterhooks until we knew that Jim was all right."

on the warpath   Someone who is "on the warpath" is very angry and inclined to take some hostile action. "Watch out! Alicia just heard that her vacation plans were canceled and she's on the warpath today."

once in a blue moon   When you do something "once in a blue moon," you do it very rarely. "Sarah only writes to me once in a blue moon."

out of the frying pan into the fire   When you go "out of the frying pan into the fire," you're going from a bad situation to one that is even worse. "It was bad enough that Mrs. Norris scolded me, but now I have to go see the principal — it's out of the frying pan into the fire."

P.M.   P.M. is the abbreviation for the Latin words *post meridiem*, meaning "after noon." Compare A.M.

pot calling the kettle black, the   A person who criticizes someone else for the very faults he or she possesses is "the pot calling the kettle black." "Jeff says Priscilla talks too much, but he never shuts up himself. It's the pot calling the kettle black."

All pots and kettles were black when this idiom first appeared, because they were made of blackened iron.

raining cats and dogs, it's   When "it's raining cats and dogs," it's raining very hard. "We wanted to play touch football, but now it's raining cats and dogs, so I guess we'll stay inside."

read between the lines   When you "read between the lines," you try to figure out what somebody really means. "You can't take everything Hannah says literally. You have to read between the lines."

R.I.P.   R.I.P. is an abbreviation for the Latin words *requiescat in pace*, which mean "May he or she rest in peace." These letters are often found on tombstones.

R.S.V.P.   The abbreviation R.S.V.P. (from the French *répondez s'il vous plaît* — "reply, if you please") is often written at the bottom of invitations, meaning "Please let us know if you plan to come."

rule the roost   A person who dominates a group of people may be said to "rule the roost." "Even though she's the youngest child, Sally really rules the roost in her family."

rule of thumb   A "rule of thumb" is an inexact but useful rule for doing something. "As a rule of thumb, figure three cookies per person when you are planning the picnic."

run-of-the-mill   "Run-of-the-mill" means common, ordinary, or average. "The food at our school isn't bad, but it isn't great, either; it's run-of-the-mill cafeteria food."

señor   *Señor* is the Spanish word for "Mr."

señora   *Señora* is the Spanish word for "Mrs."

señorita   *Señorita* is the Spanish word for "Miss."

shipshape   *Shipshape* means very neat and tidy (the way that sailors must keep a ship). "His mother warned him that he couldn't go out until his room was shipshape."

sit on the fence   When you "sit on the fence," you refuse to take sides in some argument. "You can't sit on the fence forever. Sooner or later you'll have to make a choice."

sour grapes   When you want something and don't get it and then pretend that what you wanted was no good, you are like the fox who spoke of sour grapes when he couldn't reach them in AESOP'S FABLE "THE FOX AND THE GRAPES." "When Bill said that running was a silly sport after he lost the race, it was just sour grapes."

steal someone's thunder   When someone is planning to do something impressive and you do it first, you are "stealing that person's thunder." "Dad was planning to tell us about the vacation plans at dinner, but Mom was so excited that she told us first and stole his thunder."

take the bull by the horns   When you "take the bull by the horns," you face up to a difficult situation. "You can't always run away from your problems; sometimes you just have to take the bull by the horns."

tall tale   A "tall tale" is an unbelievable story that is full of exaggerations. "My grandfather says he used to walk barefoot through the snow to get to school, but I'm sure that's just one of his tall tales."

tempest in a teapot, a   "A tempest in a teapot" is a big fuss that is made over something unimportant. "Herman is throwing a fit because he can't go to the movies tonight. It's just a tempest in a teapot."

tenderfoot   A "tenderfoot" is a beginner. "Joe may have made a few mistakes on the job, but he's only a tenderfoot."

through thick and thin   When you stay with someone "through thick and thin," you stay loyal to that person no matter what happens. "She stood beside her friend through thick and thin."

till the cows come home   If you do something "till the cows come home," you do it for a long time. "Mr. Rowland said that as far as he was concerned, the students could stay there washing blackboards till the cows came home."

"**T**ill the cows come home" originally meant until the early morning hours, when the cows would come to the gate to be milked. ❧

Timbuktu   Timbuktu, a city in Africa, is sometimes used to mean a faraway place. "Mr. Carver wants to stay in this area, but he's afraid that his company will send him to Timbuktu."

tit for tat   When you give "tit for tat," you are giving back exactly what you receive. "If you support me I'll support you; it's tit for tat."

Tom, Dick, and Harry   "Tom, Dick, and Harry" means everyone or just anyone. "I asked you to keep my plans secret, but you've told them to every Tom, Dick, and Harry."

touch and go   A "touch and go" situation is dangerous or uncertain. "Aunt Mary is home from the hospital, but her doctor said it will be touch and go for a while."

touché   *Touché* is a French word used in the sport of fencing when a fencing sword touches a fencer and a point is scored. The term is used to admit that someone has made a good point against you in an argument. "I had to admit that he demolished my idea, so I said, 'Touché!' "

turn over a new leaf   Someone who begins anew or changes his or her ways is said to "turn over a new leaf." "Since he was grounded, Larry has turned over a new leaf and does his homework every night."

vice versa   *Vice versa* is Latin for "the other way around." "We'll go to the museum this Saturday and the aquarium next Saturday or vice versa; you can decide where we'll go first."

The reference to "a wolf in sheep's clothing" is taken from one of Aesop's fables, the story of a wolf who puts on a sheepskin in order to fool the sheep he wants to steal. 🐾

wolf in sheep's clothing   A "wolf in sheep's clothing" is a person who seems kind or friendly but is in fact the opposite. "Mark seems nice, but I think he's really a wolf in sheep's clothing."

English

In order to express and explain your ideas, you must be able to write good, clear English. Writing and speaking well involve knowing the rules of grammar, spelling, punctuation, and style. Using these rules skillfully, you can communicate your ideas effectively. If you want to write well, you need to practice often and show your writing to other people for their advice. Here we explain some of the terms you should be familiar with in order to learn the rules of written English.

abbreviation An abbreviation is a shortened form of a word and is usually followed by a PERIOD. For instance, *Mr.* is the abbreviation of Mister; *Jan.* is the abbreviation of January.

adjective An adjective is a part of speech that modifies (acts upon) a NOUN or PRONOUN. In these PHRASES, the words in italics are adjectives: the *red* raincoat; a *shy* boy; the *next* street; *those* apples.

adverb An adverb is a part of speech that modifies (acts upon) a VERB, an ADJECTIVE, or another adverb and often ends in *ly*. In these examples, the words in italics are adverbs:

Sam works *quickly*.
(*Quickly* modifies the verb *works*.)

My father drives *carefully*.
(*Carefully* modifies the verb *drives*.)

The trees look *very* old.
(*Very* modifies the adjective *old*.)

Please speak *more softly*.
(*More* modifies the adverb *softly*, and *softly* modifies the verb *speak*.)

agreement In every sentence, the SUBJECT must agree with (or match up with) the VERB. A singular subject takes a singular verb, and a plural subject takes a plural verb. For instance, the following sentence is wrong because the verb and subject do not agree:

My grandparents *is* coming to visit us.

It should read:

My grandparents *are* coming to visit us.

In addition, a PRONOUN must always agree with the NOUN it refers to. A singular noun takes a singular pronoun, and a plural noun takes a plural pronoun. For instance, the example that follows is wrong because the noun and pronoun do not agree:

Each boy will have to buy *their* own uniform.

It should read:

Each boy will have to buy *his* own uniform.

A pronoun must also agree with its function as a SUBJECT or OBJECT in a sentence:

They (subject) gave *them* (object) a warning.

13

antonyms Antonyms are words of opposite meaning. For example, *cold* and *hot*, *little* and *big*, are antonyms. *Compare* SYNONYMS.

apostrophe An apostrophe is a punctuation mark ['] used with a NOUN and some PRONOUNS to indicate possession:

> Sarah*'s* book
> my mother*'s* car
> anyone*'s* guess

An apostrophe is also used to indicate missing letters in a CONTRACTION, as in these examples:

> Paul can*'t* come to the phone right now.
> I*'m* getting impatient with you.

See also POSSESSIVE.

article The words *the*, *a*, and *an* are called articles. *The* is the definite article because it refers to specific (or definite) items:

> Look at *the* boats.
> *The* apples look good.

A and *an* are indefinite articles because they refer to any one of a general group of items:

> My father wants to buy *a* boat.
> Give me *an* apple. (*An* is used before a VOWEL.)

auxiliary verb When a phrase has more than one VERB, one is the main verb and the others are auxiliary (or "helping") verbs. In the examples that follow, the auxiliary verbs are in italics:

> The show *will* start in ten minutes.
> Gail *should have* won that race.

bibliography A bibliography is a list of books and articles on a particular subject. For instance, if you wanted to read about the Civil War, you would find titles of works on the subject listed in a bibliography on the Civil War.

capital letter A capital letter indicates the beginning of a sentence and a PROPER NOUN. In the examples that follow, the capital letters are in italics:

> *S*tudents should not throw food in the cafeteria.
> *M*artin *F*isher moved here from *T*oledo.

Capital letters are also called UPPER-CASE LETTERS. *Compare* LOWER-CASE LETTER.

clause A clause is a group of words that contains a SUBJECT and a PREDICATE. A sentence may contain one or more clauses. Some clauses can stand alone as sentences: *Alfred caught the biggest fish*. Other clauses cannot stand alone: *Because he caught the biggest fish*, Alfred won the trophy. A clause that can stand alone as a sentence is called an *independent* clause. A clause that cannot stand alone as a sentence is called a *dependent* clause.

colon A colon is a punctuation mark [:] used to introduce a list, a description, or an example:

> She only wanted one present for her birthday: a new bicycle.

> Before the camping trip, I had to buy several things: a backpack, a pocket knife, a canteen, and some boots.

comma A comma is a punctuation mark [,] that separates the parts of a sentence and indicates where to pause when reading a sentence:

> First we'll go to the zoo, and then the bus will take us to the museum.

Commas are also used in dates and place names:

> July 4, 1776, is the official birthday of the United States.
> Paris, France, is known for the Eiffel Tower.

conjunction A conjunction is a word that joins words or groups of words, such as *and*, *but*, *or*, and *because*.

consonant   The alphabet contains two kinds of letters, VOWELS and consonants. The letters that follow are vowels:

a, e, i, o, u

These letters are consonants:

b, c, d, f, g, h, j, k, l, m,
n, p, q, r, s, t, v, w, x, z

The letter *y* is sometimes a vowel, as in *good-bye*, and sometimes a consonant, as in *yo-yo*.

contraction   A contraction is one word made up of two words that have been shortened. For instance, *I'm* is a contraction of *I am*; *shouldn't* is a contraction of *should not*. An APOSTROPHE shows where letters or sounds have been left out.

declarative sentence   A declarative sentence makes a statement (declares something). The sentences that follow are declarative:

He loves ice cream.
That is the new train station.
My mother will be coming home soon.

Compare IMPERATIVE SENTENCE; INTERROGATIVE SENTENCE.

definite article   *See* ARTICLE.

dependent clause   *See* CLAUSE.

direct object   The noun that directly receives the action of a verb in a sentence is called the direct object. In the sentences that follow, the direct object is in italics:

Roger is eating *lunch*.
Karen threw the *ball* to Joe.

Compare INDIRECT OBJECT.

exclamation   An exclamation is a word or sentence that expresses excitement or gives a command:

Hey!
Help!
Let's go!
Get away from the fire!

exclamation point   An exclamation point is the punctuation mark [!] that comes at the end of an EXCLAMATION.

grammar   Grammar is the study of the structure of language. It also refers to the rules of correct writing and speaking.

imperative sentence   An imperative sentence requests or commands someone to do something. The following sentences are imperative:

Come to the blackboard.
Please turn off the light.

Compare DECLARATIVE SENTENCE; INTERROGATIVE SENTENCE.

indefinite article   *See* ARTICLE.

independent clause   *See* CLAUSE; SEMICOLON.

indirect object   When a verb has more than one object, the noun that *directly* receives the action of the verb is called the direct object. The noun that *indirectly* receives the action is called the indirect object. In the following sentences, the direct object is in italics and the indirect object is in boldface:

Throw the *ball* to **him**.
Throw **him** the *ball*.
He gave **Jennifer** the *ticket*.

interjection   An interjection is a brief EXCLAMATION, often containing only one word: Ouch! Hey! Gosh!

interrogative sentence   An interrogative sentence asks a question:

Can Janet come along?
Have you read that book?

Compare DECLARATIVE SENTENCE; IMPERATIVE SENTENCE.

irregular verb   In English, verbs that add *ed* in the past tense are called REGULAR VERBS. For instance, *walk* is a regular verb because it becomes *walked* in the past tense. Verbs that do not add *ed* in the past tense are called irregular verbs. Below are some irregular verbs, listed first in the present and then in the past tense:

swim swam
ring rang
teach taught
fly flew
feel felt

italics   Italics are a special kind of type used to set off a particular word or group of words. *Italics look like this.* The titles of books, magazines, and newspapers are often printed in italics.

lower-case letter   A lower-case letter is a small (not capital) letter. For instance, all the letters in this sentence except the first letter ("F") are lower-case. *Compare* CAPITAL LETTER.

modifier   A modifier is a word that acts upon, or tells about, another word. ADJECTIVES and ADVERBS are modifiers.

noun   A noun is a part of speech that names a person, place, thing, or idea, such as cat, child, river, knife, friendship, Margaret, Lincoln. *Compare* PROPER NOUN.

object   The noun, pronoun, or group of words that receives the action of a verb is called the object of the verb. *Compare* DIRECT OBJECT; INDIRECT OBJECT.

paragraph   A paragraph is a group of sentences organized around a main idea. Most writing is broken up into paragraphs. The first line of a paragraph is usually indented (moved to the right) to indicate that a new paragraph has started.

parentheses   Parentheses are punctuation marks ( ) that set off certain words inside a sentence. The information they contain does not always forward the main idea, but it may be helpful: "Aunt Sarah (my mother's sister) will visit us over the holidays."

parts of speech   In grammar, a part of speech is a class of words that have the same grammatical function: NOUNS, VERBS, ADJECTIVES, ADVERBS, PRONOUNS, ARTICLES, PREPOSITIONS, CONJUNCTIONS, and INTERJECTIONS.

period   A period is a punctuation mark [.] that comes at the end of an ABBREVIATION or a sentence.

person   Every PERSONAL PRONOUN is in either the first, the second, or the third person. The first-person pronouns (*I, me, we,* and *us*) refer to the person or persons who are speaking. The second-person pronoun (*you*) refers to the person who is being spoken to. The third-person pronouns (*he, him, she, her, it, they,* and *them*) refer to the persons or things being discussed.

personal pronoun   Personal pronouns represent a person in a sentence. They are: *I, me, we, us, you, he, him, she, her, it, they,* and *them. Compare* PERSON.

phrase   A phrase is a group of related words that cannot stand alone as a sentence, such as: a flock of birds; Mr. Hayakawa's class; crossing the street; on top of the refrigerator. Unlike a CLAUSE, a phrase does not have both a subject and a predicate.

plot   Plot is the sequence of events, or story line, in a story.

plural   Nouns, pronouns, and verbs have both SINGULAR and plural forms. The singular form refers to only one thing, while the plural form refers to more than one thing. *See also* AGREEMENT.

possessive   The possessive form of a noun or pronoun shows who owns (or possesses) something. Singular nouns become possessive when they add an apostrophe followed by an "s":

She borrowed her friend*'s* tennis racket.

Plural nouns that already end in "s" become possessive by adding an apostrophe:

Those are the student*s'* books.

predicate Every sentence contains a SUBJECT and a predicate. The subject is a noun or a group of words that tells what the sentence is about. The predicate contains a verb and sometimes a group of words related to the verb. It describes something about the subject. In the following sentences, the subject is in italics and the predicate is in boldface:

The bell **rang**.
Pigs **are intelligent**.
My father **couldn't find a parking place**.

prefix A prefix is one or more letters added to the beginning of a word to change its meaning. In the following words, the prefixes are in italics: *un*happy, *dis*qualify, *pre*school, *mis*understood, *over*eat, *post*script, *sub*terranean, *ultra*modern. *Compare* SUFFIX.

preposition A preposition is a part of speech that shows how a particular word is related to other words in a sentence. Common prepositions include: *at, in, into, on, by, from, for, to,* and *with*.

pronoun A pronoun is the part of speech that can take the place of a noun in a sentence. The following words are all pronouns: *he, you, ours, herself, what, that, who,* and *which*. *Compare* PERSONAL PRONOUN.

punctuation marks Punctuation marks are standard signs used in writing to clarify the meaning. The most important punctuation marks are the PERIOD, the COMMA, QUOTATION MARKS, the COLON, the SEMICOLON, the QUESTION MARK, and the EXCLAMATION POINT.

question mark A question mark is a punctuation mark [?] used at the end of a question.

regular verb A regular verb is a verb whose past tense is formed by adding *ed* to the present tense. For example, the verb *walk* becomes *walked* in the past tense, and the verb *open* becomes *opened*. Most verbs in English are regular verbs. *Compare* IRREGULAR VERB.

semicolon A semicolon is a punctuation mark [;] that is used to join two independent CLAUSES: Jim likes to run; Martha prefers swimming.

sentence A sentence is a group of words that expresses a complete thought. Every sentence contains at least one SUBJECT and PREDICATE.

singular Nouns, pronouns, and verbs have both singular and PLURAL forms. The singular form refers to only one thing, while the plural form refers to more than one thing. *See also* AGREEMENT.

style Style, when applied to writing, means the characteristic manner of the writing. Long or short sentences, plain or fancy words, and serious or comic tones are some of the traits that define a writer's style.

subject Every sentence contains a subject and a PREDICATE. The subject consists of the main noun (or a group of words acting like the main noun) and tells what the sentence is about. In the following sentences, the subject is in italics:

My sister and her friends joined the Girl Scouts.
The river looks too wide to swim across.
Squirrels are afraid of cats.
Running is good exercise.

suffix A suffix is one or more letters added to the end of a word to change its meaning. In the following words, the suffixes are in italics: disappoint*ment*, kind*ness*, usual*ly*, machin*ist*, port*able*. *Compare* PREFIX.

synonyms   Synonyms are words of similar meaning. For instance, *small* is a synonym of *little*. *Compare* ANTONYMS.

tense   Tense is the form of a verb that expresses when the action of the verb takes place. For example, in the sentence "He *runs*," the verb is in the present tense. In the sentence "He *ran*," the verb is in the past tense. In the sentence "He *will run*," the verb is in the future tense.

topic sentence   The most important sentence in a paragraph is the topic sentence because it states the main idea of the paragraph.

upper-case letter   An upper-case (capital) letter is used at the beginning of a sentence or a proper noun. *Compare* LOWER-CASE LETTER.

verb   A verb is a word that expresses action or a state of being. *Walk, fly, read, catch, turn, complain, grow, hold, smile, notice, play, decide, rattle, get,* and *release* are all action verbs. The verb *to be* expresses states of being; it tells what something *is* rather than what it *does*. Every sentence must contain (or imply) at least one verb.

vowels   The alphabet contains two kinds of letters, vowels and CONSONANTS. The letters *a, e, i, o,* and *u* are vowels. The letter *y* is sometimes a vowel, as in *try*, and sometimes a consonant, as in *your*. All the other letters in the alphabet are consonants.

Literature

Literature is a category of writing that includes such works as novels, poems, and plays. The names of different literary works as well as terms that apply to them are listed and explained here.

Some of the works listed were written by well-known authors. Others — especially the stories we call folk tales, fairy tales, and fables, and the children's poems known as nursery rhymes — have been handed down from generation to generation for so long that the original writer has been forgotten. All of these works have one thing in common, however: they have been read and remembered over many years for the stories they tell, the experiences they describe, and the wisdom they contain.

Included here are the literary works that people often refer to in writing and conversation. There is no substitute for reading literature in its original form or in a good translation. Many of the works mentioned below are useful and enjoyable to everyone.

Aesop's fables (EE-sops, EE-suhps) Aesop's fables are stories thought to have been written by Aesop, a Greek storyteller. In many of the fables, animals are the main characters. They act like people, and their actions are used to teach a lesson, or moral, about human life. Two of Aesop's best-known fables are "The FOX AND THE GRAPES" and "The HARE AND THE TORTOISE." *See also* FABLE.

> **A**esop is thought to have been a slave who lived in the sixth century B.C. His fables were passed on to us by later Greek and Latin writers. ❧

Aladdin's Lamp Aladdin's Lamp is a magical lamp that appears in one of the stories of the *ARABIAN NIGHTS*. When Aladdin rubs the lamp, a magic spirit called a genie appears and offers to do anything that Aladdin asks. The genie makes Aladdin rich and powerful.

Alcott, Louisa May Louisa May Alcott was a popular American author of the 1800s who wrote novels for children, including *LITTLE WOMEN* and *Little Men*.

Ali Baba Ali Baba is a character in one of the stories of the *ARABIAN NIGHTS*. Ali is a poor man. One day he overhears a band of robbers enter a secret cave by saying, "Open, Sesame." When the robbers leave, Ali Baba repeats the magic words and enters the cave. He becomes rich by taking the treasure left by the thieves.

Alice in Wonderland. Alice with the March Hare, the Dormouse, and the Mad Hatter.

Alice in Wonderland   Alice appears in two books by Lewis Carroll. In the first book, *Alice's Adventures in Wonderland*, Alice falls down a rabbit hole and finds herself in Wonderland, where she meets the White Rabbit, the Cheshire Cat, the Mad Hatter, and the Queen of Hearts. In the second book, *Through the Looking-Glass*, Alice climbs through a looking-glass, or mirror, to see what is on the other side. There she meets Humpty Dumpty, the twins Tweedledum and Tweedledee, and other strange characters.

Andersen, Hans Christian   Hans Christian Andersen was a Danish author of the 1800s. He wrote many popular fairy tales, such as "The Ugly Duckling," "The Emperor's New Clothes," and "The Princess and the Pea."

Androcles and the Lion   According to legend, Androcles, a Greek slave, escaped from his cruel master, but as he was running away, he stopped to remove a thorn from the paw of a lion. Some time later Androcles was caught and, as punishment, was sent into an arena before the emperor, to be attacked by a wild beast. The animal turned out to be the very lion he had helped and it greeted him joyously.

Angelou, Maya   Maya Angelou is a modern American writer known for her autobiography, *I Know Why the Caged Bird Sings*.

Arabian Nights   The *Arabian Nights*, also known as *The Thousand and One Nights*, is a collection of old stories from India and the Middle East. Some of the most familiar stories are about Ali Baba, Aladdin's Lamp, and Sinbad the Sailor.

autobiography   An autobiography is a book about the author's own life. Some important autobiographies are *The Autobiography of Benjamin Franklin*, *The Story of My Life*, by Helen Keller, and *I Know Why the Caged Bird Sings*, by Maya Angelou. *See also* Franklin, Benjamin.

"Baa, baa, black sheep"   "Baa, baa, black sheep" is a nursery rhyme:

Baa, baa, black sheep,
Have you any wool?
Yes, sir, yes, sir,
Three bags full;
One for my master,
And one for my dame,
And one for the little boy
Who lives down the lane.

Babar   Babar is an elephant in a series of children's books by the French writers and illustrators Jean de Brunhoff and his son, Laurent de Brunhoff.

"Beauty and the Beast"   "Beauty and the Beast" is a fairy tale. Beauty is a young woman who is taken to live with the Beast, an ugly monster, in return for a favor he did for her father. Because the Beast is kind to her, Beauty eventually falls in love with him. Her love frees him from an evil spell. He turns into a handsome prince, and they are married.

Big Bad Wolf   The Big Bad Wolf is a character in the fairy tale "The Three Little Pigs." In the Walt Disney cartoon film, the little pigs sing a song, "Who's Afraid of the Big Bad Wolf?"

Brer Rabbit. Brer Fox and Brer Rabbit. Drawing by A. B. Frost.

biography   A biography is a book that tells the story of a person's life. Some good biographies are *Traitor: The Case of Benedict Arnold*, by Jean Fritz, and *Laura Ingalls Wilder: Growing Up in the Little House*, by Patricia Riley Giff.

"Blind Men and the Elephant, The" "The Blind Men and the Elephant" is a fable in which six blind men describe an elephant. Each one touches a different part of the elephant and says what he finds. But all they do is argue and argue because no one will listen to the others. Each foolishly believes that his idea about the elephant is the only correct one.

"Boy Who Cried Wolf, The"   The boy who cried wolf is a character in one of AESOP'S FABLES. He is a shepherd boy who often tricked the people of his village by pretending that a wolf was attacking his sheep. The villagers came to help him chase away the wolf, only to find that he was lying. One day a wolf really did come. The boy ran to the village for help, but he had cried "Wolf!" so many times that nobody believed him, and the wolf ate his sheep.

Brer Rabbit   Brer Rabbit is a character in the UNCLE REMUS stories, by Joel Chandler Harris. He is a wily rabbit who outsmarts his rival, Brer Fox. (*Brer* means "brother.")

Brothers Grimm   *See* GRIMM BROTHERS.

Camelot   Camelot was the place where KING ARTHUR and his Knights of the Round Table gathered.

Captain Hook   In the story of PETER PAN, Captain Hook is an evil pirate whose hand has been bitten off by a crocodile and replaced by a hook.

Carroll, Lewis   Lewis Carroll was the PEN NAME of an English writer of the late 1800s, Charles Lutwidge Dodgson. He is known for his books about ALICE IN WONDERLAND.

character   A character is any person who appears in works of FICTION (made-up, or imaginary, stories), such as novels, poems, plays, movies, cartoons and comic books, and television shows.

The names of many important characters in literary works have come to stand for the type of person described in the story. A mean, miserly person, for example, might be called a "grinch" (from *How the Grinch Stole Christmas*) or a "scrooge" (from *A Christmas Carol*).

Cheshire Cat.
Alice meeting
the Cheshire Cat.
Drawing by
John Tenniel.

Cinderella

Cheshire Cat (CHESH-uhr) The Cheshire Cat is one of the characters that Alice meets in Wonderland. He can make himself slowly disappear until all that can be seen is his big grin. *See also* ALICE IN WONDERLAND.

Chicken Little Chicken Little is a character in a children's story. One day she is hit on the head by an acorn that falls from a tree. She then tells the other animals she meets that the sky is falling. The foolish animals set off to tell the king, but on the way they meet a clever fox, who catches them for his dinner.

Christmas Carol, A *A Christmas Carol* is a book by CHARLES DICKENS, an English writer of the 1800s, that tells the story of Ebenezer SCROOGE, a mean old miser. Whenever someone wishes him a merry Christmas, he says, "Bah, humbug." On Christmas Eve, Scrooge is haunted by three spirits who show him what an empty life he has led. Scrooge awakens on Christmas Day and becomes a generous and friendly man.

"Cinderella" "Cinderella" is a fairy tale about a young girl who is badly treated by her stepmother and stepsisters. On the day of a ball (dance), Cinderella helps her stepsisters get ready but must stay at home herself. Later, Cinderella's fairy godmother appears and sends her to the ball, warning her that she must leave before midnight. That night, the prince falls in love with Cinderella, but at the first stroke of midnight she leaves, dropping one of her glass slippers in her haste. Soon after, the prince finds Cinderella, for hers is the only foot that will fit the slipper, and they are married.

comedy A comedy is a type of FICTION, whether a PLAY, story, or movie, that ends happily for the main character and contains at least some humor.

Crane, Ichabod Ichabod Crane is the tall, skinny schoolteacher in the story "The LEGEND OF SLEEPY HOLLOW," by Washington Irving. *See also* HEADLESS HORSEMAN.

Emily Dickinson

Don Quixote. Don Quixote, on the right, and his squire Sancho Panza.

David Copperfield *David Copperfield* is a novel by the English author CHARLES DICKENS about David's life as a boy and young man. Many of the incidents in the book are based on Dickens's own life, especially his boyhood, when he had to go to work in a FACTORY.

Dickens, Charles Charles Dickens was an English author of the 1800s who wrote many popular novels and stories, including OLIVER TWIST, DAVID COPPERFIELD, *A Tale of Two Cities*, and *A CHRISTMAS CAROL*.

> **D**ickens wrote of the problems of working-class people at the time of the Industrial Revolution. ❧

Dickinson, Emily Emily Dickinson was an American poet of the 1800s whose verse is known for its short, simple lines, such as "I'm Nobody! Who are you?/Are you — Nobody — too?"

Dr. Jekyll and Mr. Hyde (JEK-uhl)　In a book called *The Strange Case of Dr. Jekyll and Mr. Hyde*, by the Scottish writer ROBERT LOUIS STEVENSON, Dr. Jekyll is a kind doctor who develops a drug that changes him into an evil man called Mr. Hyde. A person who is sometimes kind and sometimes nasty may be said to have a Jekyll and Hyde personality.

Don Quixote (don-kee-HOH-tay)　*Don Quixote* is a novel by the Spanish writer Miguel de Cervantes. Its hero, Don Quixote, has read so many stories about knights and their adventures he begins to think he must travel about the world to fight evil and injustice. In his madness, he attacks a windmill, thinking it is a giant. He has many other comic adventures with his servant, SANCHO PANZA.

Dracula Dracula is a vampire in a famous horror story. (A vampire is a dead man who comes out of his coffin at night in search of human blood.) The vampire can only be killed by driving a wooden stake through its heart.

Emerson, Ralph Waldo Ralph Waldo Emerson was an American thinker and writer of the 1800s. In his poem about the first battle of the Revolutionary War, "Concord Hymn," is the famous phrase "the shot heard round the world." The poem begins:

> By the rude bridge that arched the flood,
> Their flag to April's breeze unfurled,
> Here once the embattled farmers stood,
> And fired the shot heard round the world.

In his essay "Self-Reliance" and other works, Emerson stressed the importance of the individual and encouraged people to rely on their own judgment. ❧

"Emperor's New Clothes, The" "The Emperor's New Clothes" is a story by the Danish writer HANS CHRISTIAN ANDERSEN about an emperor who loves to wear fine new clothes. Two swindlers tell him that they can make clothes out of a very unusual cloth that can only be seen by people who are very intelligent or very good at their jobs. The swindlers only pretend to make this cloth, so that when the emperor puts on his new clothes and walks down the street, he is actually naked. Everyone acts as though he has on a fine new outfit until a child speaks up, "But he hasn't got any clothes on!"

epic An epic is a long poem that describes heroic deeds and adventures, such as the *ILIAD* and the *ODYSSEY*. HOMER, who wrote these epics, is called an epic poet.

fable A fable is a brief story that ends with a moral (a short message about how people should behave). *See also* AESOP'S FABLES.

fairy tale A fairy tale is a story in which the hero or heroine triumphs over adversity, often with the aid of a fairy or other supernatural creature. "CINDERELLA" is a fairy tale.

Faulkner, William William Faulkner was an American author of the 1900s who wrote mostly about the American South. Two of his novels are *The Sound and the Fury* and *As I Lay Dying.*

fiction Fiction is a term that refers to imaginary stories, events that did not really happen as described. It can take the form of novels, plays, poetry, or short stories, such as fairy tales.

folk tale A folk tale is a story that has been told by many generations of people before it is written down. Often the names of the people who made up the folk tales are not known. The stories of PAUL BUNYAN are American folk tales. Many fairy tales, such as "JACK AND THE BEANSTALK," are folk tales.

The Fox and the Grapes

"Fox and the Grapes, The" "The Fox and the Grapes" is one of AESOP'S FABLES. A fox sees some grapes hanging from a vine, but he cannot reach them. He gives up, saying, "They were sour, anyway." This fable has given us the expression *sour grapes*, which refers to anything we criticize because it is something we want but cannot get.

Frankenstein   *Frankenstein* is a novel by Mary Shelley about a scientist named Dr. Victor Frankenstein, who creates a monster that looks like a gigantic, hideous human being. The monster has human feelings and thoughts, but because he is so deformed he terrifies everyone who sees him. Today, people often use the name Frankenstein when they really mean Frankenstein's monster.

frog prince   The frog prince is a character in fairy tales. In these stories, a frog is really a handsome prince who has been put under a spell. In order to break the spell, a beautiful lady must be kind to the frog or give it a kiss.

Frost, Robert   Robert Frost was an American poet of the 1900s who is best known for his verse about rural New England. Two of his best-known poems are "The Road Not Taken" and "Stopping by Woods on a Snowy Evening."

Galahad, Sir   Sir Galahad was the finest and most noble of KING ARTHUR's knights.

"Georgie Porgie"   "Georgie Porgie" is a nursery rhyme:

> Georgie Porgie, pudding and pie,
> Kissed the girls and made them cry;
> When the boys came out to play,
> Georgie Porgie ran away.

"God bless us, every one!"   "God bless us, every one!" is a line from CHARLES DICKENS's book *A CHRISTMAS CAROL*. The words are spoken at Christmas dinner by a young crippled boy, Tiny Tim.

"Goldilocks and the Three Bears"   "Goldilocks and the Three Bears" is a story for children about a little girl who visits the bears' house while they are out. She enjoys the little bear's porridge and eventually falls asleep in his bed. When the bears come home, the little bear sees Goldilocks asleep in his bed and says, "Somebody has been lying in my bed — and here she is!" Goldilocks wakes up and runs all the way home.

"Goose That Laid the Golden Eggs, The"   "The Goose That Laid the Golden Eggs" is a fable. A man discovers that his goose lays a golden egg every morning. He grows rich, but he also grows greedy. He decides to cut open the goose so that he can take all the golden eggs at once. But when he cuts the goose open, he finds that it is empty, and he is left with no gold and no goose. When we say, "Don't kill the goose that lays the golden eggs," it means that we shouldn't lose what we have by trying to get more.

Grimm Brothers   Jacob and Wilhelm Grimm were two brothers who lived in Germany in the early 1800s. They heard many stories from peasants and wrote them down, making a large, eventually famous, collection called *Grimm's Fairy Tales*. "HANSEL AND GRETEL" and "SNOW WHITE" are two of the fairy tales from that book.

Grinch   The Grinch is a nasty creature in the children's story *How the Grinch Stole Christmas*, by the American writer DR. SEUSS. The Grinch is so mean that he does not want anyone else to enjoy Christmas, so he spends Christmas Eve stealing everyone's presents, decorations, and holiday food. But on Christmas morning he hears everyone singing and celebrating in spite of their losses. He realizes that the spirit of Christmas is something within each person that cannot be stolen, and he becomes a happier and wiser creature.

Gulliver's Travels   *Gulliver's Travels* is a book by the Irish author Jonathan Swift that describes the adventures of Lemuel Gulliver,

Gulliver's Travels. Gulliver in Lilliput.

who makes several sea journeys to strange lands. In the first he is washed ashore in LIL- LIPUT, where the people are six inches tall. The second voyage is to a land of giants. The third takes him to a flying island peopled by odd scientists and thinkers. In his final voyage, he arrives at a land where talking horses are superior beings. The story is a fantasy, but it is also meant to expose the faults and stupidities of humankind.

Hamlet   *Hamlet* is a tragedy by WILLIAM SHAKESPEARE. The main character, Hamlet, is a Danish prince whose father, the king, has been murdered. The king's ghost appears and says that he was murdered by his own brother, Hamlet's uncle Claudius. The ghost demands

The character Hamlet has come to represent a person whose thoughts and feelings stop him from being able to act quickly. 🐚

that Hamlet kill Claudius, who has already married Hamlet's mother and become king. Much of the play is about Hamlet's thoughts as he prepares to avenge his father's death. Many familiar speeches and phrases come from this play, such as: "To be, or not to be, that is the question" and "Neither a borrower, nor a lender be."

"Hansel and Gretel"   "Hansel and Gretel" is a FAIRY TALE in the collection of the GRIMM BROTHERS about a brother and sister who are abandoned in the forest when their family has no more food. They come upon a cottage made of gingerbread and sugar candy and begin to eat it until an old woman comes out. She invites them in and gives them food. But she is really a wicked witch who plans to fatten them up and cook them in the oven. Gretel tricks her, however, pushing her into the oven instead. The witch burns to death, and Hansel and Gretel escape and find their way home.

"Hare and the Tortoise, The"   "The Hare and the Tortoise," one of AESOP'S FABLES, tells about a race between the two animals. The hare runs so fast that he is sure he will win, so he takes a nap halfway through the race. The tortoise keeps plodding along until he is ahead of the hare. By the time the hare wakes up, the tortoise is almost at the finish line. He wins because he kept going even though he was slow. From this fable we get the expression "Slow and steady wins the race."

Hawthorne, Nathaniel   Nathaniel Hawthorne was an American author of the 1800s who wrote short stories and novels, among them *The Scarlet Letter*. Two of his books for children retell some of the best-known Greek myths.

Headless Horseman   The Headless Horseman is a legendary ghost rider that appears in the story "The LEGEND OF SLEEPY HOLLOW," by Washington Irving. *See also* CRANE, ICHABOD.

The Hare and the Tortoise

Homer. Courtesy, Museum of Fine Arts, Boston.

Hemingway, Ernest Ernest Hemingway was an American author of the 1900s who wrote novels and short stories about war, hunting, fishing, and bullfighting. Two of his novels are *The Sun Also Rises* and *The Old Man and the Sea*.

"Hey Diddle Diddle" "Hey Diddle Diddle" is a nursery rhyme:

> Hey diddle diddle,
> The cat and the fiddle,
> The cow jumped over the moon;
> The little dog laughed
> To see such sport,
> And the dish ran away with the spoon.

Hiawatha Hiawatha was an American Indian chief of the 1500s. A poem by HENRY WADSWORTH LONGFELLOW, "The Song of Hiawatha," tells some of the legends that have been passed down about Hiawatha's life.

"Hickory, Dickory, Dock" "Hickory, Dickory, Dock" is a nursery rhyme:

> Hickory, dickory, dock,
> The mouse ran up the clock.
> The clock struck one,
> The mouse ran down,
> Hickory, dickory, dock.

Homer Homer was a great poet of ancient Greece who wrote two EPICS, or long poems: the *ILIAD*, about the TROJAN WAR, and the *ODYSSEY*, about the adventures of the Greek hero Odysseus. Homer is said to have been blind.

"Hot Cross Buns" "Hot Cross Buns" is a nursery rhyme:

> Hot cross buns! Hot cross buns!
> One a penny, two a penny,
> Hot cross buns!

"House That Jack Built, The" "The House That Jack Built" is a nursery tale. It begins with the single line, "This is the house that Jack built," and a new line is added to make each verse:

> This is the malt
> That lay in the house that Jack built.

> This is the rat,
> That ate the malt
> That lay in the house that Jack built.

This is the cat,
That killed the rat,
That ate the malt
That lay in the house that Jack built.

The story continues until there are eleven lines in the final verse.

Huckleberry Finn, The Adventures of

The Adventures of Huckleberry Finn is a novel by MARK TWAIN, an American writer of the 1800s. Huck Finn escapes from his cruel father and travels down the Mississippi River on a raft with an escaped slave, Jim, and together they have many adventures.

Humpty Dumpty

"Humpty Dumpty"

"Humpty Dumpty" is a nursery rhyme:

Humpty Dumpty sat on a wall,
Humpty Dumpty had a great fall.
All the king's horses,
And all the king's men,
Couldn't put Humpty together again.

This rhyme is also a riddle. If you are asked, "What is Humpty Dumpty?" the answer is, "An egg," because no one can put an egg back together once it is broken. In the book THROUGH THE LOOKING GLASS, Alice meets Humpty Dumpty, a character who actually is a large egg.

Hunchback of Notre Dame, The

The Hunchback of Notre Dame is a novel by Victor Hugo, a French writer of the 1800s. It tells the story of Quasimodo, a physically deformed man who works as a bellringer in the great cathedral of Notre Dame in Paris.

I think I can, I think I can *See* "LITTLE ENGINE THAT COULD, THE."

Iliad (IL-ee-uhd, IL-ee-ad) The *Iliad* is an EPIC by the ancient Greek poet HOMER that tells the story of the TROJAN WAR.

"Jack Be Nimble"

"Jack Be Nimble" is a nursery rhyme:

Jack be nimble,
Jack be quick,
Jack jump over
The candlestick.

"Jack and the Beanstalk"

"Jack and the Beanstalk" is a fairy tale about a boy who finds a huge magic beanstalk in his garden. He climbs it until he comes to a strange land in the sky. There he finds the castle of a giant, who cries, "Fee fie fo fum, I smell the blood of an Englishman!" The giant chases Jack down the beanstalk, but Jack gets to the bottom first and chops it down. The giant falls from the sky and is killed.

"Jack and Jill"

"Jack and Jill" is a nursery rhyme that begins:

Jack and Jill went up the hill,
To fetch a pail of water;
Jack fell down, and broke his crown,
And Jill came tumbling after.

(*Crown* means "head.")

"Jack Sprat"

"Jack Sprat" is a nursery rhyme:

Jack Sprat could eat no fat,
His wife could eat no lean,
And so betwixt them both,
They licked the platter clean.

Jekyll and Hyde   *See* DR. JEKYLL AND MR. HYDE.

Julius Caesar   *Julius Caesar* is a play by WILLIAM SHAKESPEARE that tells the story of a group of men who killed Caesar, the Roman ruler, and took over the empire.

> **A** famous line from *Julius Caesar* is Caesar's last line, "Et tu, Brute?" ("Even you, Brutus?"), spoken when he discovers his friend Brutus among the assassins. ❧

King Arthur   King Arthur is the legendary hero of a group of stories about ancient England. He proved that he was a king because he was the only one who could pull a magic sword out of the stone that held it in the ground. The leader of the KNIGHTS OF THE ROUND TABLE, he was known as a just ruler who fought many battles and had many wonderful adventures.

Kipling, Rudyard   Rudyard Kipling was an English author of the late 1800s and early 1900s who is known for his stories, poems, and several children's books, such as *The Jungle Book* and *Just So Stories.*

Knights of the Round Table   The Knights of the Round Table were the knights of KING ARTHUR's court.

"Ladybug, Ladybug, Fly Away Home"   "Ladybug, Ladybug, Fly Away Home" is a nursery rhyme. It has many versions, but it is often recited as follows:

> Ladybug, ladybug,
> Fly away home,
> Your house is on fire,
> Your children all gone.

Lancelot, Sir   Sir Lancelot is the bravest and most famous of KING ARTHUR's knights.

King Arthur

The Legend of Sleepy Hollow. Ichabod Crane meets the Headless Horseman.

"Legend of Sleepy Hollow, The"   "The Legend of Sleepy Hollow" is a short story written in the early 1800s by the American author Washington Irving. The story is about a village schoolteacher, ICHABOD CRANE, who wants to marry a pretty farmgirl. One night he meets a terrifying ghost called the HEADLESS HORSEMAN, who chases him through the woods of Sleepy Hollow. Crane disappears and is never seen again. Some people think he has been carried off by the ghost, but others know that the Headless Horseman was really another man who wanted to marry the young farmgirl himself.

Lilliput   Lilliput is a land of tiny people that is one of the places that Lemuel Gulliver visits in the book *GULLIVER'S TRAVELS*, by Jonathan Swift.

limerick   A limerick is a humorous poem with five lines. One familiar limerick is:

A fly and a flea in a flue
Were imprisoned, so what could they do?
Said the fly, "Let us flee!"
Said the flea, "Let us fly."
So they flew through a flaw in the flue.

"Little Bo-peep"   "Little Bo-peep" is a nursery rhyme that begins:

Little Bo-peep has lost her sheep,
And can't tell where to find them:
Let them alone, and they'll come home,
Wagging their tails behind them.

"Little Boy Blue"   "Little Boy Blue" is a nursery rhyme that begins:

Little boy blue, come blow your horn,
The sheep's in the meadow, the cow's in the corn.

"Little Engine That Could, The"   "The Little Engine That Could" is a children's story by Watty Piper. The Little Engine is a train engine that tries to pull a load of toys over the top of the mountain. Even though it is not very powerful, it keeps saying, "I think I can, I think I can," as it struggles up the mountain. It finally succeeds where other engines had refused even to try.

"Little Jack Horner"   "Little Jack Horner" is a nursery rhyme:

Little Jack Horner sat in the corner,
Eating a Christmas pie;
He put in his thumb, and pulled out a plum,
And said, "What a good boy am I!"

"Little Miss Muffet"   "Little Miss Muffet" is a nursery rhyme:

Little Miss Muffet
Sat on a tuffet,
Eating her curds and whey;
There came a big spider,
Who sat down beside her
And frightened Miss Muffet away.

(A *tuffet* is a low seat.)

Little Red Hen, the   The Little Red Hen is a character in a FOLK TALE. She works hard to plant, hoe, and harvest wheat, and then grinds it into flour and bakes it into bread. At every stage she asks, "Who will help me?" but her animal companions always reply, "Not I." When the bread is baked, the hen asks, "Who will help me eat the bread?" and the others call out, "I will!" But the hen says that she has done each step alone, and she will eat the bread alone.

Little Red Riding Hood. Red Riding Hood with the wolf disguised as Grandmother.

"Little Red Riding Hood"   "Little Red Riding Hood" is a fairy tale. A little girl named Red Riding Hood sets off for her grandmother's house. In the woods, she meets a wolf and tells him where she is going. The wolf gets to the house first and eats up the grandmother. He then puts on her clothes and gets into her bed. When Little Red Riding Hood comes in, the wolf pretends to be the grandmother. The little girl is fooled and is soon eaten up by the wolf. But a huntsman passing by runs in and chops the wolf open. Out step Red Riding Hood and her grandmother, alive and well.

Little Women *Little Women* is a novel by LOUISA MAY ALCOTT about the four March sisters, Jo, Meg, Beth, and Amy, in a New England family of the 1800s.

> **O**ne of the most popular children's stories, *Little Women* is mostly autobiographical; that is, it tells about many things that happened to Louisa May Alcott and her family. ❧

Longfellow, Henry Wadsworth Henry Wadsworth Longfellow was a well-known American poet of the 1800s. Among his works are "The Song of HIAWATHA," about a real Indian hero, and "PAUL REVERE'S RIDE."

Macbeth *Macbeth* is a TRAGEDY by WILLIAM SHAKESPEARE. The nobleman Macbeth is told by three witches that he will become the king of Scotland. His wife persuades him to murder the king and take the throne himself. In order to stay in power, he must keep killing the people who oppose him. Finally, Macbeth himself is killed in battle.

magic carpet A magic carpet is a rug that can carry people wherever they wish to go. Magic carpets appear in Middle Eastern stories, such as those in the ARABIAN NIGHTS.

"Mary Had a Little Lamb" "Mary Had a Little Lamb" is a nursery rhyme that begins:

Mary had a little lamb,
Its fleece was white as snow,
And everywhere that Mary went,
The lamb was sure to go.

"Mary, Mary, Quite Contrary" "Mary, Mary, Quite Contrary" is a nursery rhyme:

Mary, Mary, quite contrary,
How does your garden grow?
With silver bells, and cockle shells,
And pretty maids all in a row.

Melville, Herman Herman Melville was an American author of the 1800s who wrote short stories and novels, among them *MOBY DICK*.

Merlin In the stories about KING ARTHUR, Merlin is a magician and the king's chief adviser.

metaphor A metaphor is a way of describing something by comparing it to something else, but without using the words *like* or *as*. For example, Christina Rossetti, an English writer of the 1800s, uses metaphors to describe the clouds and the sky in the poem "Clouds":

White sheep, white sheep,
On a blue hill,
When the wind stops
You all stand still.

If Rossetti had written, "The clouds are *like* white sheep," she would have been using a SIMILE.

"Mirror, mirror, on the wall" In the fairy tale about SNOW WHITE, Snow White's stepmother, the wicked queen, says these words to her mirror: "Mirror, mirror, on the wall, who is fairest of them all?"

Moby Dick In HERMAN MELVILLE's novel *Moby Dick*, Moby Dick is a huge white whale, so fierce that he can sink the boats of the sailors who try to hunt and kill him.

moral The moral is the lesson that a story or a fable is meant to teach. *See also* AESOP'S FABLES.

Mother Goose Mother Goose is the name used in English for the make-believe person who is supposed to have first told many famil-

Mother Goose. Drawing by Arthur Rackham.

iar nursery rhymes to children. They are often called Mother Goose rhymes, but in fact several people collected and told these songs and poems. Many nursery rhymes have been repeated by so many generations of people that we no longer know who first made them up.

narrator In a work of FICTION, the narrator is the person who tells the story.

Never-Never Land Never-Never Land is where PETER PAN's adventures take place.

Night before Christmas, 'Twas the These are the first words of a favorite Christmas poem by Clement C. Moore. It begins:

> 'Twas the night before Christmas, when all through the house
> Not a creature was stirring, not even a mouse.
> The stockings were hung by the chimney with care,
> In hopes that Saint Nicholas soon would be there.

novel A novel is a long story, written in prose. *THE ADVENTURES OF HUCKLEBERRY FINN, LITTLE WOMEN, MOBY DICK,* and *DAVID COPPERFIELD* are all novels. A person who writes novels is called a novelist.

"Now I Lay Me Down to Sleep" "Now I Lay Me Down to Sleep" is a child's prayer:

> Now I lay me down to sleep,
> I pray the Lord my soul to keep;
> If I should die before I wake,
> I pray the Lord my soul to take.

Odyssey (OD-i-see) The *Odyssey* is an EPIC by the ancient Greek poet HOMER. It is about the adventures of the Greek hero ODYSSEUS as he journeys back to his kingdom after the TROJAN WAR.

"Old King Cole" "Old King Cole" is a nursery rhyme that begins:

> Old King Cole was a merry old soul,
> And a merry old soul was he;
> He called for his pipe, and he called for his bowl,
> And he called for his fiddlers three.

"Old Mother Hubbard" "Old Mother Hubbard" is a nursery rhyme that begins:

> Old Mother Hubbard
> Went to the cupboard,
> To fetch her poor dog a bone;
> But when she got there
> The cupboard was bare,
> And so the poor dog had none.

Oliver Twist *Oliver Twist* is a novel by CHARLES DICKENS, an English writer of the 1800s. Oliver is a boy who does not know who his parents are. He runs away from a workhouse where he is badly treated. To survive, he has to join a gang of thieves. Oliver finally discovers his real family and escapes a life of crime.

One, if by land, and two, if by sea *See* "PAUL REVERE'S RIDE."

"One, two, buckle my shoe" "One, two, buckle my shoe" is a nursery rhyme that begins:

> One, two, buckle my shoe;
> Three, four, shut the door;

Five, six, pick up sticks;
Seven, eight, lay them straight;
Nine, ten, a big fat hen.

Open, Sesame "Open, Sesame" is the magic expression used in one of the tales of the ARABIAN NIGHTS. ALI BABA says, "Open, Sesame," to get into a secret cave where thieves have stored their treasure.

Othello *Othello* is a tragedy by WILLIAM SHAKESPEARE. Othello is a Moor, or dark-skinned MOSLEM, who is tricked by an evil soldier, Iago, into thinking that his wife has been unfaithful to him, and he kills her in a jealous rage. When he realizes that his wife had been innocent, he kills himself in his grief.

A line that is often quoted from the play is Othello's description of himself as "one that loved not wisely, but too well." ❧

"Owl and the Pussycat, The" "The Owl and the Pussycat" is a poem for children by Edward Lear. It begins:

The Owl and the Pussycat went to sea
In a beautiful pea-green boat.
They took some honey, and plenty of money,
Wrapped up in a five-pound note.

Paul Bunyan Paul Bunyan is a gigantic, powerful lumberjack who appears in many "tall tales," or legends, about the forests of the American North and Northwest. He is usually shown carrying an ax and wearing a flannel shirt and a knitted cap. His pet is a huge blue ox named Babe.

"Paul Revere's Ride" "Paul Revere's Ride," by HENRY WADSWORTH LONGFELLOW, is a poem based on a patriot of the REVOLUTIONARY WAR. Paul Revere rode to warn the villages of Lexington and Concord, near Boston, Massachusetts, that British troops were coming. The poem begins:

Listen, my children, and you shall hear,
Of the midnight ride of Paul Revere,
On the eighteenth of April, in Seventy-five;
Hardly a man is now alive
Who remembers that famous day and year.

The poem goes on to tell how Revere waited for a friend to hang one or two lamps in a church steeple to signal how the British were traveling: "One if by land, and two if by sea." When he saw two lamps, Revere began his ride.

pen name A pen name is a fictitious name, or pseudonym, used by a writer. It may be completely made up or may come from the writer's middle name or someone else's name. MARK TWAIN was the pen name of Samuel Langhorne Clemens; DR. SEUSS is the pen name of Theodore Seuss Geisel.

Peter Pan *Peter Pan* is a favorite children's play by the Scottish author J. M. Barrie. Peter Pan is a young boy in Never-Never Land who never wants to grow up. He lives with the fairy TINKER BELL, who teaches him to fly and protects him and his friends from danger. His enemy is the evil CAPTAIN HOOK, the leader of a band of pirates.

Peter Rabbit, The Tale of *The Tale of Peter Rabbit*, by the English illustrator and writer Beatrix Potter, is a favorite children's story about a mischievous little rabbit who gets into a farmer's garden and is almost caught.

"Pied Piper of Hamelin, The" "The Pied Piper of Hamelin" is an old folk story about a man who gets rid of all the rats in the town of Hamelin. He plays enchanting music on his pipe (a kind of flute), and the rats all follow him down to the river, where they drown. When the townspeople refuse to pay the pied piper, he uses his pipe to lure the children away from the town, and they are never seen again. Many people know this story from a long poem of the same name written by Robert Browning in the 1800s.

Pinocchio   *Pinocchio* is a book by the Italian writer C. Collodi. Pinocchio is a wooden puppet who wants to be a real boy. He is watched over by a good fairy, but he has many adventures before he proves himself worthy of becoming a real child. The fairy provides that whenever Pinocchio tells a lie, his nose grows longer, and everyone can see that he has been lying.

play   A play is a story that is performed by actors and actresses on a stage. It may consist only of dialogue (spoken words) or include music and dance. Plays are often presented in a building called a theater, but they can also be staged outdoors or in television programs. *See also* MUSICAL COMEDY.

plot   The plot is the structure of a story. Almost every story has a plot, whether it is a novel, short story, play, movie, or television show.

Poe, Edgar Allan   Edgar Allan Poe was an American author of the 1800s who wrote poems, horror stories, and detective stories, such as "The RAVEN" and "The Murders in the Rue Morgue."

poem   A poem is a work of literature that is written in lines, like songs. Poems often have a particular rhythm, or repeated beat. Sometimes the word at the end of one line RHYMES with the word at the end of another line. Poems that have no rhyme or regular rhythm are called free verse. A person who writes poems is called a poet.

Pollyanna   *Pollyanna*, by the American author Eleanor Porter, is a book about a young girl who always looks on the bright side of things.

Someone who is overly optimistic even when things are very difficult is called a pollyanna.

Pooh   *See* WINNIE-THE-POOH.

"Princess and the Pea, The"   "The Princess and the Pea," by the Danish writer HANS CHRISTIAN ANDERSEN, is a story about a prince who is searching for a true princess to marry. A young, bedraggled woman comes to his door and claims to be a true princess. To see whether she is telling the truth, the prince's mother covers a pea with many mattresses and offers this bed to the young woman. The next morning, the young woman says she couldn't sleep because there was something very hard in her bed. The queen then knows that the young woman is telling the truth, for only a true princess could be so sensitive.

"Puss-in-Boots"   "Puss-in-Boots" is a fairy tale about a clever cat who brings good fortune to its master.

"Rain, rain, go away"   "Rain, rain, go away" is a RHYME chanted by children when it rains:

> Rain, rain, go away,
> Come again another day.

"Rapunzel"   "Rapunzel" is a fairy tale about a girl who has long, beautiful hair. She is locked in a high tower, and the only way anyone can get into the tower is by calling, "Rapunzel, Rapunzel, let down your hair."

"Raven, The"   "The Raven" is a poem by EDGAR ALLAN POE, an American writer of the 1800s. A mysterious black bird visits the poet, who is mourning the loss of his beloved, and repeats, "Nevermore."

rhyme   When a word or the last part of a word sounds like another word or the last part

Rapunzel. Drawing by Walter Crane.

of another word, those words are said to rhyme; for example, *part* rhymes with *heart*, *rougher* rhymes with *tougher*, and *believable* rhymes with *inconceivable*.

"Ride a Cock-Horse"   "Ride a Cock-Horse" is a nursery rhyme:

> Ride a cock-horse to Banbury Cross,
> To see a fine lady upon a white horse;
> Rings on her fingers and bells on her toes,
> She shall have music wherever she goes.

"Rip Van Winkle"   "Rip Van Winkle" is a short story written in the early 1800s by the American author Washington Irving about a man who goes hunting in the mountains one day and falls asleep for twenty years.

Robin Hood   Robin Hood is a legendary English outlaw who stole from the rich to give to the poor. He and his band of men, including Friar Tuck and Little John, lived in Sherwood Forest.

Robinson Crusoe   *Robinson Crusoe* is a novel written in the 1700s by the English author Daniel Defoe. It tells how Robinson Crusoe, an English sailor, is shipwrecked on a desert island and lives there alone for many years. He survives with the help of his man, Friday, by making, finding, or growing everything he needs.

"Rock-a-Bye Baby"   "Rock-a-Bye Baby" is a nursery rhyme and lullaby:

> Rock-a-bye, baby, on the tree top;
> When the wind blows, the cradle will rock;
> When the bough breaks, the cradle will fall,
> And down will come baby, cradle and all!

Romeo and Juliet   *Romeo and Juliet* is a tragedy by WILLIAM SHAKESPEARE. Two young lovers, Romeo and Juliet, are kept apart by their families, who hate each other. When Romeo kills a cousin of Juliet's for killing one of his friends, he is forced to leave the city. Juliet's family tries to make her marry another man, but she drinks a potion to make it look as if she were dead. Romeo hears that she is dead and believes it. He goes to her tomb and kills himself by drinking poison. When Juliet awakens to find her lover dead beside her, she stabs herself.

Roses are red   "Roses are red" are the first words of a Valentine's Day poem. The poem has many forms, but in the United States it is often recited as follows:

> Roses are red, violets are blue,
> Sugar is sweet, and so are you.

"Rub-A-Dub-Dub"   "Rub-A-Dub-Dub" is a nursery rhyme that begins: "Rub-a-dub-dub,/Three men in a tub."

"Rumpelstiltskin"   "Rumpelstiltskin" is a fairy tale from the collection of the GRIMM BROTHERS. A little man named Rumpelstiltskin helps the beautiful young wife of a prince to spin straw into gold thread in exchange for her firstborn child. In order to keep her baby, she has to guess his name. When she discovers it, the dwarf destroys himself in a rage.

Sancho Panza   Sancho Panza is the companion of DON QUIXOTE and is his opposite in every way. He is short and fat while Don Quixote is tall and thin, he is uneducated while Quixote is well read, and he is practical and has common sense while Quixote is an idealist and a dreamer. Still, he agrees to be Don Quixote's squire (the assistant to a KNIGHT) and follows him on his adventures.

Scrooge   Scrooge is the stingy old man in CHARLES DICKENS's *A CHRISTMAS CAROL* whose life is changed when he meets a series of ghosts on Christmas Eve.

The name "Scrooge," meaning someone who is miserly, has become very common in English. The cartoonist Walt Disney even used the name for Donald Duck's stingy uncle, Scrooge McDuck. 🎸

Secret Garden, The   *The Secret Garden*, a book by Frances Hodgson Burnett, tells the story of Mary Lennox, a miserable girl who is sent to England to live with her uncle after the death of her parents in India. Mary discovers a garden on her uncle's property that has been locked up for years. She and her friends secretly restore the garden and become happy and healthy.

Seuss, Dr.   Dr. Seuss is the PEN NAME of the American writer Theodore Seuss Geisel. His picture books (for example, *The Cat in the Hat* and *How the Grinch Stole Christmas*) have fantastical characters and are written in humorous verse.

Seven Dwarfs   The Seven Dwarfs are the characters who take care of SNOW WHITE when she comes into their house. In the Walt Disney cartoon film of the story, the Seven Dwarfs are given the names Happy, Sleepy, Doc, Bashful, Sneezy, Grumpy, and Dopey.

Shakespeare, William   William Shakespeare was a great English writer of the late 1500s and early 1600s. His plays and poems are considered to be among the best literary works ever written. Some of his most familiar plays are *HAMLET*, *ROMEO AND JULIET*, *MACBETH*, *OTHELLO*, *JULIUS CAESAR*, and *A Midsummer Night's Dream*.

Sherlock Holmes   Sherlock Holmes is a famous fictional detective who appears in a series of novels and stories by the English writer Sir Arthur Conan Doyle. When investigating a crime, Holmes finds clues that other people have not noticed or understood. He always amazes the other people in the stories by cleverly getting to the bottom of any mystery.

Sherwood Forest   Sherwood Forest was where ROBIN HOOD and his men lived.

short story   A short story is a work of fiction in prose that is shorter than a novel. Often, a number of short stories are brought together to make a book.

simile   A simile describes something by comparing it to something else. Many common expressions are similes, such as, "He is as strong as an ox" and "He eats like a pig." Similes usually use the word *like* or *as*. In the poem "My Bed Is a Boat," by Robert Louis Stevenson, the first line contains a simile: "My bed is like a little boat." *Compare* METAPHOR.

"Simple Simon"   "Simple Simon" is a nursery rhyme. The first verse goes:

Simple Simon met a pieman
Going to the fair;
Says Simple Simon to the pieman,
"Let me taste your ware."

Sinbad the Sailor   Sinbad the Sailor is a merchant in one of the stories of the *ARABIAN*

NIGHTS. He sails around the world and has many fantastic adventures.

"Sing a Song of Sixpence" "Sing a Song of Sixpence" is a nursery rhyme. The first verses go:

> Sing a song of sixpence,
> A pocket full of rye;
> Four and twenty blackbirds
> Baked in a pie;
>
> When the pie was opened,
> The birds began to sing;
> Was not that a dainty dish,
> To set before the king?

"Sleeping Beauty" "Sleeping Beauty" is a fairy tale about a beautiful princess who is put under a curse that makes her sleep for one hundred years. When a handsome prince finds her and falls in love with her, his kiss releases her from the evil spell, and she awakens.

"Snow White" "Snow White" is a fairy tale in the collection of the GRIMM BROTHERS. Snow White is a beautiful girl with a wicked stepmother. The stepmother owns a magic mirror, and every day she asks it, "Mirror, mirror, on the wall, who is the fairest of them all?" At first the mirror always answers, "You are, my queen," but when Snow White grows to be a young woman, the mirror says that Snow White is the fairest. Enraged, the queen sends Snow White into the woods to be killed. Instead, the queen's servant lets the girl go. In the woods, Snow White finds the home of the SEVEN DWARFS, and she hides in their tiny cottage. The queen finds her, however, and tricks her into eating a poisoned apple, which makes the girl fall into a deep sleep. Finally Snow White is rescued by a prince, awakens, and becomes his wife.

stanza A stanza is a unit of lines in a poem usually arranged in a recurring pattern of RHYME or rhythm.

"Star Light, Star Bright" "Star Light, Star Bright" is a nursery rhyme:

> Star light, star bright
> First star I see tonight,
> I wish I may, I wish I might,
> Have the wish I wish tonight.

Superman Superman is a comic book hero who has also appeared in a television show and movies. He can fly, run faster than a speeding bullet, and leap tall buildings in a single bound. He uses these superhuman powers to protect people from evil and injustice.

Tarzan Tarzan is a character who has appeared in many books, comic books, and movies. As a baby, he is abandoned in the African jungle and raised by a family of apes. He grows up to become a strong hero.

"There is no joy in Mudville" "There is no joy in Mudville" is a line from the poem "Casey at the Bat," which tells the story of a baseball player on the team from Mudville. Casey comes to bat in the ninth inning with his team behind. He confidently lets two strikes go by before he swings mightily at the third pitch. The poem ends: "But there is no joy in Mudville — mighty Casey has struck out."

"There was a little girl" These are the first words of a poem by HENRY WADSWORTH LONGFELLOW. It begins:

> There was a little girl
> Who had a little curl
> Right in the middle of her forehead;
> And when she was good
> She was very, very good,
> But when she was bad she was horrid.

"There Was an Old Woman Who Lived in a Shoe" "There Was an Old Woman Who Lived in a Shoe" is a nursery rhyme:

> There was an old woman who lived in a shoe,
> She had so many children she didn't know
>   what to do;

She gave them some broth without any bread;
She whipped them all soundly and put them to bed.

"Thirty Days Hath September"   "Thirty Days Hath September" is a rhyme that helps us remember how many days there are in each month:

Thirty days hath September,
April, June, and November;
All the rest have thirty-one,
Excepting February alone,
And that has twenty-eight days clear
And twenty-nine in each leap year.

This little piggy went to market   These words are the first line of a toe-counting game. It is often recited as follows:

This little piggy went to market,
This little piggy stayed home,
This little piggy had roast beef,
This little piggy had none,
And this little piggy cried, "Wee-wee-wee-wee,"
All the way home.

Thoreau, Henry David   Henry David Thoreau was an American writer of the 1800s. In *Walden*, the book for which he is known, he tells about living in a cabin that he built in the woods on Walden Pond, in Concord, Massachusetts.

> Thoreau wrote a well-known essay, "Civil Disobedience," in which he says that people should follow their own conscience. If that means they must break the laws of their government, he says, they should be prepared to take the punishment given to them. ❧

"Three Bears, The"   *See* "Goldilocks and the Three Bears."

"Three Blind Mice"   "Three Blind Mice" is a nursery rhyme:

Three blind mice, see how they run!
They all ran after the farmer's wife,
She cut off their tails with a carving knife,
Did you ever see such a sight in your life,
As three blind mice?

"Three Little Pigs, The"   "The Three Little Pigs" is a children's story about three pigs who leave home to make their own way in the world. The first one builds a house of straw, the second a house of twigs, and the third a house of bricks. A wolf comes along and is able to blow the first two houses down, but the third is too strong, so the third little pig lives happily ever after. *See also* Big Bad Wolf.

Tinker Bell   In the story *Peter Pan*, Tinker Bell is a fairy who teaches Peter to fly and helps him and his friends.

Tolkien, J. R. R.   J. R. R. Tolkien was an English scholar of the 1900s. In *The Hobbit* and a series of three books, *The Lord of the Rings*, he wrote about the adventures of some small creatures called Hobbits.

Tom Sawyer, The Adventures of   *The Adventures of Tom Sawyer* is a novel by Mark Twain, an American writer of the 1800s. Tom is a clever boy with a strong imagination and a desire for adventure. In one famous scene, he tricks his friends into painting a fence that he was supposed to paint by himself.

Tom Thumb   Tom Thumb is the tiny hero of a fairy tale. When he is born, he is no bigger than his father's thumb, and he never grows any bigger.

"Tortoise and the Hare, The"   *See* "Hare and the Tortoise, The."

tragedy   A tragedy is a serious play in which the main character (usually an important, heroic person) meets with disaster, either

Mark Twain

Tweedledum and Tweedledee.
Drawing by John Tenniel.

because of a personal fault or through events that cannot be helped.

Treasure Island *Treasure Island* is an adventure story about a boy who finds a treasure map. Two men hire a ship to search for the treasure on an island. Among the ship's crew are the pirate Long John Silver and his men, who try to get the treasure for themselves. The story was written by Robert Louis Stevenson, a Scottish author of the 1800s.

"Trees" "Trees" is a poem by the American poet Joyce Kilmer. It is famous for these lines: "I think that I shall never see/A poem as lovely as a tree."

Twain, Mark Mark Twain was the PEN NAME of an American writer of the 1800s whose real name was Samuel Langhorne Clemens. *See also* HUCKLEBERRY FINN, THE ADVENTURES OF; TOM SAWYER, THE ADVENTURES OF.

Tweedledum and Tweedledee Tweedledum and Tweedledee are two identical fat twins that Alice meets in the story *Through*

the Looking Glass. See also ALICE IN WONDERLAND.

"Twinkle, twinkle, little star" "Twinkle, twinkle, little star" is a poem for children that is often sung. The first verse goes:

Twinkle, twinkle, little star,
How I wonder what you are!
Up above the world so high,
Like a diamond in the sky.

> **A**n ugly duckling is someone who turns out wonderfully after an unpromising beginning. ❧

"Ugly Duckling, The" "The Ugly Duckling," by the Danish writer HANS CHRISTIAN ANDERSEN, is a story about a baby bird who is hatched into a family of ducks. He is bigger and uglier than the rest of the ducklings, and the other barnyard creatures mock him. He leaves, but everywhere he goes he is threatened or laughed at. When spring comes, however, he finds he has grown up to be a beautiful swan.

Uncle Remus   Uncle Remus is a character in a series of stories by the American writer Joel Chandler Harris. He is an old black man who tells the folk tales of black people to a young white boy. Some of the stories about animals, such as the wily BRER RABBIT and his enemy, Brer Fox, are well known.

> **M**any of the Uncle Remus stories, such as the story of Brer Rabbit, were originally Afro-American folk tales. 🐾

Uncle Tom's Cabin   *Uncle Tom's Cabin*, by the American writer Harriet Beecher Stowe, was a famous novel of the 1800s that exposed the evils of slavery.

verse   Verse can be used to mean poetry in general or to refer to a stanza of a poem or song.

"Village Blacksmith, The"   "The Village Blacksmith" is a poem about a strong and hard-working man. It was written in the 1800s by the American poet HENRY WADSWORTH LONGFELLOW. The first lines of the poem are well known: "Under the spreading chestnut tree/The village smithy stands." (A *smithy* is where a blacksmith works.)

Whitman, Walt   Walt Whitman was an American poet of the 1800s whose chief work is called *Leaves of Grass*, a collection of poems. One of his poems, "O Captain! My Captain!," remembers the death of ABRAHAM LINCOLN.

Wilder, Laura Ingalls   Laura Ingalls Wilder was an American writer who was born in the pioneer days (the 1800s). In *The Little House in the Big Woods* and eight other books, she

gives many details about the everyday activities and adventures of the settlers.

William Tell   William Tell is a legendary hero of Switzerland who was able to shoot an apple off his son's head with an arrow.

Wind in the Willows, The   *The Wind in the Willows* is a book by the English author Kenneth Grahame. It describes the adventures of three animals, Toad, Mole, and Rat, and their friend Badger.

Winnie-the-Pooh   Winnie-the-Pooh is a toy bear who is the main character in several books for children by the English writer A. A. Milne. The author's son, Christopher Robin, is also a character in the books.

The Wizard of Oz. From left to right: Dorothy, the Cowardly Lion, the Tin Woodman, and the Scarecrow.

Wizard of Oz, The Wonderful   *The Wonderful Wizard of Oz*, by the American writer L. Frank Baum, tells about the adventure of a little girl, Dorothy. Dorothy and her dog, Toto, are carried by a tornado from Kansas to the land of Oz. There she meets many strange characters, including a scarecrow who wants a brain, a cowardly lion who wants courage, and a tin woodman who wants a heart. Many people know the story from the 1939 movie *The Wizard of Oz*, starring Judy Garland.

Wright, Richard   Richard Wright was an American novelist of the 1900s whose best-known book is *Native Son*.

"Wynken, Blynken and Nod"   "Wynken, Blynken and Nod" is a poem by the American author Eugene Field about a child falling asleep. It begins:

> Wynken, Blynken and Nod one night
> Sailed off in a wooden shoe —
> Sailed on a river of crystal light,
> Into a sea of dew.

Wynken and Blynken are eyes, Nod means the head, and the wooden shoe means the bed.

Mythology

Myths are traditional stories about gods, goddesses, and mortals with special powers, and they were an important part of the religious belief of many ancient peoples. Although we do not believe that the events in these stories actually took place as they are described, myths are still an important part of our culture. They often speak about the beginning of the world, about the forces of nature, about good and evil, and about universal human qualities and emotions. Every culture has some form of myths. The ones we are most familiar with are those of classical mythology (from the ancient Greek and Roman civilizations) and, to some extent, those of the Norse (Scandinavian and North German) peoples as well.

Many of the gods and goddesses listed here have two names, a Greek name and a Roman name. When the Greek civilization declined and the Romans conquered much of Europe and parts of Asia, they took over many of the Greek myths and gave the gods and goddesses new names in their own language, Latin. When two names are given together in the following entries, the *Greek* name is given first and the *Roman* name follows it in parentheses.

Achilles (uh-KIL-eez)   Achilles was the greatest Greek warrior in the TROJAN WAR. The only way to kill him was to attack his one weak spot, his heel. Today we use the term "Achilles' heel" to describe the one weakness in a person's character.

Adonis   Adonis was a Greek youth who was so handsome that even APHRODITE, the goddess of love, fell in love with him. Today we call any young man who is extremely handsome an Adonis.

Agamemnon (ag-uh-MEM-non) Agamemnon was the king who led the Greek forces in the TROJAN WAR.

Adonis. Detail of *Venus and Adonis* by Titian. National Gallery of Art, Washington; Widener Collection.

42

Amazons In Greek mythology, the Amazons were a tribe of female warriors who were known for their great size, strength, and fierceness.

Aphrodite (af-ruh-DEYE-tee) **(Venus)** Aphrodite was the beautiful goddess of love and beauty. *See also* HEPHAESTUS; VENUS.

> **A**phrodite was said to have been born from the sea foam. A famous picture by Botticelli, *The Birth of Venus*, shows her rising from the water on a seashell. ❧

Apollo (uh-POL-oh) Apollo was the god of prophecy, music, poetry, medicine, and light. He was a very important god for both the Greeks and the Romans because he controlled many of the activities necessary for civilized life. People often visited his oracle, or shrine, in the city of Delphi to ask him questions through a priestess. *See also* DELPHIC ORACLE.

Ares (AIR-eez) **(Mars)** Ares was the god of war. *See also* MARS.

Artemis (AHR-tuh-muhs) **(Diana)** Artemis was the goddess of the hunt. She is often pictured with a deer.

Arthur, King *See* KING ARTHUR *under "Literature."*

Athena (Minerva) Athena was the goddess of wisdom as well as the protector of Athens and other cities. Her birth was unusual: she sprang fully grown and in full armor from the head of ZEUS. The Parthenon, a beautiful temple overlooking the city of Athens, was dedicated to her.

Atlas Atlas was a TITAN, or giant, who rebelled against the gods. He was punished by being forced to hold up the earth and sky on

Athena

his shoulders for eternity. Today, a person who is very strong is sometimes called an Atlas.

Bacchus (BAK-uhs) Bacchus is the Roman name for DIONYSUS, god of wine.

Cerberus (SUR-buh-ruhs) Cerberus was the three-headed dog that guarded the gates of the underworld, HADES. He allowed all dead souls to enter but none to leave.

Ceres (SEER-eez) Ceres is the Roman name for DEMETER, goddess of farming. The word *cereal* comes from her name because cereal is made of grain and Ceres made the grain grow.

chimera (keye-MEER-uh) The chimera was a monster with the head of a lion, the body of a goat, and the tail of a dragon or serpent.

Cupid Cupid was the Roman god of love. When he shot his arrows into people's hearts, they fell in love. Cupid is now often pictured

Cupid

on Valentine's Day cards as a baby dressed in red or pink and carrying his bow and arrows.

Cyclops (SEYE-klops)   The Cyclopes (seye-KLOH-peez) were giants with only one eye, set in the middle of the forehead. The best-known Cyclops imprisoned the Greek hero ODYSSEUS and his men, but Odysseus finally escaped by tricking the giant and putting out his eye.

Daedalus (DED-l-uhs)   Daedalus was a famous Greek inventor who built the LABYRINTH, a great maze from which no one could escape. He was the father of ICARUS. *See also* MINOTAUR.

> **D**aedalus stands for inventiveness and great skill. 🙠

Delphic oracle   The Delphic oracle was a temple at the city of Delphi, in Greece, where people tried to find guidance and advice about the future. A priestess, who was also called an oracle, sat in the temple and uttered puzzling messages from the god APOLLO. These messages, also called oracles, prophesied (or predicted) the future. Priests heard the oracles and explained them.

Demeter (di-MEE-tuhr) **(Ceres)**   Demeter was the goddess of grain and of farming. When her daughter PERSEPHONE was kidnapped and taken to the underworld by HADES, she caused all the crops to wither and die as she searched the earth for her daughter. Finally, ZEUS allowed Persephone to join Demeter for eight months each year. Every year, when Demeter finds her daughter, her happiness brings the spring. But when she loses her again, the four months of winter begin. *See also* CERES.

Diana   Diana is the Roman name for ARTEMIS, goddess of the hunt.

Dionysus (deye-oh-NEYE-suhs) **(Bacchus)**   Dionysus was the god of wine. Because he showed people how to turn grapes into wine, he was often pictured with a wreath of grape leaves on his head. The religious groups, or cults, who worshiped him performed ceremonies in his honor.

Diana

Fates   The Fates were three old women who decided how long everybody would live and what would happen during their lifetimes. Every person's life was represented by a thread. One Fate spun the thread of life, one measured it, and one cut it at death.

Furies   The Furies were horribly ugly goddesses of revenge who had snakes for hair. They pursued people who were guilty of terrible crimes and drove them mad.

Golden Fleece   The Golden Fleece was the gold wool coat that had been taken from a magical, winged ram. It was the prize sought by the hero Jason in one of the quests, or journeys, of Greek mythology. *See also* Jason and the Golden Fleece.

Hades (HAY-deez) **(Pluto)**   Hades was the Greek and Roman god of the underworld. Hades is also the Greek name for the underworld, the gray and gloomy kingdom where the dead lived. *See also* Pluto.

Hector   Hector was the noblest of the Trojan warriors and the leader of the Trojan army. He was slain by Achilles, who dragged his body around the walls of Troy. *See also* Trojan War.

Helen of Troy   Helen was the most beautiful woman in the world. Even though she was Greek by birth, she was called Helen of Troy because Paris, a prince of Troy, kidnapped her and made her his princess. The Trojan War began when the Greeks sent a huge fleet of ships to attack Troy and win her back.

Hephaestus (hi-FES-tuhs, hi-FEE-stuhs) **(Vulcan)**   Hephaestus was the god of fire. He was also the blacksmith of the gods and used fire to make their tools and weapons. *See also* Aphrodite.

Hera (HEER-uh) **(Juno)**   Hera was the wife of Zeus and the queen of the Greek gods and goddesses. She was also the goddess of marriage. *See also* Juno.

Hercules. One of his Twelve Labors was to kill the Nemean lion. From its skin Hercules fashioned a garment that made him invulnerable. Courtesy, Museum of Fine Arts, Boston.

Hercules (HUR-kyuh-leez)   Hercules was the strongest man in the world and one of the greatest Greek heroes. He proved his strength by performing a series of supposedly impossible tasks called the Twelve Labors of Hercules. He is sometimes referred to as Herakles.

Hermes (HUR-meez) **(Mercury)**   Hermes was the messenger of the gods. He wore winged sandals and a winged cap, which allowed him to travel very fast, and carried a magic wand. *See also* Mercury.

hero   A hero is the important figure in a myth or legend and is usually especially strong and able. The word "hero" is also used to mean the main character in a literary or dramatic work.

Juno

Icarus (IK-uh-ruhs)   Icarus was the son of DAEDALUS, the great inventor. Daedalus made wings of wax that he and Icarus used to escape from the island where they were imprisoned. Daedalus warned his son not to fly too close to the sun, but Icarus ignored his warning. The heat of the sun melted the wings, and Icarus fell into the sea and drowned.

Jason and the Golden Fleece   Jason was one of the first great heroes of Greek mythology. In order to claim his rightful throne, he had to sail off in search of the GOLDEN FLEECE, the coat of a magical ram. This task was though to be impossible because the fleece was far away and guarded by a terrible snake. Jason sailed in his ship, the *Argo*, with other Greek heroes, called the Argonauts. He survived many perilous adventures and recovered the fleece.

Juno (JOOH-noh)   Juno is the Roman name for HERA, the wife of JUPITER and therefore queen of the gods and goddesses and the goddess of marriage. The month of June is named after her.

Jupiter   Jupiter is the Roman name for ZEUS, king of all the gods and goddesses. The largest planet in our solar system is named Jupiter.

Labyrinth (LAB-uh-rinth)   The Labyrinth was a large maze (a building full of confusing hallways and dead ends) designed by the inventor DAEDALUS. Those who entered the Labyrinth would get lost in the endless passages and could never escape. A monster, the MINOTAUR, was kept in the center of the Labyrinth.

leprechaun   In the folklore of Ireland, leprechauns are little men who look like elves. It is said that they will reveal (to anyone who catches them) a buried treasure — usually a crock of gold at the end of the rainbow.

Mars   Mars is the Roman name for ARES, the god of war. The planet Mars is named for him, possibly because it is red, the color of blood. The month of March is also named for Mars.

Medusa   Medusa was a Gorgon, a horrible monster with snakes for hair. Whoever looked at her directly was turned to stone. A hero, Perseus, was able to kill her by looking at her reflection in a polished shield as he aimed his sword.

Mercury   Mercury is the Roman name for HERMES, messenger of the gods. The planet closest to the sun is named Mercury because it moves swiftly in its orbit.

Midas (MEYE-duhs)   Midas was a greedy king who wished that everything he touched would turn to gold. The gods granted his wish, but he soon found that he could not eat because his food turned to gold as soon as he touched it. Midas asked the gods to take away his power so that he would not starve, and he was allowed to live a normal life again.

Mars. Courtesy, Museum of Fine Arts, Boston.

Minerva   Minerva is the Roman name for ATHENA, goddess of wisdom.

Minotaur   The Minotaur was a terrible monster, half man and half bull, who was kept in the LABYRINTH to kill anyone who entered. Finally, he was destroyed by the hero Theseus.

Mount Olympus   *See* OLYMPUS.

Narcissus (nar-SIS-uhs)   Narcissus was a beautiful youth who gazed into a pool and fell in love with his own reflection. He wasted away staring into the pool, and the gods turned him into the flower now called the narcissus.

> **N**arcissists are people who are interested only in themselves. ❧

Neptune   Neptune is the Roman name for POSEIDON, the god of the sea. He is often pictured as a bearded giant with a fish's tail and holding a trident (a three-pronged spear). The large planet that is eighth in order from the sun is named Neptune.

Odin (OH-din)   In Norse (Scandinavian and North German) mythology, Odin is the ruler of the gods as well as the god of wisdom, poetry, farming, and war. Wednesday is named after Odin, using a form of his name that begins with *W*. Friday is named after Odin's wife, Frigg, the Norse goddess of love.

Odysseus (oh-DIS-yoohs, oh-DIS-ee-uhs) **(Ulysses)**   Odysseus was a Greek hero who fought in the TROJAN WAR. Making his way home to Ithaca, he encountered many adventures and was imprisoned several times. His journey, or odyssey, took ten years, but he was finally reunited with his wife, PENELOPE, and his son. The story of this journey is told in the *ODYSSEY*, an EPIC (long poem) by the Greek poet HOMER. *See also* SIRENS.

Odysseus. Odysseus tied to the mast to keep from being lured to death by the Sirens' singing.

Oedipus (ED-uh-puhs)   Oedipus was a great but tragic king. He saved the city of Thebes by solving the riddle of the SPHINX. However, the

47

DELPHIC ORACLE predicted that he would kill his father and marry his mother. Because Oedipus had been abandoned as a child, he did not know his true parents. He argued with an old man on the road to Thebes and killed him; the man was his father. After he saved the city of Thebes, he married its queen, his mother. When he found out that the prophecy had come true, Oedipus blinded himself.

Olympus   Olympus is the legendary home of the Greek gods. It is an actual mountain in Greece, the highest in the country. The ancient Olympic games were a celebration held every four years on the plain of Olympus in honor of ZEUS. Our modern Olympic games are modeled after them.

Orpheus (AWR-fyoos, AWR-fee-uhs)   Orpheus was an outstanding musician who could play and sing nearly as well as the gods. When his wife, Eurydice, died, he went down to the underworld to find her. His music was so beautiful that HADES, the ruler of the underworld, was charmed into releasing her on the condition that Orpheus would go ahead and not look back at Eurydice until they had returned to earth. At the last moment, however, Orpheus turned around and looked. As a result, Eurydice vanished forever.

Pan   Pan was the god of shepherds and their flocks. He was half man and half goat, and he often played tunes on his musical pipes.

Pandora's box   Pandora's box was a box that ZEUS gave to Pandora, the first woman. Zeus warned her never to open it, but her curiosity was too strong. When she opened the box, all the evils and miseries of the world (such as

> **T**o open a Pandora's box is to create a situation that will cause great unhappiness. ❧

sorrow, disease, and hatred) flew out and have made us suffer ever since. At the bottom of the box, however, was one good thing: hope.

Paris   Paris was the prince of Troy who kidnapped HELEN and thus started the TROJAN WAR. Paris killed ACHILLES by piercing his heel with an arrow.

Pegasus. Drawing by Peter Paul Rubens.

Pegasus   Pegasus was a magnificent winged horse that could fly above the earth.

Penelope (puh-NEL-uh-pee)   Penelope was the wife of ODYSSEUS. Many men tried to convince her to marry them while Odysseus was making his ten-year journey home. But Penelope had faith that he would return and remained true to him.

Persephone (pur-SEF-uh-nee) **(Proserpina)** Persephone was the goddess of spring and the daughter of DEMETER. When she was kidnapped by HADES, she became queen of the underworld.

phoenix (FEE-niks)   The phoenix is a mythical bird that burns itself to death and arises from its ashes as a new phoenix.

Pluto   Pluto is the Roman name for HADES, the king of the underworld. The cold, dark planet that is farthest from the sun is named Pluto.

Poseidon (puh-SEYED-n) **(Neptune)** Poseidon was the god of the sea, one of the most powerful gods, after ZEUS. *See also* NEPTUNE.

Prometheus (pruh-MEETH-yoohs, pruh-MEE-thee-uhs) Prometheus was a TITAN, or giant, who stole fire from the gods and gave it to humans.

Prometheus was punished for his theft by Zeus, who had him chained to a rock while a great eagle gnawed at his liver. The giant was later rescued by Hercules. ❧

Proserpina (proh-SUR-puh-nuh)   Proserpina, the daughter of CERES, is the Roman name for PERSEPHONE, the goddess of spring. She is also called Proserpine.

Romulus and Remus

Romulus and Remus   Romulus and Remus were twin brothers who were taken from their mother and abandoned when they were

babies. A she-wolf found them and cared for them until they were taken in by a shepherd. Romulus later founded the city that was named for him — Rome, the capital of the Roman Empire.

Saturn   Saturn is the Roman name for the king of the TITANS. He was the father of JUPITER. The second largest planet in the solar system is named Saturn.

Sirens   The Sirens were evil creatures who lived on a rocky island. Their beautiful singing lured many passing sailors to their deaths. The wanderer ODYSSEUS wanted to hear the Sirens' song, so before he sailed past them he plugged his sailors' ears with wax and had them tie him to the mast of his ship.

Sphinx   The Sphinx was a terrible monster with the body of a winged lion and the head of a woman. She devoured anyone who could not answer this riddle: "What goes on four feet in the morning, on two at noon, and on three in the evening?" The answer is "man," because human beings crawl when they are babies, stand up and walk when they are grown, and walk with a cane (the third foot) when they are old. When OEDIPUS solved the riddle, the Sphinx killed herself. The most famous statue of a sphinx is the huge Great Sphinx of Egypt, near the PYRAMIDS.

Styx (STIKS)   The Styx was the river that dead souls crossed to get to the underworld. *See also* HADES.

Thor   In Norse (Scandinavian and North German) mythology, Thor is the god of thunder. His weapon is a hammer, which makes the sound of thunder. Thursday (Thor's Day) is named after him.

Titans (TEYET-ns)   The Titans were a race of immensely strong giants who ruled the universe until ZEUS and the other Greek gods overthrew them.

Trojan horse. An engraving showing the Greek army emerging from the Trojan horse.

Trojan horse   The Trojan horse was a gigantic wooden horse left by the Greek army outside the walls of TROY. Inside the horse were hidden the Greeks' best soldiers. Another Greek soldier, pretending to have deserted his comrades, tricked the Trojans into bringing the horse inside the city walls. That night the Greeks crept out of the horse and conquered Troy. *See also* TROJAN WAR.

Trojan War   The Trojan War was fought by the Greek cities against the walled city of TROY. It began when PARIS, a Trojan prince, kidnapped HELEN, a beautiful woman who was supposed to marry one of the Greek rulers. The Greeks sent a fleet of one thousand ships full of soldiers to attack Troy. After ten years, the Greeks still had not taken the city. ODYSSEUS, a Greek leader, finally made up a plan to trick the Trojans. He and his best soldiers hid inside the TROJAN HORSE, sur-

The story of the Trojan horse is the source of the saying "Beware Greeks bearing gifts"; that is, don't trust an enemy who brings you a present—it could be a trick. ❧

prised the Trojan army, and set fire to the city. After fierce fighting, Troy was conquered and destroyed. The story of the Trojan War is told in the *Iliad* of HOMER.

troll   In Norse (Scandinavian and North German) mythology, trolls were horrible dwarfs who lived in caves or other hidden places. They were very nasty and often hoarded treasure.

Troy   Troy was a powerful city in ancient Turkey. It sat on a hill overlooking the sea and was protected by high walls. Its people were called Trojans. *See also* TROJAN WAR.

Ulysses (yoo-LIS-eez)   Ulysses is the Roman name for ODYSSEUS.

unicorn   The unicorn is a mythical animal that looks like a small white horse with a long, straight, pointed horn growing from its forehead.

Venus   Venus is the Roman name for APHRODITE, goddess of love and beauty. The brightest planet in the sky is named Venus.

Vulcan   Vulcan is the Roman name for HEPHAESTUS, god of fire.

Zeus (ZOOHS) **(Jupiter)**   Zeus was the supreme ruler of the gods and goddesses of ancient Greece. He controlled the thunder and lightning and often used thunderbolts as weapons. He was more powerful than all the other gods and goddesses. *See also* JUPITER.

Music, Art, and Architecture

Many well-known songs, monuments, buildings, paintings, and artists are listed here. There are also a number of terms that will help you learn about the arts of music, painting, drawing, sculpture, and architecture. Some of the entries are the lyrics (words) of familiar songs. It is hard to appreciate them fully without their tunes, but the words themselves are an important part of American culture.

Acropolis

Abstract art   Abstract art is a kind of PAINTING, DRAWING, and SCULPTURE that has flourished in the twentieth century. It does not present objects as they appear to the eye but rather is an arrangement of colors and forms as imagined by the artist. PABLO PICASSO, Alexander Calder, and Henry Moore all created this form of art.

Acropolis   The Acropolis is the hill that overlooks the city of Athens, Greece. The ruins of ancient buildings, including the PAR-THENON, are on top of this hill. *Acropolis* means "high city" in Greek.

"Ain't Going to Study War No More"   *See* "DOWN BY THE RIVERSIDE."

alto   Alto is a singing voice that is lower than SOPRANO. It is sometimes called contralto.

"Amazing Grace"   "Amazing Grace" is a popular HYMN:

> Amazing Grace! How sweet the sound
> That saved a wretch like me!
> I once was lost, but now am found,
> Was blind, but now I see.

"America"   "America" is a patriotic song:

> My country, 'tis of thee,
> Sweet land of liberty,
> Of thee I sing:
> Land where my fathers died,
> Land of the pilgrims' pride,
> From every mountainside
> Let freedom ring.

51

"America the Beautiful"   "America the Beautiful" is a patriotic song that begins:

> O beautiful for spacious skies,
> For amber waves of grain,
> For purple mountain majesties
> Above the fruited plain!
> America! America!
> God shed his grace on thee
> And crown thy good with brotherhood
> From sea to shining sea!

Arch. The Arch of Triumph in Paris, France.

arch   An arch is a curved, sometimes pointed, opening. It can be part of a building's doorway or window or it can stand by itself, like the Gateway Arch in St. Louis, Missouri, or the Arch of Triumph in Paris, France.

architecture   Architecture is the art of designing buildings and other structures, including fortresses and walls (the BASTILLE and the GREAT WALL OF CHINA), and towers (the EIFFEL TOWER and SKYSCRAPERS). The person who practices this art is called an architect.

"Auld Lang Syne"   "Auld Lang Syne" is a Scottish poem by Robert Burns that is sung on New Year's Eve to mark the passing of the old year:

> Should auld acquaintance be forgot,
> And never brought to min'?
> Should auld acquaintance be forgot,
> And days of auld lang syne?

> For auld lang syne, my dear,
> For auld lang syne,
> We'll tak a cup o' kindness yet,
> For auld lang syne!

(*Auld lang syne* is Scottish for "long ago." *Tak* means "take.")

Bach, Johann Sebastian   Johann Sebastian Bach was a German composer, organist, and choirmaster of the 1700s. He composed a large number of instrumental and choral (singing) works, including "Jesu, Joy of Man's Desiring" and the *Brandenburg Concertos*.

ballad   A ballad is a simple song or poem that tells a story, such as "CLEMENTINE" and "CASEY JONES."

ballerina   A ballerina is a female dancer in a BALLET.

Ballet. Boston Ballet principal dancers Carla Stallings and Serge Lavoie in George Balanchine's *Theme and Variations*. Photograph copyright © by Jack Mitchell. Courtesy, the Boston Ballet.

Ludwig van Beethoven. Composing the *Missa Solemnis.*

Big Ben

ballet　A ballet is an elaborate dance presented on a stage set to instrumental music. It usually tells a story or sets a mood and is performed by a group of highly trained dancers, both male and female. The nineteenth-century Russian composer Peter Tchaikovsky wrote three ballets that are still performed today, *The Nutcracker* (frequently presented during the Christmas season), *Sleeping Beauty*, and *Swan Lake*.

bass　A bass voice is the lowest male singing voice.

"Battle Hymn of the Republic, The"
"The Battle Hymn of the Republic" is a patriotic HYMN from the CIVIL WAR:

> Mine eyes have seen the glory of the coming of the Lord;
> He is trampling out the vintage where the grapes of wrath are stored;
> He hath loosed the fateful lightning of his terrible swift sword;
> His truth is marching on.

Beethoven, Ludwig van　Ludwig van Beethoven was a German musician of the 1700s and 1800s who is considered one of the greatest composers of all time. The *Moonlight Sonata* and the "Ode to Joy" from the Ninth Symphony are two of his more familiar works. Although he began to grow deaf midway in his career, he continued to compose music.

Big Ben　Big Ben is the nickname for the bell in the clock tower of the Houses of Parliament in London, England.

blues　Blues are a kind of sad, slow music, usually with words, that developed among blacks in the southern United States. Major blues artists include Bessie Smith and Billie Holiday.

brass　The brass are a family of musical instruments that are often made of brass. Each instrument has a mouthpiece that the player blows through and a horn that produces the

53

Brooklyn Bridge

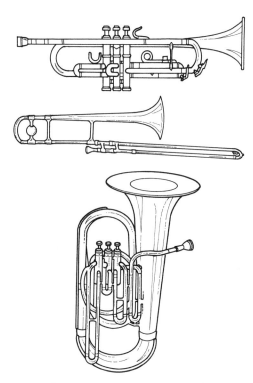

Brass instruments. From top to bottom: Trumpet, trombone, and tuba.

sound. The brass instruments are trumpets, trombones, tubas, bugles, cornets, and French horns.

Brooklyn Bridge   The Brooklyn Bridge spans the East River between Manhattan and Brooklyn in New York City. When it was built in the late 1800s, it was one of the longest bridges in the world.

If a person is described as someone who "tries to sell the Brooklyn Bridge," it means that the person is extremely dishonest (since the bridge is actually public property). ❧

"Camptown Races"   "Camptown Races" is an American FOLK SONG by Stephen Foster:

The Camptown ladies sing this song,
Doo-da, doo-da,
The Camptown racetrack's five miles long,
Oh, doo-da day.
Goin' to run all night!
Goin' to run all day!
I'll bet my money on the bob-tail nag —
Somebody bet on the bay.

Capitol   *See* CAPITOL *under "Politics and Economics."*

carol   A carol is a FOLK SONG that expresses happiness or joy and is often sung on festive holidays, such as Christmas. "Silent Night," "O Come, All Ye Faithful," and "Deck the Halls" are Christmas carols.

"Casey Jones"   "Casey Jones" is a popular American FOLK SONG about a railroad engineer who died in a train crash. It starts:

Come all you rounders, for I want you to hear
The story of a brave engineer.
Casey Jones was the rounder's name,
On a big eight-wheeler of a mighty fame.

cathedral   A cathedral is a Christian church that is usually the home church of a BISHOP. Cathedrals are often large, impressive buildings with high arches, domed ceilings, and stained-glass windows.

classical music   Classical music is complex music written for an ORCHESTRA or for smaller groups of instruments. Some of the most notable composers of classical music are BACH, BEETHOVEN, Brahms, Haydn, MOZART, and Tchaikovsky.

"Clementine"   "Clementine" is an American FOLK SONG that begins:

In a cavern, in a canyon,
Excavating for a mine,
Dwelt a miner, forty-niner,
And his daughter, Clementine.

Colosseum

Conductor. Arthur Fiedler conducting the Boston Symphony Orchestra.

Oh, my darling, oh, my darling,
Oh, my darling Clementine,
You are lost and gone forever,
Dreadful sorry, Clementine.

(A FORTY-NINER is someone who took part in the California gold rush of 1849.)

Colosseum   The Colosseum was a large stadium where competitions were held in ancient Rome. Its ruins are still standing. Today, sports arenas called coliseums are named after this building.

conductor   A conductor directs a group of musicians to make sure that they are playing at the right speed and volume.

country and western music   Songs about love and everyday life that have a regular beat and usually rhymed lyrics are examples of country and western music. It is especially popular in the southeastern United States. Well-known country and western singers are Hank Williams, Loretta Lynn, and Johnny Cash.

Disney, Walt   *See* WALT DISNEY *under "American History Since 1865."*

"Dixie"   "Dixie" is a battle song that was sung by Confederate soldiers during the CIVIL WAR. It begins:

I wish I was in the land of cotton,
Old times there are not forgotten.
Look away, look away,
Look away, Dixie land.

The word *Dixie* has been used as a nickname for the SOUTH since the Civil War.

dome   A dome is a roof that is shaped like an upside-down bowl. The CAPITOL in Washington, D.C., has a dome.

"Down by the Riverside"   "Down by the Riverside" is an American SPIRITUAL:

Gonna lay down my burden,
Down by the riverside, down by the riverside.
Down by the riverside,
Gonna lay down my burden,
Down by the riverside,
Going to study war no more.

"Down in the Valley"   "Down in the Valley" is an American FOLK SONG:

Down in the valley, the valley so low,
Hang your head over, hear the wind blow.
Hear the wind blow, dear, hear the wind blow,
Hang your head over, hear the wind blow.

drawing   Drawing is the creation of an image by producing lines on a surface, usually with pencils, pens, or crayons. In drawing, the outline of a figure is marked by a noticeable line, whereas in PAINTING, lines are usually blended. Cartoons are examples of drawings.

"Drunken Sailor, The"   "The Drunken Sailor" is a sea chantey, a sailors' work song, that is set to an Irish dance tune:

Oh, what shall we do with a drunken sailor,
What shall we do with a drunken sailor,
What shall we do with a drunken sailor,
Early in the morning?

Way, hay, and up she rises,
Way, hay, and up she rises,
Way, hay, and up she rises,
Early in the morning!

Eiffel Tower (EYE-fuhl) The Eiffel Tower is a tall structure that is probably the most familiar landmark in Paris, France. It is made of steel girders that curve from the ground upward into a long thin tower.

Empire State Building The Empire State Building is an office building in New York City that was built in the 1930s. It was the tallest building in the world for many years.

filmmaking A very popular art form, used by such artists as Charlie Chaplin, an early actor in silent movies, and WALT DISNEY.

folk song A folk song is a simple song, like a BALLAD, that is passed down from generation to generation by word of mouth. More recent songs, composed in this century by Pete Seeger and Woody Guthrie, for example, are called folk songs because they were inspired by the older tradition.

"God Bless America" "God Bless America" is a patriotic American song that begins: "God bless America, / Land that I love."

Golden Gate Bridge   The Golden Gate Bridge, in San Francisco, California, is noted for its graceful design and is the second longest suspension bridge in the world.

"Gonna Lay Down My Burden"   *See* "DOWN BY THE RIVERSIDE."

Eiffel Tower

Golden Gate Bridge

gospel music   Gospel music is strong and rhythmic religious music that is especially popular in the southern United States.

Great Wall of China   The Great Wall of China is an ancient stone wall that runs for 1500 miles along the northern border of China.

harmony   Harmony is the pleasing sound that results when different musical notes are played or sung together.

"Here We Go 'Round the Mulberry Bush"   "Here We Go 'Round the Mulberry Bush" is a children's singing game:

Here we go round the mulberry bush,
The mulberry bush, the mulberry bush;
Here we go round the mulberry bush,
So early in the morning.

"Home on the Range"   "Home on the Range" is a cowboy song about life in the old American West:

Oh, give me a home where the buffalo roam,
Where the deer and the antelope play,
Where seldom is heard a discouraging word
And the skies are not cloudy all day.

"Hush, little baby"   These are the first words of a well-known lullaby (a song used to soothe a baby to sleep). The first few verses go:

Hush, little baby, don't say a word,
Papa's going to buy you a mocking bird.
If that mocking bird won't sing,
Papa's going to buy you a diamond ring.

hymn   A hymn is a song that is sung as part of a religious service as well as at school assemblies and family gatherings. "God of Our Fathers," "A Mighty Fortress Is Our God" (by MARTIN LUTHER), "For All the Saints," and "Praise to the Lord, the Almighty" are favorite hymns. They are collected in books called hymnals.

"I've Been Working on the Railroad"   "I've Been Working on the Railroad" is an American FOLK SONG:

I've been working on the railroad
All the livelong day,
I've been working on the railroad
Just to pass the time away.
Don't you hear the whistle blowing?
Rise up so early in the morn.
Don't you hear the Captain shouting,
"Dinah blow your horn."

igloo   An igloo is a domed house built of ice or hard snow in which Eskimos live. (An Eskimo is a native of the far northern regions of North America.)

jazz   Jazz is a form of American music invented by black musicians in New Orleans, Louisiana, early in the twentieth century. It is America's most important contribution to the world of music. Prominent jazz musicians include Louis Armstrong, Duke Ellington, Benny Goodman, and Ella Fitzgerald.

> **F**amous American jazz musicians include Duke Ellington, Count Basie, Louis Armstrong, Benny Goodman, and Ella Fitzgerald. ❧

"John Brown's Body"   "John Brown's Body" is a song written during the CIVIL WAR in honor of John Brown, who fought against slavery. It begins: "John Brown's body lies a-moldering in the grave." "The BATTLE HYMN OF THE REPUBLIC" was written to this tune.

"John Henry"   "John Henry" is an American FOLK SONG about a race to build a railroad between a machine and a strong black man with a hammer. John Henry tried to build more track than the machine and died from his heroic effort. One verse goes:

John Henry told his captain,
Says, "A man ain't nothin' but a man,
And before I'd let your steam drill beat me
   down, Lord,
I'd die with the hammer in my hand."

Leaning Tower of Pisa

"Joshua Fit the Battle of Jericho"
"Joshua Fit the Battle of Jericho" is an American SPIRITUAL based on the biblical story of Joshua:

> Joshua fit the battle of Jericho,
> Jericho, Jericho,
> Joshua fit the battle of Jericho,
> And the walls come tumbling down.

("Fit" means "fought.") *See also* JERICHO.

Leaning Tower of Pisa   The Leaning Tower of Pisa is a tall, round building in Pisa, Italy, that was constructed during the RENAISSANCE. Soon after it was built, its foundation sank, causing it to lean.

Leonardo da Vinci   Leonardo da Vinci was a great Italian artist, scientist, and inventor who lived during the RENAISSANCE. He

> Leonardo kept notebooks of his sketches, including designs for flying machines and other technological inventions. ❧

painted such works as *The Last Supper* and the *MONA LISA*, perhaps the most famous painting in the world.

Lincoln Memorial   *See* LINCOLN MEMORIAL *under "Politics and Economics."*

"London Bridge Is Falling Down"
"London Bridge Is Falling Down" is a children's singing game:

> London Bridge is falling down,
> Falling down, falling down,
> London Bridge is falling down,
> My fair lady.

lyrics   Lyrics are words that are set to music.

melody   A melody is a recognizable tune.

Michelangelo   Michelangelo was an Italian painter and sculptor of the RENAISSANCE. Considered one of the greatest artists of all time, he is best known for his Sistine Chapel frescoes (wall paintings) and for his sculptures *David* (the boy who slew the giant Goliath in the Old Testament) and the *Pietà* (a pietà is the figure of Mary, the mother of Jesus, holding Jesus' dead body).

Mona Lisa   The *Mona Lisa* is a painting by LEONARDO DA VINCI that portrays a woman sitting with her hands crossed and with a curious half-smile on her face. Probably the most famous painting in the world, it hangs in the Louvre, in Paris, France.

Mozart, Wolfgang Amadeus   Wolfgang Amadeus Mozart was an Austrian musician of the 1700s who began composing music when he was only five years old. Among the great

Mona Lisa. Painting by Leonardo da Vinci.

Musical notation. The first few bars from *The Return Quick Step.*

variety of choral (singing) and orchestral music he wrote, two operas, *The Magic Flute* and *The Marriage of Figaro,* are especially well known.

museum   A museum is a building that displays objects considered to be of lasting interest and value in a particular subject, such as art, history, science, and sports. There are museums in almost every city; some especially notable ones, such as the Metropolitan Museum of Art, in New York City, the Louvre, in Paris, France, the British Museum, in London, England, and the Hermitage, in Leningrad, USSR, exhibit paintings, drawings, and sculpture. The National Air and Space Museum, part of the Smithsonian Institution in Washington, D.C., displays aircraft, old and new. The National Baseball Hall of Fame, in Cooperstown, New York, is devoted to the history of baseball.

musical comedy   A musical comedy, sometimes called a musical, is a play or film that includes song and dance as major elements. *The Sound of Music, My Fair Lady, Annie,* and *Cats* are all musicals.

musical instruments   Musical instruments are the devices used to make music. They are divided into four main groups, often called families: BRASS, PERCUSSION, STRINGS, and WOODWINDS.

musical notation   The standard way of writing music so that it can be played or sung is called musical notation.

"My country, 'tis of thee"   These words are the first line of the patriotic song "AMERICA."

national anthem   A national anthem is the official song of a country. The national anthem of the United States is "The STAR-SPANGLED BANNER." It is sometimes called "The National Anthem." Two other familiar

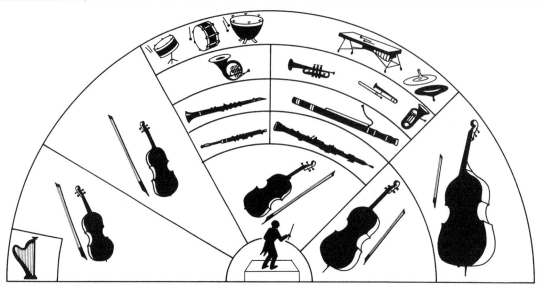

Orchestra. One arrangement of families of instruments in a symphony orchestra.

national anthems are those of Canada, "O Canada," and France, "La Marseillaise."

"Nobody Knows the Trouble I've Seen" "Nobody Knows the Trouble I've Seen" is an American SPIRITUAL. It begins: "Nobody knows the trouble I've seen, / Nobody knows but Jesus."

"O beautiful for spacious skies" These words are the first line of the patriotic song "AMERICA THE BEAUTIFUL."

"O Susanna" "O Susanna" is an American FOLK SONG. The refrain is:

O, Susanna! O, don't you cry for me,
I've come from Alabama, with my banjo on my knee.

"On Top of Old Smoky" "On Top of Old Smoky" is an American FOLK SONG:

> **S**ome well-known operas are *Aïda, Carmen,* and *The Magic Flute.* 🎵

On top of old Smoky
All covered with snow,
I lost my true lover
By courtin' too slow.

opera An opera is a play set to music in which the lines are all sung instead of spoken and is performed by an ORCHESTRA, singers, and sometimes dancers. Operas usually have many characters, dramatic action, and elaborate stage sets. *Don Giovanni, Madame Butterfly,* and *Aïda* are all operas.

orchestra An orchestra is a large group of musicians who play STRING, WOODWIND, BRASS, and PERCUSSION instruments. The musicians are led by a CONDUCTOR.

organ The organ is a keyboard instrument that produces sound through large pipes. Large organs are found in churches and SYNAGOGUES. Smaller, electronic organs can be played at home.

painting A painting is an artwork that is created by the application of paints to a surface. There are several different types of paintings. A portrait is a painting of a person; for example, the *MONA LISA.* A landscape repre-

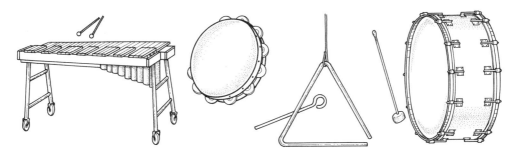

Percussion instruments. From left to right: Xylophone, tambourine, triangle, and bass drum.

sents scenery. A still life shows inanimate objects (things that do not move), such as a bowl of fruit on a table. Other types of painting are examples of ABSTRACT ART.

Parthenon   The Parthenon was a beautiful temple overlooking the city of Athens, Greece. It is now in ruins, but its white marble columns are often visited by tourists. *See also* ACROPOLIS.

"Pat-a-Cake, Pat-a-Cake"   "Pat-a-Cake, Pat-a-Cake" is a hand-clapping song enjoyed by young children:

> Pat-a-cake, pat-a-cake, baker's man,
> Bake me a cake as fast as you can;
> Pat it and prick it, and mark it with B,
> Put it in the oven for baby and me.

percussion   Percussion describes the family of musical instruments that are played by striking them. They include all kinds of drums, such as snare, bass, and kettle drums (also called timpanies), as well as triangles, tambourines, wood-blocks, and xylophones. Pianos are also considered percussion instruments because the keys control hammers that hit strings.

Peter and the Wolf   *Peter and the Wolf* is a piece of music for an ORCHESTRA by the Russian composer Sergei Prokofiev. Through the music, it tells the story of a disobedient boy's encounter with a wolf.

Picasso, Pablo   Pablo Picasso was a Spanish painter of the twentieth century and one of the most influential contemporary artists.

printmaking   Printmaking is an art form in which a design is created on a surface, then covered with ink or dye and stamped or pressed on a piece of paper, thus printing a copy of the design on the paper. Many copies of the original design can be made in this fashion. Posters are often made this way.

Pyramids

Pyramids   The Pyramids are huge stone structures, shaped like four triangles that rise to a point, that were built as tombs for the rulers of ancient Egypt. Three of the greatest Pyramids are still standing at Giza, near Cairo, Egypt.

Rembrandt   Rembrandt was a Dutch painter of the seventeenth century and is considered one of the greatest European painters. He is especially known for his fine portraits and for *The Night Watch*, which hangs in the Rijksmuseum in Amsterdam, the Netherlands.

rhythm   Rhythm is the pattern of stressed and unstressed notes in music and poetry. The *down beat* is the name for the main stress in rhythm.

"Ring Around the Rosies"   "Ring Around the Rosies" is a children's singing game:

> Ring around the rosies,
> A pocket full of posies,
> Ashes, ashes,
> We all fall down.

There are many ways of singing this song. Sometimes it begins: "Ring-a-ring o' roses." Sometimes the children say, "A-tishoo! A-tishoo," before they all fall down.

rock 'n' roll   Rock 'n' roll is a form of popular music that grew out of GOSPEL MUSIC and COUNTRY AND WESTERN MUSIC in the 1950s. Elvis Presley, the Supremes, and the Beatles were early rock 'n' roll stars.

round   A round is a song that is begun at different times by different voices and results in harmonious singing. Two rounds are "Row, Row, Row Your Boat" and "Frère Jacques."

"Row, Row, Row Your Boat"   "Row, Row, Row Your Boat" is a popular round:

> Row, row, row your boat,
> Gently down the stream,
> Merrily, merrily, merrily, merrily,
> Life is but a dream.

sculpture   Sculpture is the art of creating three-dimensional figures or designs out of wood, stone, clay, or metal. Two common types of sculpture are statues and busts. A statue usually represents a person, such as the STATUE OF LIBERTY or MICHELANGELO's *David*. A bust portrays just the head and shoulders of a person. Modern sculpture sometimes represents only a shape rather than people or things.

skyscraper   Skyscrapers are extremely tall buildings. Two cities known for their skyscrapers are New York (the EMPIRE STATE BUILDING, the World Trade Center) and Chicago (the Sears Tower, the John Hancock Building).

soprano   A soprano voice is the highest female singing voice.

spiritual   A spiritual is a religious FOLK SONG, such as "SWING LOW, SWEET CHARIOT" and "WHEN THE SAINTS GO MARCHING IN." Many spirituals were first composed and sung by African slaves.

Francis Scott Key wrote the words to "The Star-Spangled Banner" during the War of 1812, when he saw the U.S. flag still flying over Fort McHenry, in Maryland, after the British troops had attacked all night. ❧

"Star-Spangled Banner, The"   "The Star-Spangled Banner," which was written by Francis Scott Key during the War of 1812, is the NATIONAL ANTHEM of the United States:

> Oh, say, can you see by the dawn's early light,
> What so proudly we hailed at the twilight's last gleaming?
> Whose broad stripes and bright stars, through the perilous fight,
> O'er the ramparts we watched were so gallantly streaming?
> And the rockets' red glare, the bombs bursting in air,

String instruments. Top: Violin. Bottom, from left to right: Harp and cello.

Gave proof through the night that our flag was still there.
Oh, say, does that star-spangled banner yet wave
O'er the land of the free and the home of the brave?

Statue of Liberty   *See* STATUE OF LIBERTY *under "Politics and Economics."*

strings   The strings are the family of musical instruments that use strings to produce sound. Some are played by drawing a bow over their strings, such as violins, cellos, violas, and double basses. Others are plucked with the fingers or a pick; these include harps, guitars, banjos, and mandolins.

"Swing Low, Sweet Chariot"   "Swing Low, Sweet Chariot" is an American SPIRITUAL:

I looked over Jordan, and what did I see,
Coming for to carry me home?
A band of angels coming after me,
Coming for to carry me home.
Swing low, sweet chariot,
Coming for to carry me home.

symphony   A symphony is a long piece of music usually with four parts, called movements, that is played by an ORCHESTRA. Haydn, MOZART, BEETHOVEN, and Brahms composed some of the greatest symphonies.

> **T**hree composers known for their symphonies are Beethoven, Haydn, and Mozart. ❧

symphony orchestra   A symphony orchestra is a full-size ORCHESTRA usually devoted to playing CLASSICAL MUSIC.

Taj Mahal   The Taj Mahal is a marble building in India built by an Indian ruler in memory of his wife. It is one of the world's most beautiful buildings and a popular tourist attraction.

Taj Mahal

63

"Take Me Out to the Ball Game" "Take Me Out to the Ball Game" is a popular song about baseball. It begins:

Take me out to the ball game,
Take me out with the crowd.
Buy me some peanuts and Cracker Jack,
I don't care if I never come back.

tenor A tenor is the highest adult male singing voice.

tepee A tepee is a tent shaped like a cone that is made of skins or bark. It is used by North American Indians.

"This Land Is Your Land" "This Land Is Your Land" is an American FOLK SONG by Woody Guthrie. It begins: "This land is your land, this land is my land."

"Turkey in the Straw" "Turkey in the Straw" is an American folk dance tune, usually played on a fiddle:

Turkey in the straw, turkey in the hay,
Roll 'em up and twist 'em up a high tuckahaw,
And hit 'em up a tune called Turkey in the Straw.

"Twelve Days of Christmas, The" "The Twelve Days of Christmas" is a Christmas CAROL that begins:

On the first day of Christmas,
My true love sent to me
A partridge in a pear tree.

Each verse of the song adds a line, and a new gift, for each of the twelve days of the Christmas season.

Venus de Milo *Venus de Milo* is a Greek statue of Venus that is known for its beauty. It is in the Louvre, in Paris, France.

Washington Monument *See* WASHINGTON MONUMENT *under "Politics and Economics."*

"Way down upon the Swanee River, / Far, far away" These words are the first lines of

Venus de Milo

an American FOLK SONG called "The Old Folks at Home," by Stephen Foster:

Way down upon the Swanee River,
Far, far away,
There's where my heart is turning ever;
There's where the old folks stay.

"We Shall Overcome" *See* "WE SHALL OVERCOME" *under "Politics and Economics."*

"When Johnny Comes Marching Home" "When Johnny Comes Marching Home" is a song from the CIVIL WAR:

When Johnny comes marching home again,
Hurrah! hurrah!
We'll give him a hearty welcome then,
Hurrah! hurrah!
The men will cheer, the boys will shout,
The ladies, they will all turn out,
And we'll all feel gay
When Johnny comes marching home.

"When the Saints Go Marching In"

"When the Saints Go Marching In" is an American SPIRITUAL about entering heaven that was played by New Orleans JAZZ musicians:

Oh, when the saints go marching in,
Oh, when the saints go marching in,
Lord, I want to be in that number,
When the saints go marching in.

Whistler's Mother   Whistler's Mother is the popular name of a well-known painting of the mother of the artist James Whistler. (Its real name is *Arrangement in Grey and Black*.)

White House   *See* WHITE HOUSE *under "Politics and Economics."*

woodwinds   Woodwinds are the family of long, thin musical instruments that make a softer sound than the brass instruments. (All woodwinds used to be made of wood, but now many are made of metal.) Many woodwinds use reeds, which are thin pieces of wood that vibrate when a musician blows air through them. The woodwinds include piccolos, flutes, clarinets, oboes, English horns, saxophones, recorders, fifes, and bassoons.

Wright, Frank Lloyd   Frank Lloyd Wright was an American architect known for his highly original methods of uniting structures with their surroundings. He designed both houses and public buildings, such as Fallingwater, in Bear Run, Pennsylvania, and the Guggenheim Museum, in New York City.

"Yankee Doodle"

"Yankee Doodle" is an American song sung during the REVOLUTIONARY WAR. The British soldiers first sang it to make fun of the Americans, but the American

Woodwind instruments. Top: Flute. Bottom, from left to right: Clarinet and tenor saxophone.

soldiers liked it and began to sing it themselves:

Yankee Doodle came to town
Riding on a pony,
He stuck a feather in his hat
And called it macaroni.
Yankee Doodle, keep it up,
Yankee Doodle dandy,
Mind the music and the step,
And with the girls be handy.

The early settlers of New York were Dutch, and the Dutch name for Johnny is Janke, pronounced "Yankee." In the 1600s *doodle* meant "a simple, foolish person." ❧

The Bible

The Bible is the holy book of the Jewish and Christian religions. It is really two sets of books, one, the Old Testament, stemming from an earlier period of history than the other, the New Testament. For Christians, both sets are the basis of their beliefs. For Jews, only the earlier set is valid, and they use the terms *old* and *new* only as a matter of convenience. The Old Testament, principally written in Hebrew, tells the story of the ancient Israelites and their special relationship with God. The later set was originally written in Greek and is the story of the life and teachings of Jesus Christ and the early Christian church.

The Bible is by far the best-known book in our culture. Hundreds of its sayings have become part of our everyday speech. Biblical stories are frequently referred to in books, newspapers, magazines, and on television. Many paintings and other works of art portray people or scenes from the Bible. Furthermore, the Bible is the basis of some of our most important ideas about law and government. Because it is such a basic part of our culture, it is important for you to know something about the Bible, regardless of your individual religious belief.

Abraham and Isaac   According to the Old Testament, Abraham was the first of the Israelites. Once God decided to test Abraham's faith and ordered him to kill his son Isaac and offer him to God as a sacrifice. Though Abraham loved Isaac very much, he started to obey God's command, but an angel appeared and told him not to hurt Isaac. The angel said that Abraham already proved his faith in God when he was willing to give up the son he loved.

Adam and Eve   According to the Old Testament, Adam and Eve were the first man and the first woman in the world. After God created Adam, he made Eve out of one of Adam's ribs. He placed Adam and Eve in a beautiful garden, called EDEN, where all kinds of fruit grew on the trees. God warned Adam not to eat the fruit on one particular tree. One day a serpent came up to Eve and told her that if she ate the forbidden fruit, she would know good and evil. Eve ate some of the fruit and then gave some to Adam. When God learned that Adam and Eve had disobeyed him, he punished them by forcing them to leave Eden.

apostles   In the New Testament, Jesus had twelve main followers who traveled with him as he spread his religious beliefs. They have become known as the apostles.

Adam and Eve. Albrecht Dürer's engraving *The Fall of Man.* Courtesy, Museum of Fine Arts, Boston.

Hebrew Scriptures

Genesis	II Kings	Nahum	Ruth
Exodus	Isaiah	Habakkuk	Lamentations
Leviticus	Jeremiah	Zephaniah	Ecclesiastes
Numbers	Ezekiel	Haggai	Esther
Deuteronomy	Hosea	Zechariah	Daniel
Joshua	Joel	Malachi	Ezra
Judges	Amos	Psalms	Nehemiah
I Samuel	Obadiah	Proverbs	I Chronicles
II Samuel	Jonah	Job	II Chronicles
I Kings	Micah	Song of Songs	

Old Testament

Jerusalem Version	King James Version	Jerusalem Version	King James Version
Genesis	Genesis	Song of Solomon	Song of Solomon
Exodus	Exodus	Wisdom	
Leviticus	Leviticus	Ecclesiasticus	
Numbers	Numbers	Isaiah	Isaiah
Deuteronomy	Deuteronomy	Jeremiah	Jeremiah
Joshua	Joshua	Lamentations	Lamentations
Judges	Judges	Baruch	
Ruth	Ruth	Ezekiel	Ezekiel
I Samuel	I Samuel	Daniel	Daniel
II Samuel	II Samuel	Hosea	Hosea
I Kings	I Kings	Joel	Joel
II Kings	II Kings	Amos	Amos
I Chronicles	I Chronicles	Obadiah	Obadiah
II Chronicles	II Chronicles	Jonah	Jonah
Ezra	Ezra	Micah	Micah
Nehemiah	Nehemiah	Nahum	Nahum
Tobit		Habakkuk	Habakkuk
Judith		Zephaniah	Zephaniah
Esther	Esther	Haggai	Haggai
Job	Job	Zechariah	Zechariah
Psalms	Psalms	Malachi	Malachi
Proverbs	Proverbs	I Maccabees	
Ecclesiastes	Ecclesiastes	II Maccabees	

New Testament

Matthew	II Corinthians	I Timothy	II Peter
Mark	Galatians	II Timothy	I John
Luke	Ephesians	Titus	II John
John	Philippians	Philemon	III John
Acts	Colossians	Hebrews	Jude
Romans	I Thessalonians	James	Revelation
I Corinthians	II Thessalonians	I Peter	

Books of the Bible

Babel, Tower of The building of the Tower of Babel is described in the Old Testament. The people who built it tried to make it so tall that it would reach up to heaven, but God punished them for their pride by making each of them speak a different language. Since they could not understand each other, they could not work together, and the tower was never finished.

Sometimes the apostles are referred to as Jesus' disciples. Four of the apostles, Matthew, Mark, Luke, and John, are said to have written the first four books of the New Testament. ❧

beginning, In the The first words in the Bible are: "In the beginning God created the heaven and the earth." *See also* CREATION.

Bethlehem The New Testament says that Jesus Christ was born in the town of Bethlehem. *See also* NATIVITY.

brother's keeper In an Old Testament narration, Cain killed his brother Abel. When God asked Cain where Abel was, Cain said, "I know not: Am I my brother's keeper?" (In other words, "Am I supposed to look after my brother?") *See also* CAIN AND ABEL.

Cain and Abel   According to the Old Testament, Cain and Abel were sons of Adam and Eve. Once, when they both offered gifts to God, God liked Abel's gift but not Cain's. Cain was so jealous and angry that he killed Abel, thus committing the first murder. God punished Cain by sending him to a distant land. *See also* BROTHER'S KEEPER.

Calvary   According to the New Testament, Jesus was crucified on a hill named Calvary. *See also* CRUCIFIXION.

chosen people   The Old Testament says that God chose the Israelites as his special people. He promised that they would possess a land of their own and grow into a great nation. *See also* HOLY LAND; ISRAELITES.

Christ   *See* JESUS CHRIST.

coat of many colors   In an Old Testament narration, Joseph was a young man whose father gave him a beautiful coat of many colors. This coat made Joseph's brothers so envious that they decided to sell him as a slave. *See also* JOSEPH AND HIS BROTHERS.

Creation   The Old Testament says that God created the world in seven days. Because God rested on the seventh day, Jews and Christians take the seventh day of each week as a day of prayer and rest. For Jews it is Saturday, and for Christians, Sunday. *See also* SABBATH.

crown of thorns   The New Testament says that before Jesus was crucified, he was handed over to some soldiers who laughed at him, saying that he wanted to be king of the Jews. They made a king's crown out of some thorny branches and forced Jesus to wear this crown of thorns. *See also* CRUCIFIXION.

Crucifixion   The Crucifixion is the name for the death of Jesus, as described in the New Testament. After being sentenced to death, Jesus was beaten and mocked. Then he was forced to carry his own cross to the place

Crown of thorns

Daniel in the lions' den

where people were crucified, a hill called CALVARY. Christians believe that Jesus died to make up for the sins of all people. The cross on which he died has become a symbol of the Christian faith.

Daniel in the lions' den   Daniel was an Israelite who, according to the Old Testament, was captured and taken to a foreign country. The king of that land made it illegal to pray to anyone but the king himself. But Daniel prayed only to God. One day he was caught saying his prayers, and he was punished by being thrown into a den of lions. God sent an angel to keep the lions from attacking him. When the king saw that Daniel was unharmed, he let him go free.

David and Goliath   In an Old Testament narration, the Israelites were at war. Their enemies had a great fighter, a giant named Goliath, who stood almost ten feet tall. All of the Israelites were afraid of him except a boy named David. David went out to fight Goliath armed with only a slingshot and some stones. Because God was on his side, David was able to kill the giant. Later, David became one of the greatest kings of the Israelites.

Many of the psalms are thought to have been written by David, who was famed as a harp player. ❧

Day of Judgment   According to the New Testament, on the last day of the world, the Day of Judgment, Jesus will return to judge all the living and the dead. The good will be sent to heaven and the wicked to hell.

Eden, Garden of   According to the Old Testament, the Garden of Eden was a beautiful place where ADAM AND EVE lived until they disobeyed God by eating the forbidden fruit. Eden has come to mean a place where life is perfect.

Exodus   The Old Testament describes how MOSES led the Israelites out of Egypt, where they were being kept in slavery, across the Red Sea to their new home in the PROMISED LAND. This journey is called the Exodus, which means "going out."

Garden of Eden   *See* EDEN, GARDEN OF.

Genesis   Genesis is the first book of the Bible. The word genesis means "beginning" or "origin."

golden calf   According to the Old Testament, MOSES went up to the top of a mountain to receive the TEN COMMANDMENTS from God. While he was gone, the Israelites made a golden statue in the shape of a calf and began to worship it. When Moses came down from the mountain, he was very angry. He destroyed the statue and scolded the people for abandoning their God for an idol.

Good Samaritan   Jesus tells the story of the Good Samaritan in the New Testament. Once a man traveling along a road was attacked by robbers, who beat him up and left him to die. Other people passed on the same road, but they ignored the injured man. Then a man from another country, a Samaritan, came along. He took care of the injured man, bandaging his wounds and helping him to an inn. Jesus then tells his followers that they should act like this good Samaritan.

Gospel   The four books that tell about the life and teachings of Jesus — Matthew, Mark, Luke, and John — are called the Gospels. They are named after the four apostles who are traditionally considered to have written these books.

Holy Land   Most of the events described in the Bible happened in a region in the Middle East called the Holy Land. It is bordered on the west by the Mediterranean Sea, on the east by the Jordan River, on the north by Lebanon, and on the south by the Sinai Peninsula. This area has also been known as the PROMISED LAND, since, according to the Old Testament, God promised it to the Israelites.

Israelites   The Old Testament is the story of the Israelites, or the Hebrews, a people who lived in the HOLY LAND in ancient times and were considered God's CHOSEN PEOPLE. Later, they became known as the Jews.

Jehovah   In English translations of the Old Testament, Jehovah is another name for God.

Jericho, Battle of   In an Old Testament story, the Israelites were trying to capture the city of Jericho when God told Joshua, their leader, that he should order his priests to blow their trumpets and his soldiers to give a great shout. At the noise, the walls of the city fell, and Joshua's soldiers were triumphant.

Jerusalem   Jerusalem, a city in the HOLY LAND, is a spiritual center of Judaism and the capital of modern Israel. The Old Testament describes how Solomon built a great temple in Jerusalem. According to the New Testament, Jesus was crucified in Jerusalem.

Jesus Christ   The main figure in the New Testament, Jesus of Nazareth, is worshiped by Christians as Jesus Christ, the Son of God. According to the Gospels, Jesus was born and brought up in the HOLY LAND. His mother, MARY, was the wife of a carpenter named JOSEPH. When Jesus was a grown man, he was baptized by JOHN THE BAPTIST. Afterward, he traveled across the Holy Land, teaching about the coming kingdom of God. The most important teachings of Jesus are given in the SERMON ON THE MOUNT. In his travels, Jesus healed the sick and performed miracles. Soon many people became his followers. However, some powerful people thought that he was stirring up trouble among the people and breaking religious laws. Finally, his enemies had him arrested and sentenced to death. On

Jerusalem. View of Jerusalem with Solomon's Temple in the forefront.

a hill called CALVARY, Jesus was crucified (nailed to a cross and left to die). The New Testament says that, after lying in his tomb for three days, Jesus arose and appeared to his followers. Christians often refer to Jesus as Jesus Christ or simply Christ. In fact, *Christ* is a title, not a name, and means "the anointed one"; that is, the one chosen by God. *See also* APOSTLES; CRUCIFIXION; JUDAS; LAST SUPPER; LOAVES AND FISHES; NATIVITY; PILATE; RESURRECTION.

Job   Job is the central figure in the Old Testament Book of Job, which tells the story of a man whose faith in God is tested by great suffering.

A person who suffers for a long time without complaining is sometimes said to be as patient as Job. ❧

John the Baptist John the Baptist was a religious teacher who lived at the time of Jesus. According to the New Testament, he was sent by God to prepare for Jesus' coming. After he baptized Jesus, he was arrested and beheaded for speaking out against the country's leaders.

Jonah According to the Old Testament, God commanded Jonah to preach to foreigners. Jonah tried to escape God's will by going on a voyage. God then raised a great storm, which nearly sank Jonah's ship. The sailors, knowing that his disobedience had caused the storm, threw Jonah into the sea, where he was swallowed by a "great fish" (often thought of as a whale). After staying in the fish's belly for three days, he prayed to God for forgiveness. God then pardoned Jonah, and the fish coughed him up onto dry land.

Jonah. Being swallowed by a "great fish."

Joseph In the New Testament, Joseph was the husband of MARY, the mother of JESUS. Some Christians refer to him as Saint Joseph.

Joseph and his brothers The Old Testament tells the story of Joseph, whose brothers envied him because he was their father's favorite son. One day, his brothers sold Joseph into slavery in Egypt. Joseph became a servant of the pharaoh, who suffered from strange and frightening dreams he did not understand. Joseph was the only one who could explain the dreams; he showed the king how they predicted the future. To reward Joseph, the king made him rich and powerful. Years later, a famine broke out in Joseph's own country. When Joseph's brothers came to Egypt to ask for food, Joseph was the official who heard their request. At first, they did not recognize their brother, but in time Joseph revealed his identity. He forgave his brothers, and they had a joyous reunion. *See also* COAT OF MANY COLORS.

Joshua *See* JERICHO.

Judas Iscariot Judas Iscariot was one of the APOSTLES, the twelve closest followers of JESUS, in the New Testament. By kissing Jesus, Judas betrayed him to his enemies, who arrested and crucified him. Judas felt so much guilt that he hanged himself.

> **A** "Judas" is someone who betrays another person, especially a friend. ❧

Judge not, that ye be not judged In the SERMON ON THE MOUNT in the New Testament, Jesus says, "Judge not, that ye be not judged," thus warning his followers that all humans have weaknesses and shortcomings.

The Last Supper. Leonardo da Vinci's fresco, in the refectory of Santa Maria delle Grazie in Milan, Italy.

land flowing with milk and honey   In the Old Testament, God calls the PROMISED LAND "the land flowing with milk and honey."

Last Supper   The night before Jesus was crucified, according to the New Testament, he ate a meal with the APOSTLES that has become known as the Last Supper. During the meal, he announced that one of his followers would betray him. His prediction came true, when JUDAS ISCARIOT identified him to his enemies by a kiss.

The Last Supper is the subject of a famous painting by Leonardo da Vinci. It depicts events described in the twenty-sixth chapter of the Book of Matthew. ❧

Let there be light   According to the Old Testament story of the CREATION, the world was completely dark until God said, "Let there be light."

loaves and fishes   The New Testament describes the miracle of the loaves and fishes. One day five thousand people gathered to see Jesus heal the sick. At dinnertime there were only five loaves of bread and two fishes to feed the huge crowd. After Jesus blessed the loaves and fishes, they multiplied until there was plenty of food for everyone.

Lord's Prayer   The Lord's Prayer, in the New Testament, is the most important Christian prayer:

"Our Father, which art in heaven, hallowed be thy name; thy kingdom come; thy will be done, in earth as it is in heaven. Give us this day our daily bread. And forgive us our debts as we forgive our debtors. And lead us not into temptation, but deliver us from evil."

Some versions of the Bible add words of praise at the end: "For thine is the kingdom, and the power, and the glory, forever. Amen." Jesus taught his followers this prayer in the SERMON ON THE MOUNT.

Mary. *The Small Cowper Madonna* by Raphael. National Gallery of Art, Washington; Widener Collection.

Moses

Lot's Wife   In the Old Testament story, there was once a city so full of wicked people that God decided to destroy it, but he wanted to save one good man, named Lot. God told Lot and his family to leave their home, but he warned them not to look back at the city. Lot's wife looked back, and God punished her by changing her into a pillar of salt.

Magi   The Magi, or Wise Men, visited the infant JESUS in Bethlehem. According to the GOSPELS, they followed a star and arrived on the twelfth day after his birth, which is now called the feast of Epiphany. They brought three gifts: gold, frankincense, and myrrh.

Mary   The mother of JESUS CHRIST was named Mary. According to the New Testament, she gave birth to Jesus while she was still a virgin.

Moses   Moses was the greatest leader of the ancient Israelites. As told in the Old Testament, he was born in Egypt, where the Israelites were living as slaves. When he was still a baby, the Egyptian ruler, the pharaoh, ordered his soldiers to kill all the male children of the Israelites. Moses' mother saved his life by placing him in a marsh, where he was found by the daughter of the pharaoh and raised as if he were her own son. When Moses was grown, God spoke to him out of a burning bush and commanded him to lead the Israelites out of Egypt. When the pharaoh refused to free the Israelites from slavery, Moses appealed to God, who sent a series of disasters, or plagues, to persuade the Egyptians. Eventually the pharaoh gave in, and the Israelites began their long journey, known as the EXODUS. It was during this journey that God gave Moses the TEN COMMANDMENTS, the laws God expected the Israelites to follow. Moses and his people wandered in the wilderness for forty years. Just as they came within sight of the PROMISED LAND, Moses died. *See also* PLAGUES OF EGYPT; RED SEA, PARTING OF THE.

Countries in the Western world have traditionally dated historical time beginning with the birth of Jesus. The years before his birth are indicated by the abbreviation B.C. (before Christ), and the years after his death are indicated by A.D. (*anno Domini*, Latin for "in the year of our Lord"). ❧

Noah and the Flood. Noah, his family, and pairs of animals leaving the Ark after the Flood.

Nativity   The birth of JESUS, described in the New Testament, is also called the Nativity. Jesus was born in BETHLEHEM, where his parents, MARY and JOSEPH, were visiting. Because there was no room for them in the inn, the couple spent the night in a stable, and it was there that Jesus was born. Mary had no cradle for the infant, so she placed him in a manger (a box that holds food for animals). While Jesus and his parents were still in the stable, they were visited by three wise men from the East, also called MAGI, who brought valuable gifts for the child.

New Testament   The New Testament, originally written in Greek, is the second part of the Christian Bible. It tells the story of JESUS' life and presents the main ideas of Christianity. *See also* OLD TESTAMENT.

Noah and the Flood   The Old Testament describes a time when people everywhere were living in evil ways. This made God so angry that he decided to send a great flood to destroy the world. Noah, however, had always lived a good life. God told Noah to build a great ship, or ark, so that he and his family would survive the flood, and to take into the ark a pair of every kind of animal on earth. Then God made it rain for forty days and forty nights, until the whole world was flooded. Every living creature on earth drowned except

the people and animals in the ark, which eventually came to rest on the top of a mountain. When the rain ended, Noah sent out a dove from the ark. The bird returned with an olive branch in its mouth, so Noah knew that the water was disappearing from the land and he could begin a new life on earth. God promised that he would never again destroy the world by flood, and as a sign, he placed a rainbow in the sky.

Old Testament   The Old Testament is the name commonly used to refer to the first part of the Bible, which was written principally in Hebrew. For Jews, the books of the Old Testament are the whole Bible. They tell the stories of the ancient Israelites, including such figures as NOAH, MOSES, Joshua, Deborah, RUTH, and SAMSON. *See also* NEW TESTAMENT.

Paul   Paul, known also as the Apostle Paul and as Saint Paul, was an influential religious leader who converted to Christianity and

Plagues of Egypt. The plague of flies.

helped spread the new religion through his activities as a missionary. He wrote some of the books of the New Testament in the form of letters to the churches he helped to found.

Peter   Peter was one of the twelve APOSTLES of JESUS. On the night before the CRUCIFIXION, the New Testament says, Jesus predicted that before the cock crowed, Peter would deny three times that he was one of Jesus' followers. That night, after Jesus' arrest, Peter did as Jesus had said because he was afraid of being arrested. Despite his momentary cowardice, Peter went on to become the greatest leader of the early Christians. Some Christians call him Saint Peter.

> The Apostle Peter was originally a fisherman named Simon. Jesus gave him the name Peter (which means "rock") and said that Peter would be the rock on which he would build his church. 🐝

Pilate, Pontius   As told in the New Testament, Pontius Pilate was the Roman official who sentenced JESUS to death. Before delivering the sentence, Pilate washed his hands and said that he was not responsible for Jesus' death.

plagues of Egypt   In the time of MOSES, the Old Testament says that God was angry with the Egyptians because they were keeping the Israelites in slavery. So he punished them by inflicting ten disasters, or plagues, on their land. He turned the waters of the rivers into blood; he sent swarms of insects to destroy the crops; he covered the Egyptians' bodies with painful sores. Eventually he sent the most terrible plague of all: he killed the oldest child in each family. After this plague, the Israelites were permitted to leave Egypt. *See also* PASSOVER.

prodigal son, the   In the New Testament, JESUS tells the story of a father who divided all he had between his two sons. One of the sons left home and went to a foreign country, where he lived in a wild and foolish way,

75

thinking only of his own enjoyment. Soon he had wasted all his father's money. Poor and hungry, he returned to his father and begged his forgiveness. The father was so pleased to see his son that he forgave him and joyfully ordered a feast to celebrate his return.

Promised Land   God promised the ancient Israelites, in the Old Testament, that they would rule a great and beautiful country. When Moses led them out of Egypt, they began their search for this Promised Land. After forty years, they found it in the region occupied today by Israel. *See also* Holy Land.

psalms   The psalms are songs and prayers that have been part of Jewish and Christian worship services for thousands of years. These songs are collected in the Old Testament in the Book of Psalms. *See also* Twenty-third Psalm.

Red Sea, parting of the   According to the Old Testament, when Moses led the Israelites out of Egypt, they were chased by an Egyptian army. When they reached the Red Sea, God parted the waves, making a path of dry land. When the Egyptians tried to follow, God sent back the water to stop them.

Resurrection   Christians believe in the Resurrection (or rising) of Jesus Christ. The New Testament says that after he was crucified, he lay in his tomb for three days. On the third day he rose from the dead and appeared again to his followers.

Ruth   According to the book named for her in the Old Testament, Ruth was a Moabite who married an Israelite who had come to her country. When he died, she returned to his land with her mother-in-law, Naomi. Ruth then married Boaz, a relative of her husband's, and became known for her kindness and faithfulness. She was the great-grandmother of King David. *See also* David and Goliath.

> **T**he Sabbath celebrates the last of the seven days of Creation, when God rested after creating the heavens and the earth. ❧

Sabbath   In Judaism and Christianity, the Sabbath is a holy day, one day each week that is set aside for rest and worship. For Jews, it falls on Saturday, and for Christians, on Sunday. *See also* Creation.

Samson   The Old Testament tells the story of Samson, a leader of the Israelites and the strongest man in the world. The secret of his strength lay in his long hair, which had never been cut. The enemies of the Israelites paid Delilah to cut off Samson's hair and make him helpless. Then they captured Samson, forcing him into slavery. Eventually, though, Samson's hair grew back, and his strength returned. He took his revenge on his enemies by pulling down the pillars that held up their largest temple. When the building collapsed, Samson was killed along with great numbers of the Israelites' enemies.

Satan. Presiding over hell.

Satan In the New Testament, Satan is another name for the devil, the spirit of evil. Satan always tries to work against God's plan.

Sermon on the Mount The most important sermon that Jesus preached is known as the Sermon on the Mount, in the New Testament. It contains the LORD'S PRAYER and many other well-known teachings, such as: "Blessed are the meek, for they shall inherit the earth" (part of the Beatitudes) and "Whosoever shall smite thee on the right cheek, turn to him the other also."

Solomon One of the greatest kings of the Israelites in the Old Testament, Solomon built a great temple in Jerusalem. He was famous for the wisdom with which he ruled his people.

Ten Commandments The Ten Commandments are the ten most important laws, or rules, that Jews and Christians are supposed to follow. According to the Old Testament, God gave the commandments to MOSES on tablets of stone. Among the commandments are: "Thou shalt not kill" and "Thou shalt not steal."

Twenty-third Psalm The Twenty-third Psalm is the most familiar song in the Old Testament:

> The Lord is my shepherd; I shall not want.
> He maketh me to lie down in green pastures;
> He leadeth me beside the still waters.
> He restoreth my soul;
> He leadeth me in the paths of righteousness for his name's sake.
> Yea, though I walk through the valley of the shadow of death,
> I will fear no evil;
> For thou art with me;
> Thy rod and thy staff, they comfort me.
> Thou preparest a table for me in the presence of mine enemies;
> Thou anointest my head with oil; my cup runneth over.
> Surely goodness and mercy will follow me all the days of my life:
> And I will dwell in the house of the Lord for ever.

See also PSALMS.

Religion
and Philosophy

Some of the important words, names, and ideas that will help you begin to understand religion and philosophy are explained below. A *religion* is a set of beliefs about a supernatural power that created the universe, about why we are here on earth, and about how we should conduct our lives.

Philosophy, which means "love of wisdom," answers questions about the nature of reality and about how to lead a good life. Philosophy is more concerned with the nature of the world than with religious beliefs about God. People who write about and study philosophy are called philosophers. Both philosophy and religion try to provide wise answers to our most important questions.

Allah   In the religion of IsLAM, Allah is the name for God, the Supreme Being.

Aristotle   Aristotle was a great philosopher of ancient Greece. He was a student of PLATO's and studied and wrote about many subjects, including politics, science, and literature. He placed particular importance on the direct observation of the natural and political world.

> **F**or nearly one thousand years Aristotle was known as "the Philosopher." ❧

asceticism   Asceticism is a way of life that opposes fancy clothes, expensive possessions, fine food and drink, and physical pleasures. It favors a simple, thoughtful way of life devoted to God and helping other people.

baptism   Baptism is a religious ceremony practiced by Christians. The person being baptized is sprinkled with water, though some churches immerse the person completely. The water represents God's power to cleanse a person's soul. A person being baptized as a Christian is being accepted into the Christian faith and is thought to be united with God and Jesus Christ. *See also* CHRISTIANITY.

bar mitzvah   A bar mitzvah, a Jewish religious ceremony for thirteen-year-old boys, marks the point at which a boy takes on adult religious and social responsibilities. *See also* BAT MITZVAH; JUDAISM. *Compare* CONFIRMATION.

bat mitzvah   A bat mitzvah, a religious ceremony for thirteen-year-old girls, is performed by some Reform Jews to mark the time when girls take on adult religious and social responsibilities. *See also* BAR MITZVAH; JUDAISM. *Compare* CONFIRMATION.

Bible   The Bible is the sacred book of JUDAISM and CHRISTIANITY. *See also the section called "The Bible."*

bishop   A bishop is a high church official who directs the activities of other religious officials. The ROMAN CATHOLIC CHURCH, the EASTERN ORTHODOX CHURCHES, and some PROTESTANT CHURCHES have bishops.

Buddha (BOOH-duh)   The Buddha was a holy man in ancient India. His teachings form the basis of BUDDHISM, a major Eastern religion.

Buddhism (BOOH-diz-uhm)   Buddhism is a major religion of Asia based on the teachings of the BUDDHA. Buddhists seek wisdom, meaning, inner peace, and freedom from desire through physical and spiritual discipline. Meditation, a way of thinking deeply and calmly that takes many years to learn, is one Buddhist discipline.

Catholicism   *See* ROMAN CATHOLIC CHURCH.

charity   Charity in the New Testament means love of others and is considered one of the greatest virtues. It has also come to mean helping people in need.

Christianity   Christianity is a religion based on the life and teachings of JESUS CHRIST. Its main ethical belief is love of others. There are many different Christian churches and forms of worship, but all Christians believe that Jesus Christ is the Son of God and that he was sent by God to redeem, or save, humankind. Christianity is the major religion of Europe and of North and South America. *See also* EASTERN ORTHODOX

Buddha. Statue of the Great Buddha in Kamakura, Japan.

CHURCHES; PROTESTANT CHURCHES; ROMAN CATHOLIC CHURCH.

Christmas   Christmas is the holiday on which Christians celebrate the birth of JESUS CHRIST. For most Christians, it falls on December 25. In the countries where CHRISTIANITY is the dominant faith, such as the United States, it is a national holiday as well.

Communion   Communion is a part of the religious service practiced by many Christians. It is also called the Eucharist. A priest or minister gives bread to the church members. Some churches also use wine in the ceremony. When the worshipers eat the bread and drink the wine, they are celebrating their union with JESUS CHRIST. *See also* CHRISTIANITY; MINISTER; PRIEST.

confession   Confession is a religious ceremony that is especially important in the ROMAN CATHOLIC CHURCH. A person speaks privately to a PRIEST, admits (confesses) to having done wrong in some way, and asks to be forgiven.

confirmation   Confirmation is the ceremony in Christian churches that marks the point at which a person becomes a full member of the church after receiving religious education. Some Reform Jewish temples also confirm fifteen- or sixteen-year-olds when they have completed their religious study. *Compare* BAR MITZVAH; BAT MITZVAH.

Confucianism   Confucianism is an important religion in China and Japan based on the teachings of CONFUCIUS.

Confucius   Confucius was an ancient Chinese teacher known for his wisdom. He developed a system of ethics that is still influential in China and other parts of Asia.

Devil   In CHRISTIANITY and other religions, the Devil is the source of evil in the universe, for he tries to lead people away from God and goodness. Also called Satan, he is often pictured with horns on his head, a tail, and hooves like a goat's. Some religions believe in lesser devils or demons as well.

Easter   Easter is the holiday on which Christians celebrate the return to life, or Resurrection, of JESUS CHRIST. According to the New Testament, Jesus was crucified (nailed to a wooden cross), died, and was buried, but after three days he rose from the dead. The Easter holiday is observed every spring. *See also* LENT.

Eastern Orthodox churches   The Eastern Orthodox churches, which include the Greek, Russian, and Syrian Orthodox churches, among others, form one of the three branches of CHRISTIANITY. (The others are the ROMAN CATHOLIC CHURCH and the PROTESTANT CHURCHES.) The buildings used by Orthodox Christians are usually square, with domes, and have likenesses of holy people, called

Confucius

icons, on their walls. Eastern Orthodoxy is the dominant form of Christianity in most of Eastern Europe and in Greece. There are also many Orthodox Christians in the United States.

ethics   Ethics is a set of beliefs about what is right and wrong in people's actions. Ethical rules sometimes come from religion, for example, from the TEN COMMANDMENTS and the SERMON ON THE MOUNT, and sometimes from social traditions.

fasting   Fasting means going without food or certain foods for a period of time. In many religions, it is used to help cleanse the soul of sin and guilt.

Friends, Religious Society of   *See* QUAKER.

God   God is the name for the Supreme Being worshiped by Jews, Christians, Moslems, and followers of other religions. In the BIBLE, God created the universe and all humankind. Moslems call God by the name Allah. *See also* CHRISTIANITY; ISLAM; JUDAISM.

gods   Gods are the supernatural beings or spirits worshiped in religions that believe in many gods rather than one.

Good Friday   Good Friday is the Friday before EASTER Sunday, when Christians remember the CRUCIFIXION of JESUS CHRIST. It is called *good* because Jesus' death led to the Resurrection, or return to life, which is celebrated on Easter.

heaven   In many religions, heaven is the happy and peaceful place where good people will go to live with God after death. It is often thought to be above the clouds and is depicted as a place where angels play harps.

hell   In many religions, hell is the place of damnation where bad people will go to be punished after death. It is often thought to be below the earth and is depicted as a place with flames and devils.

> The sacred books of Hinduism include the Upanishads and the *Bhagavad-Gita.*

Hinduism   Hinduism is the ancient religion of India and is practiced by people called Hindus. Hindus believe that the soul is reborn into a new body after death through a process called reincarnation. The major religious goal of the Hindus is to escape the cycle of death and rebirth so that the soul may be released into eternity. Some Hindus worship one god or goddess while others worship many gods and goddesses. *See also* GODS; REINCARNATION.

Islam   Islam is the religion based on the teachings communicated by MOHAMMED, an Arabian prophet, in the KORAN. People who practice Islam, called Moslems or Muslims, believe in strict obedience to the will of God, or ALLAH. Religious observances such as prayer, FASTING, and giving gifts to the poor are central to the Moslem faith. Congregational prayer takes place on Fridays. Once in their lives, Moslems try to make a PILGRIMAGE (a journey made for religious purposes) to Mecca, the city where Mohammed was born. Islam is the major religion of the Arab countries, central Asia, and Indonesia.

Jesus Christ   Jesus was a religious leader from Palestine, in what is now called the Middle East. His life and teachings are the basis of CHRISTIANITY. Jesus became known as Christ, which means "the anointed one," the one who

Jesus Christ. Portrayed in a Byzantine mosaic.

is chosen by God. The important events of Jesus' life are marked by major Christian holidays. CHRISTMAS celebrates his birthday and EASTER, his Resurrection, or return to life. *See also* JESUS CHRIST *under "The Bible."*

Judaism   Judaism is a religion based on the teachings of the Jewish Bible, or Old Testament, especially the TORAH, which consists of the first five books of the BIBLE. It has three branches, Orthodox, Conservative, and Reform. People who follow Judaism are called Jews and believe in one God. Many of their laws and ideas, such as "Remember the sabbath day, to keep it holy," are shared with Christianity, which grew out of Judaism. Judaism is the dominant religion in Israel, a nation in the Middle East. There are also many Jews in the United States as well as in Europe and parts of Asia. *See also* TALMUD.

King James Bible   The King James Bible is an important English translation of the BIBLE famous for its noble language. (The Bible was first written in the ancient languages of Hebrew in the Old Testament and Greek in the New Testament.) It is named after James I, a

---

The King James Bible is considered to have the finest language and style of all the translations in English. ❧

---

king of England in the 1600s, who commissioned this particular translation. Many familiar biblical quotations come from this translation.

Koran   The Koran is the sacred book of ISLAM and contains the rules and ideals that Moslems follow. Moslems believe that God (or ALLAH) revealed the Koran to the prophet MOHAMMED and that it is the direct word of God. Koran is also spelled Qur'an.

Martin Luther

Lent   In CHRISTIANITY, Lent is the solemn period of FASTING and repentance that begins on Ash Wednesday and ends on EASTER.

logic   Logic is the science concerned with the rules of reasoning. An important logical principle is the syllogism, the most famous example of which is: All men are mortal. SOCRATES is a man. Therefore, Socrates is mortal.

Luther, Martin   Martin Luther was a German religious leader of the 1500s. He founded Protestantism after protesting against the policies of the ROMAN CATHOLIC CHURCH that he felt were wrong. *See also* PROTESTANT CHURCHES.

Madonna   The Madonna, which is Italian for "my lady," is a Christian title for the VIRGIN MARY, the mother of JESUS CHRIST. Paintings or statues of Mary holding the baby Jesus are called Madonnas.

Mary, Virgin   *See* VIRGIN MARY. *See also* MARY *under "The Bible."*

82

Mecca. The sacred Kaaba is a stone building in the courtyard of the Great Mosque. The Black Stone, a meteor believed to have been sent from heaven at the time of Adam, is enclosed within the wall of the Kaaba.

mass   The mass is the main ceremony of worship in the Roman Catholic faith. *See also* COMMUNION; ROMAN CATHOLIC CHURCH.

Mecca   Mecca, in modern Saudi Arabia, is the birthplace of the prophet MOHAMMED and thus the holy city of ISLAM. All Moslems try to make a PILGRIMAGE to Mecca at least once in their lives. The word *mecca* is often used to mean a destination that attracts many people.

minister   A minister is the leader of the congregation (worshipers) in a Protestant church. Ministers preach, celebrate COMMUNION, BAPTISMS, and marriages, and advise the members of their churches. *See also* PROTESTANT CHURCHES.

Mohammed   Mohammed was the Arabian prophet who, according to Moslems, received God's revelation and passed it on in the KORAN. These teachings form the basis of the Moslem religion, or ISLAM. He is also known as Muhammad or simply as the Prophet.

monk   A monk is a man who devotes himself to a holy life of study, prayer, and good works. Most monks live in buildings called monasteries. *See also* NUN.

Moses   *See* MOSES *under "The Bible."*

Moslems   A Moslem (or Muslim) is a person who believes in ISLAM.

mosque   A mosque is a Moslem house of worship that usually has a dome. *See also* ISLAM.

nun   A nun is a woman who devotes herself to a life of study, prayer, and good works. Nuns often live in buildings called convents. *See also* MONK.

Orthodox churches   *See* EASTERN ORTHODOX CHURCHES.

Palm Sunday   Palm Sunday is the Sunday before EASTER, when Christians remember the day Jesus entered JERUSALEM. The people of the city welcomed him by spreading palm leaves in his path. Today some churches hand out palm leaves during Palm Sunday services.

Paradise   Paradise is a place where everything is perfect and everyone is happy. *See also* EDEN, GARDEN OF; HEAVEN.

Passover   Passover is the Jewish festival that celebrates the EXODUS, the escape of the ancient ISRAELITES from slavery in Egypt. The eight-day holiday is observed in the spring. *See also* SEDER.

The Passover seder is a special meal at which the story of the Israelites' escape from Egypt is read aloud and thanks are given to God. ❧

philosopher   A philosopher is a person who thinks and writes about basic questions, such as, What is Truth? What is the Good? How should we act?

pilgrimage   A pilgrimage is a journey to a holy place.

Plato   Plato was an ancient Greek philosopher who was a student of SOCRATES and the teacher of ARISTOTLE. In his writings, he searches for answers to basic questions about human life, such as, What is the Good? and What is Truth? His best-known book is *The Republic*, which describes an ideal government.

John Paul II, who was elected in 1978, is the first Polish pope. ❧

pope   The pope is the leader and ultimate authority of the ROMAN CATHOLIC CHURCH. He lives and works in the VATICAN in Rome, Italy. The first pope was PETER, whom Catholics believe was appointed by JESUS CHRIST. Other popes were then chosen to succeed Saint Peter, and his authority was passed on to them.

prayer   Prayers are thoughts or words addressed to God. Sometimes they are spoken by several people using the same words, sometimes by individuals out loud or silently. Most often, prayers give thanks or ask for help.

priest   A priest is the person who leads worshipers in Roman Catholic, Eastern Orthodox, and Episcopalian churches. All Roman Catholic and Orthodox priests are men; some Episcopal priests are women. *See also* EASTERN ORTHODOX CHURCHES; ROMAN CATHOLIC CHURCH; SACRAMENT.

Pope. Pope John Paul II during a visit to Boston in 1980.

Protestant churches   Protestant churches as a group make up one of the three great branches of CHRISTIANITY. (The others are the ROMAN CATHOLIC CHURCH and the EASTERN ORTHODOX CHURCHES.) Protestants believe that the ultimate religious authority is the BIBLE rather than priests or the church. Protestantism originated in Germany in the 1500s when Martin Luther "protested" against certain practices of the Roman Catholic Church. Protestantism is a major religion in Western Europe as well as the United States, where the Protestant churches with the largest memberships are Baptist, Episcopal, Lutheran, Methodist, and Pentecostal.

Quaker   A Quaker is a member of the Religious Society of Friends, a Christian faith that believes in simplicity of life and worship. Services, called meetings, consist mainly of silent meditation.

Qur'an   *See* KORAN.

rabbi   A rabbi is a Jewish religious teacher and spiritual guide, similar to a PRIEST or MINISTER. Rabbis study the TORAH and TALMUD in order to pass on their teachings to others. *See also* JUDAISM.

Ramadan   (RAM-uh-dahn)   Ramadan is the holy month in the Moslem faith. In order to purify themselves, Moslems fast (eat no food) from sunrise to sunset throughout the month.

reincarnation   Reincarnation is the belief that the soul lives on after death and returns to existence in another body. Hindus and some Buddhists believe in reincarnation. *See also* HINDUISM.

Roman Catholic Church   The Roman Catholic Church, or Roman Catholicism, is one of the three branches of CHRISTIANITY. (The other two are the EASTERN ORTHODOX CHURCHES and the PROTESTANT CHURCHES.) The POPE is the leader of the Roman Catholic Church. Many Catholics look to his judgments and teachings on religious matters, which are passed on to them by their BISHOPS and PRIESTS (in contrast to Protestants, who rely more directly on the BIBLE). Catholicism is the major religion of southern Europe, Ireland, and Latin America. There are also many Catholics in the United States.

Rosh Hashanah   (rosh-huh-SHAH-nuh; rosh-huh-SHOH-nuh)   Rosh Hashanah marks the beginning of the Jewish New Year. The first ten days of the year are special days of penitence, which end on YOM KIPPUR. The holiday usually falls in September or early October. *See also* JUDAISM.

sacrament   A sacrament is a very holy religious ceremony. For many Christians, BAPTISM, COMMUNION, and marriage are considered sacraments.

sacred   Something that is sacred is worshiped or has to do with religious and spiritual life.

saint   In some Christian churches and in other religions, saints are very holy people who have died and gone to heaven and who may be called upon to ask God for help. A person who lives a holy life is sometimes called saintly.

salvation   In religion, salvation means being saved from sin and the penalties of sin. In Christianity, JESUS CHRIST promised salvation to his faithful followers.

seder   The seder is the ceremonial dinner held at the beginning and, for some observers, the end of the Jewish feast of PASSOVER. The story of the Jews' EXODUS from Egypt is read during the meal.

sermon   A sermon is a prepared talk, often based on stories from the BIBLE, given by the leaders of many religions to a group of worshipers. It is part of the service in many churches and SYNAGOGUES.

Shinto   Shinto is an ancient Japanese religion that today has been influenced by CONFUCIANISM and BUDDHISM. Its followers take PILGRIMAGES and show special reverence for their ancestors.

Socrates   Socrates was a great Greek philosopher and teacher who taught his students by asking them questions rather than by telling them what to think. In this way, his students learned to find and correct their own errors.

Socrates. Jacques-Louis David's painting *The Death of Socrates*.

This type of teaching is called the Socratic method. *See also* PHILOSOPHER; PLATO.

synagogue   A synagogue is a Jewish house of worship and study. It is also called a TEMPLE. *See also* JUDAISM.

Talmud   The Talmud is the collection of writings that contain the religious laws and traditions of JUDAISM. It includes centuries of interpretation of Jewish ideas.

Taoism   Taoism is an important religion of China based on the writings of Lao-Tzu. It stresses meditation and serenity in the face of life's troubles.

temple   A temple is a building used for religious worship. The followers of many religions, such as JUDAISM, HINDUISM, and BUDDHISM, call their houses of worship temples. *See also* SYNAGOGUE.

Torah (TOH-ruh; TAWR-uh)   The Torah is the group of religious writings sacred to

The Torah. A young man reading the Torah at his bar mitzvah.

JUDAISM. It consists of the five books of Moses, which are the first five books of the Jewish Bible (called the Old Testament by Christians). The word *torah* also refers in a general way to the sacred laws and teachings of Judaism. *See also* TALMUD.

Trinity   Many Christians think of GOD as a trinity, or a being made up of three parts, or persons: the Father, the Son, and the Holy Ghost (also called the Holy Spirit). Together, these three persons, making one God, are known as the Trinity. *See also* CHRISTIANITY.

Vatican   The Vatican is the headquarters of the ROMAN CATHOLIC CHURCH and the home of the POPE. It is an independent state within the city of Rome, Italy.

Virgin Mary   The Virgin Mary was the mother of JESUS CHRIST. She is especially honored by Roman Catholic and Orthodox Christians. *See also* ROMAN CATHOLIC CHURCH; EASTERN ORTHODOX CHURCHES. *See also* MARY *under "The Bible."*

Wailing Wall   *See* WESTERN WALL.

Western Wall   The Western Wall is a wall in Jerusalem, where the ancient temple of the

Western Wall. Men praying at the Western Wall in Jerusalem. Men and women pray separately at the wall.

Jews once stood. The area in front of the wall is the holiest place in JUDAISM, where Jewish people go to pray. Some people call it the Wailing Wall because it reminds them of the past sorrows of the Jews. *See also* JUDAISM.

Yom Kippur (YOHM ki-POOR; YOM KIP-uhr)   Yom Kippur, also called the Day of Atonement, is the most important Jewish holiday. On this day Jews atone, or make amends, for their sins through PRAYER and FASTING. *See also* JUDAISM; ROSH HASHANAH.

American History
to 1865

This section covers the period of American history up to and including the Civil War. When Columbus sailed to America in 1492 and returned to Spain to announce his discovery, Indian peoples were already well established in North America. The first British settlers did not arrive in North America until the early 1600s, and as more and more British and other Europeans settled in America, they found themselves struggling with the Indians over the land. In 1776, the colonists, who came mainly from Britain and were living under British rule, declared their independence. After the Revolutionary War against Britain, the Constitution became the foundation of the government.

From the earliest days of the colonies, soon after the first Europeans established their settlements, slaves had been brought to America from Africa. The United States gradually began to divide, North against South, over the issue of slavery, resulting in the Civil War. It ended in victory for the North, which wanted to free the slaves, and the nation was reunited. The entries below are about soldiers and battles, ideas and speeches, Indian peoples, and presidents and patriots who were an important part of the first centuries of American history.

The symbol at the beginning of most of the following entries places the events or persons described in their approximate place in time. See the legend for the span of years indicated by the symbol.

1492   In 1492, the Italian explorer CHRISTOPHER COLUMBUS discovered the American continents.

1776   The American colonies declared their independence from England in 1776. *See also* REVOLUTIONARY WAR.

1861–1865   The CIVIL WAR was fought from 1861 to 1865.

abolition   Abolition was a movement to end, or abolish, slavery. People who spoke out against slavery were called abolitionists. Abolition was an important movement leading to the Civil War.

Alamo (AL-uh-MOH)   The Alamo was a building in what is now San Antonio, Texas. A famous battle was fought there in the early 1800s, when Texas belonged to Mexico and a group of Americans, wanting to gain independence for Texas, held off a much larger Mexican army until the Americans, including Davy Crockett, were all killed. *See also* REMEMBER THE ALAMO.

all men are created equal   These words, from the DECLARATION OF INDEPENDENCE, express a basic belief held by the founders of the United States. The Declaration states: "We hold these truths to be self-evident: That all men are created equal; that they are endowed by their Creator with certain unalienable rights; that among these are life, liberty, and the pursuit of happiness." ABRAHAM LINCOLN also used the phrase "all men are created equal" in his GETTYSBURG ADDRESS.

American Revolution   *See* REVOLUTIONARY WAR.

Apaches (uh-PACH-eez)   The Apaches are an American Indian people who live in the southwestern United States. Traditionally, they were hunters and warriors who lived in tepees, a kind of tent.

Appleseed, Johnny   Johnny Appleseed was the nickname of an American pioneer and folk hero of the early 1800s. He traveled through frontier America planting apple trees and starting orchards. His real name was John Chapman.

Some well-known abolitionists were John Brown, Frederick W. Douglass, Sojourner Truth, and Harriet Tubman. 🐝

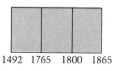

1492   1765   1800   1865

Appomattox Court House (AP-uh-MAT-uhks)   Appomattox Court House, in central Virginia, is where the CIVIL WAR came to an end in 1865 when the Southern general, ROBERT E. LEE, surrendered to the Northern general, ULYSSES S. GRANT.

Articles of Confederation   When the THIRTEEN COLONIES declared their independence from England, the Articles of Confederation formed the basis of the national government. (A confederation is a coming together of different groups for some special purpose.) This document proved to be too weak to govern the United States, and it was replaced soon after by the CONSTITUTION.

The Bill of Rights protects the freedoms of speech, religion, assembly, and the press. 🐝

Bill of Rights   The Bill of Rights is the name for the first ten amendments to the CONSTITUTION. These amendments were added soon after the Constitution was adopted because the original document did not offer enough protection for individual rights. *See also* BILL OF RIGHTS *under "Politics and Economics."*

Boone, Daniel   Daniel Boone was a pioneer of the late 1700s and early 1800s who explored and settled Kentucky.

Booth, John Wilkes   John Wilkes Booth assassinated President ABRAHAM LINCOLN in 1865. Booth, a well-known actor, supported SLAVERY and the CONFEDERACY.

Boston Tea Party

Boston Tea Party   The Boston Tea Party was one of the events that led to the REVOLUTIONARY WAR. A group of Americans who wanted to protest English taxes and other laws boarded three British ships in Boston harbor and dumped more than three hundred chests of tea overboard. The name was kind of a joke, because a tea party is really an afternoon social event at which people drink tea and eat cakes and sandwiches.

Bunker Hill, Battle of   The Battle of Bunker Hill was one of the first battles of the REVOLUTIONARY WAR. American soldiers defended a hill near Boston, Massachusetts, against two British attacks. The British took the hill on the third attack, when the Americans ran out of ammunition, but the battle proved that the Americans could fight effectively against the British.

California Gold Rush   *See* GOLD RUSH OF 1849.

Cherokees (CHER-uh-KEEZ)   The Cherokees are an American Indian people who originally farmed and hunted in the mountains of the southeastern United States. In the 1830s, the American government forced the Cherokees to move west to Oklahoma. Many died on the way, and the forced journey is now called the Trail of Tears.

Civil War   The American Civil War was fought between the Northern (Union) and Southern (Confederate) states from 1861 to 1865. The war had many causes, but the main issue dividing the country was SLAVERY. The Southern states wanted slavery to be permitted in the new territories of the western United States. The Northern states opposed the spread of slavery to these territories. The Southern states decided to secede (separate) from the United States and form a new nation, which was called the CONFEDERACY. After four years of bloody fighting, the South surrendered to the North at APPOMATTOX COURT HOUSE. *See also* LINCOLN, ABRAHAM.

Confederacy   The Confederacy was the group of states that seceded (separated) from the United States in 1860 and 1861 to form a new nation. South Carolina was the first to secede, followed by Mississippi, Florida, Alabama, Georgia, Louisiana, Texas, Virginia, Arkansas, North Carolina, and Tennessee. *See also* CIVIL WAR.

The Constitution. The opening words of the Constitution.

Constitution   The Constitution is the document that established the national government of the United States. It was written and adopted after the REVOLUTIONARY WAR and set forth the basic laws of the new nation. *See also* ARTICLES OF CONFEDERATION; BILL OF RIGHTS; FOUNDING FATHERS. *See also* CONSTITUTION *under "Politics and Economics."*

Crockett, Davy Born in Tennessee, Davy Crockett was a frontier settler, politician, and folk hero of the early 1800s. He was known for his shooting ability and died defending the ALAMO.

Davis, Jefferson Jefferson Davis was the president of the CONFEDERACY during the CIVIL WAR.

Declaration of Independence The Declaration of Independence was written in 1776 largely by THOMAS JEFFERSON. It declared that the American colonies were an independent nation, no longer ruled by the British king, and proclaimed that all people have the right to "life, liberty, and the pursuit of happiness." The Declaration was adopted on July 4, 1776, the day henceforth celebrated as the nation's birthday.

Douglass, Frederick Frederick Douglass escaped from SLAVERY before the CIVIL WAR and became an eloquent speaker and writer for the ABOLITIONIST cause.

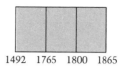

1492 1765 1800 1865

1861–1865 *See the beginning of this section.*

Emancipation Proclamation (i-MAN-suh-PAY-shuhn) The Emancipation Proclamation was the document issued during the CIVIL WAR in which President ABRAHAM LINCOLN declared that all the slaves held in the Confederate states should be freed. However, slavery was not actually abolished until the war was over. (To emancipate means to set free.) *See also* CONFEDERACY.

father of his country GEORGE WASHINGTON is often called the father of his country because he was the head of the American armies during the REVOLUTIONARY WAR and the first president of the United States.

Declaration of Independence. Left: The document. Right: A detail of John Trumbull's painting *The Declaration of Independence.*

Founding Fathers The Founding Fathers were the men who signed the DECLARATION OF INDEPENDENCE and helped write the CONSTITUTION of the United States. The most famous ones are BENJAMIN FRANKLIN, THOMAS JEFFERSON, GEORGE WASHINGTON, JAMES MADISON (sometimes called the father of the Constitution), and ALEXANDER HAMILTON.

Fourscore and seven years ago These words begin ABRAHAM LINCOLN'S GETTYSBURG ADDRESS. "Fourscore and seven" equals eighty-seven (a score equals twenty). The country was founded in 1776, eighty-seven years before Lincoln's address, which was delivered in 1863.

1492 *See the beginning of this section.*

Fourth of July The Fourth of July is the national holiday that celebrates the founding of the United States. On July 4, 1776, the DECLARATION OF INDEPENDENCE was adopted by the THIRTEEN COLONIES.

Franklin, Benjamin Benjamin Franklin, one of the FOUNDING FATHERS of the United States, was one of the most talented men in American history. He wrote a book of sayings called *Poor Richard's Almanack* and an autobiography that became famous. Many of his sayings, such as "Early to bed and early to rise makes a man healthy, wealthy, and wise" are still quoted. In addition to being a printer, patriot, statesman, and author, Franklin was a scientist and inventor. In his most famous experiment, he flew a kite in a thunderstorm to prove that lightning was electricity.

Gettysburg, Battle of The Battle of Gettysburg was the most important battle of the CIVIL WAR. The Northern troops defeated the Southern troops, thus pre-

Benjamin Franklin. Testing his theory that lightning is electricity.

venting the Confederate army from moving farther into Union territory. The battle was fought near the small town of Gettysburg, in southeastern Pennsylvania, and is often called the turning point of the war. *See also* CONFEDERACY.

Gettysburg Address The Gettysburg Address was a short speech given by President ABRAHAM LINCOLN on the battlefield at Gettysburg, Pennsylvania, four months after the battle. In the speech, Lincoln honored the men who died at Gettysburg and stated the ideals for which they fought. The speech begins: "FOURSCORE AND SEVEN YEARS AGO our fathers brought forth on this continent a new nation, conceived in liberty and dedicated to the proposition that all men are created equal." It ends with these words: "government of the people, by the people, for the people shall not perish from the earth."

Give me liberty, or give me death! These words were spoken by Patrick Henry, a Virginia patriot, in an address urging Americans to revolt against England. *See also* REVOLUTIONARY WAR.

Gold Rush of 1849 In 1849, after gold was discovered in California, thousands of people, who came to be known as forty-niners, moved west to try to make their fortunes.

Grant, Ulysses S. Ulysses S. Grant was the leader of the UNION armies at the end of the CIVIL WAR. He later became president of the United States.

I only regret that I have but one life to lose for my country These words are said to be the last spoken by Nathan Hale, an American Revolutionary War soldier who volunteered to spy on the British. He was captured and executed by British troops.

Independence Day *See* FOURTH OF JULY.

Iroquois League (IR-uh-KWOI; IR-uh-KWOIZ) The Iroquois were an alliance of five (eventually six) American Indian peoples who were warriors and fur traders in northern New York state.

> **T**he Iroquois League was founded by the Onondaga chief Hiawatha. ❧

Jackson, Andrew Andrew Jackson, who was nicknamed "Old Hickory," was a military hero and a president of the United States in the early nineteenth century. He believed in strong presidential leadership and the rights of the common people.

Jamestown Jamestown, Virginia, became the first permanent English settlement in America when English colonists arrived there early in the 1600s.

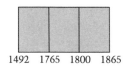

1492 1765 1800 1865

Jefferson, Thomas Thomas Jefferson was the principal author of the DECLARATION OF INDEPENDENCE and the third president of the United States. While he was president, he arranged with France for the Louisiana Purchase, a treaty that gave the United States an immense territory that stretched from the Mississippi River to the Rocky Mountains, doubling its size. Jefferson was a talented architect, scientist, and inventor and a strong defender of religious and political freedom. *See also* LEWIS AND CLARK EXPEDITION.

Lee, Robert E. Robert E. Lee was the brilliant general who commanded the Confederate armies during the CIVIL WAR. He won several victories but ultimately had to surrender to General ULYSSES S. GRANT at APPOMATTOX COURT HOUSE, ending the war.

Lewis and Clark Expedition In the early 1800s, Meriwether Lewis and William Clark were sent by President THOMAS JEFFERSON to explore the land acquired in the Louisiana Purchase. They led a group of men through the new territories west of the Mississippi River, reached the Rocky Mountains, and continued on through Oregon to the Pacific. They drew maps and claimed the Oregon Territory for the United States. Their expedition encouraged the further settlement of the West.

Liberty Bell The Liberty Bell is a symbol of American independence and freedom because it was one of the bells rung on July 4, 1776, to proclaim the signing of the DECLARATION OF INDEPENDENCE. The bell, which is on display in Independence Hall in Philadelphia, Pennsylvania, is easily recognized by the large crack in it.

life, liberty, and the pursuit of happiness These words from the DECLARATION OF INDEPENDENCE describe the rights proclaimed for all Americans.

Lincoln, Abraham Abraham Lincoln was president during the CIVIL WAR and one of the greatest American leaders. Born in a log cabin in Kentucky, he educated himself and became a politician and lawyer in Illinois who was respected for his sincerity and character. As president, he opposed the extension of slavery and fought to preserve the UNION. During the Civil War, he issued the EMANCIPATION PROCLAMATION, which led to the end of slavery in America. His GETTYSBURG ADDRESS and his Second Inaugural Address, in which he urged the nation to reunite in a spirit of forgiveness, are among the finest speeches in American history. After the war, he was assassinated by JOHN WILKES BOOTH.

Louisiana Purchase *See* JEFFERSON, THOMAS.

Madison, James James Madison is known as the father of the CONSTITUTION because of his ideas about organizing the United States government. He became the fourth president of the United States.

Mason-Dixon line The Mason-Dixon line, which runs between Pennsylvania and Maryland, is the traditional boundary between the North and the South. Before the CIVIL WAR, it was said to divide free states from slave states, and today "below the Mason-Dixon line" still refers to the South, although Maryland is also considered a Middle Atlantic state.

Mayflower The *Mayflower* was the ship that carried the PILGRIMS from England to America in the early 1600s and landed in what is now Massachusetts. *See also* PLYMOUTH COLONY.

Liberty Bell

Abraham Lincoln

94

Mexican War   The Mexican War was fought between the United States and Mexico from 1846 to 1848 and resulted in the United States' gaining territory in the Southwest. *See also* ALAMO.

minuteman   A minuteman was a volunteer soldier in the years before the REVOLUTIONARY WAR. Volunteers were organized and trained to be ready to fight "at a minute's notice."

Monroe Doctrine   The Monroe Doctrine was a foreign policy statement issued by President James Monroe in 1823. It declared that the United States would not tolerate the intervention of European nations in the affairs of countries in either North or South America.

Mormons   The Mormons are the American religious group that settled Utah under the leadership of Brigham Young and founded Salt Lake City in the 1800s.

Navajos (NAV-uh-hohz)   The Navajos are an American Indian people of the southwestern United States. Shortly after the CIVIL WAR, they were forced by the United States government to move onto a reservation, which is a piece of land set aside for Indian settlements.

> **T**he Pilgrims were not the first Europeans in New England. France, Holland, and Portugal had sent ships in the 1500s to fish and trade with the Indians. ❧

Pilgrims   The Pilgrims were the settlers who came to America in the early 1600s because their Separatist religion had been outlawed in England. The Separatists, like the Puritans, were Protestants who found the Church of England corrupt. Where

1492   1765   1800   1865

Mayflower

the Puritans sought to purify the doctrine and practice of the established Church, the Separatists sought complete separation by founding their own religious community. The first group of Pilgrims came to America on the *MAYFLOWER* and founded the PLYMOUTH COLONY, which became Massachusetts. The original meaning of *pilgrim* is "someone who goes on a pilgrimage," which is a journey in search of a sacred goal.

Plymouth Colony (PLIM-uhth)   The Plymouth Colony was the settlement started by the PILGRIMS in the early 1600s in what is now eastern Massachusetts.

Plymouth Rock (PLIM-uhth)   Plymouth Rock is a large boulder in Plymouth, Massachusetts. The PILGRIMS landed near this spot at the end of their voyage from England.

Pony Express. Frederic Remington's painting *The Coming and Going of the Pony Express.* The Thomas Gilcrease Institute of American History and Art, Tulsa, Oklahoma.

Pocahontas (poh-kuh-HON-tuhs) Pocahontas, the daughter of the Indian chief Powhatan, lived in Virginia in the early 1600s. According to the English explorer Captain JOHN SMITH, Pocahontas prevented her father from taking Smith's life.

Pony Express The Pony Express was a method of delivering mail through the western territories. Riders on fast horses carried the mail in pouches and switched to a fresh horse about every ten miles.

The Pony Express came to an end in the mid-1800s when the telegraph began to be used to send important messages and regular mail could be taken by stagecoach without danger of Indian attack. 📧

Puritans The Puritans were English Protestants who settled New England. They lived according to a strict set of rules and had a reputation for frowning on luxuries and amusements.

Quakers (KWAY-kuhrs) The Quakers were an English religious group that came to America and settled in what is now Pennsylvania in the 1600s.

Remember the Alamo! (AL-uh-MOH) "Remember the Alamo!" was the battle cry used by the Texans in their war to win independence from Mexico in the early 1800s. *See also* MEXICAN WAR.

Paul Revere. Warning of the impending attack by the British.

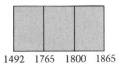

1492   1765   1800   1865

Revere, Paul Paul Revere was a REVOLUTIONARY WAR patriot. He is famous for his midnight ride from Boston to Lexington, Massachusetts, to warn the colonists that the British troops were coming. *See also* "PAUL REVERE'S RIDE."

Revolutionary War The Revolutionary War was the war for independence fought in the late 1700s by the American colonies against Great Britain. The colonists opposed the British control of American trade and resented having to pay taxes to Britain. *See also* BOSTON TEA PARTY; DECLARATION OF INDEPENDENCE; THIRTEEN COLONIES.

Ross, Betsy Betsy Ross was a Philadelphia seamstress during the REVOLUTIONARY WAR who, it is said, made the first official American flag in the form of the STARS AND STRIPES.

Salem witch trials In the late 1600s, many people believed in witchcraft. A number of people in Salem, Massachusetts, were accused of being witches and were tried, convicted, and hanged.

Seminoles The Seminoles are an American Indian people from Florida. The United States government forced most of them to move west in the early 1800s, but some kept their lands in the Everglades, a large swamp in southern Florida.

1776 *See the beginning of this section.*

Shawnees (shaw-NEEZ) The Shawnees are an American Indian people who originally inhabited parts of what is now the Midwest of the United States. They fought several wars against the white settlers.

shot heard round the world, the The phrase "the shot heard round the world" refers to the first shot fired in the REVOLUTIONARY WAR at Lexington and Concord, Massachusetts. The words come from a poem by RALPH WALDO EMERSON commemorating the event.

Sioux (SOOH) The Sioux are an American Indian people on the Great Plains of the American Midwest. They fought many battles against the white settlers and government troops until they were finally defeated and moved to reservations in the late 1800s. (Reservations are pieces of land set aside for the Indians by the United States government.) The Sioux were the people who fought against Lieutenant Colonel George A. Custer at CUSTER'S LAST STAND.

Two famous Sioux chiefs were Sitting Bull and Crazy Horse. ❧

slavery Slavery is a system in which human beings are treated as personal property and forced to work without pay. In the United States, slavery was abolished after the CIVIL WAR. *See also* EMANCIPATION PROCLAMATION.

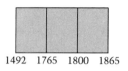

1492 1765 1800 1865

Smith, Captain John Captain John Smith was an English soldier and explorer who helped to found the settlement at JAMESTOWN, Virginia, in the early 1600s. *See also* POCAHONTAS.

Stars and Stripes The Stars and Stripes is a nickname for the official flag of the United States. The design of white stars on a blue field (one star for each state) and thirteen alternating red and white stripes (for the thirteen original colonies) was adopted during the REVOLUTIONARY WAR.

thirteen colonies Before the REVOLUTIONARY WAR, the English-speaking people on the east coast of North America were organized into thirteen colonies governed by England. On July 4, 1776, they became the original United States of America. They were Connecticut, Delaware, Georgia, Maryland, Massachusetts, New Hampshire, New Jersey, New York, North Carolina, Pennsylvania, Rhode Island, South Carolina, and Virginia.

totem pole A totem pole is a large wooden pole made by the Indians of the Pacific Northwest that often has the heads of animals, gods, and people carved on it. These carvings express a family's kinship with nonhuman creatures.

Truth, Sojourner Sojourner Truth was an escaped slave who became famous as a spokeswoman against slavery during the mid-1800s. *See also* ABOLITION.

Tubman, Harriet Harriet Tubman, an abolitionist of the 1800s, was an escaped slave who helped hundreds of other slaves gain their freedom through the UNDERGROUND RAILROAD. During the CIVIL WAR, she served in the UNION army. *See also* ABOLITION.

Turner, Nat Nat Turner was a slave in the early 1800s who led a slave revolt in Virginia. Later, he was captured and hanged.

Uncle Tom Uncle Tom is a character in a famous novel written by Harriet Beecher Stowe before the CIVIL WAR, *UNCLE TOM'S CABIN*, which exposed the terrible conditions of SLAVERY. Uncle Tom was a kind and religious slave who lived under a cruel master. A black person who accepts

Totem pole

George Washington. Emanuel Leutze's painting *Washington Crossing the Delaware.*

white domination is sometimes called an Uncle Tom.

Underground Railroad The Underground Railroad was a network of houses and other buildings used to help slaves escape to freedom in the Northern states or Canada. It operated for many years before and during the CIVIL WAR. *See also* ABOLITION; SLAVERY; TUBMAN, HARRIET.

Union, the The Union was the group of Northern states that fought against the Southern states (the CONFEDERACY) in the CIVIL WAR. "The Union" is also used in a general sense to refer to the entire United States.

Valley Forge GEORGE WASHINGTON and the American army camped at Valley Forge, Pennsylvania, near Philadelphia, during one winter early in the REVOLUTIONARY WAR. It was a harsh season, and there was not enough food or clothing. Many of the men deserted, but Washington inspired the remaining soldiers to continue the fight and shaped them into a skilled army.

War of 1812 The War of 1812 was fought between Britain and the United States. During the war, the British attacked Washington, D.C., and burned the White House and the Capitol.

Washington, George George Washington, the leader of the American armies during the REVOLUTIONARY WAR, became the first president of the United States. One of the most honored men in American history, he is called the FATHER OF HIS COUNTRY. The nation's capital, WASHINGTON, D.C., is named after him, and his picture is on the one-dollar bill. In the famous legend about the cherry tree, he says to his father, "I cannot tell a lie," and admits that he cut it down. *See also* FOUNDING FATHERS; VALLEY FORGE.

American History
Since 1865

This section covers the period of American history after the Civil War, when the United States, and the world in general, changed faster than during any other time in human history. During this period the United States fought in five wars and became a world power. Americans of African ancestry struggled against racism (prejudice against people because of their race) to secure their civil rights, which were not fully recognized until the 1960s, one hundred years after the Civil War brought slavery to an end. Americans invented the telephone, phonograph, tractor, and hand-held camera, flew the first airplane, and put a man on the moon. This section of the dictionary lists leaders and important events. It also lists outlaws and marshals of the Wild West, Indian chiefs, inventors, athletes, entertainers, and astronauts — proof of how much American culture has changed.

The symbol at the beginning of most of the following entries places the events or persons described in their approximate place in time. See the legend for the span of years indicated by the symbol.

Ali, Muhammad (MOO-ham-id al-EE) Muhammad Ali was a heavyweight boxing champion during the 1960s and 1970s known for his clever fighting style. He often boasted, "I am the Greatest," and proved it in the ring.

Anthony, Susan B. Susan B. Anthony was a reformer of the 1800s and early 1900s and an advocate of women's suffrage (right to vote). Before the CIVIL WAR, she was an ABOLITIONIST.

Armstrong, Neil In 1969, Neil Armstrong became the first man to walk on the moon. As he stepped from the spacecraft onto the moon's surface, he said, "That's one small step for a man, one giant leap for mankind."

Ask not what your country can do for you In his inaugural address, President JOHN F. KENNEDY told Americans, "Ask not what your country can do for you — ask what you can do for your country."

Susan B. Anthony

Alexander Graham Bell. Calling Chicago from New York City in 1892.

Barnum, P. T. P. T. Barnum was a showman of the 1800s. He started the Barnum and Bailey Circus and was a skillful advertiser and promoter who claimed, "There's a sucker born every minute."

Bell, Alexander Graham Alexander Graham Bell invented the telephone in the late 1800s.

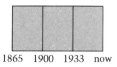

1865 1900 1933 now

Billy the Kid Billy the Kid was an outlaw, a killer, and a cattle thief who lived in New Mexico in the WILD WEST of the 1870s and 1880s.

Buffalo Bill Buffalo Bill was a buffalo hunter, Indian fighter, and scout in the western United States in the 1860s and 1870s. He later became a circus performer known for his shooting skill. His real name was William Cody.

Bush, George George Bush became president of the United States in 1988, after serving as vice president under Ronald Reagan. Born in Massachusetts, Bush was a Texas oilman before turning to politics. His positions included director of the C.I.A., U.S. representative to the People's Republic of China, U.S. ambassador to the United Nations, and member of the House of Representatives.

Carter, Jimmy President from 1977 to 1981, Jimmy Carter had been a naval officer and peanut farmer before he became governor of Georgia and then ran for the presidency.

Carver, George Washington George Washington Carver, the child of slaves, was a scientist and agricultural researcher of the late 1800s and early 1900s. He improved farming methods in the South and discovered many uses for peanuts, which increased the demand for this important southern crop.

Chaplin, Charlie Charlie Chaplin was a comedian and movie star of the early 1900s. His most famous character was the Little Tramp, a man with a small mus-

101

tache who wore a bowler hat, fancy gloves, a ragged suit, and shoes that were too big.

civil rights movement The civil rights movement was a national effort, especially during the 1950s and 1960s, to achieve equal rights for blacks. Civil rights workers used NONVIOLENCE as a method to protest against SEGREGATION. One of the principal leaders of the civil rights movement was the Reverend MARTIN LUTHER KING, JR.

The civil rights movement first won wide attention when a black woman from Alabama, Rosa Parks, refused to give up her seat on a bus to a white person. In sympathy, many other black people refused to use the buses until they could sit where they liked.

Cold War The Cold War refers to the tension between the United States and the Soviet Union between WORLD WAR II and the late 1980s. After the end of the "hot" war against Germany, the Soviet Union kept control of East Germany and much of Eastern Europe, and the United States became the leader of the free countries of Western Europe. The resulting disputes, which did not lead to open warfare between the United States and the Soviet Union, were considered to be a "cold" conflict.

Custer's Last Stand Custer's Last Stand is the nickname of the Battle of the Little Big Horn, which was fought in the Dakota Territory in the late 1800s. When United States troops led by Lieutenant Colonel George Custer were attacked by the SIOUX, Custer and all his men were killed. *See also* SITTING BULL.

D-Day D-Day was June 6, 1944, the day that British and American troops invaded German-occupied France during WORLD WAR II. The forces were led by the American general DWIGHT D. EISENHOWER. *See also* WORLD WAR II.

Depression *See* GREAT DEPRESSION.

Disney, Walt Walt Disney, who created the cartoon characters Mickey Mouse and Donald Duck, was the first person to make full-length animated cartoons, early in the 1900s. Disneyland, in California, and Walt Disney World and EPCOT Center, in Florida, are amusement parks based on his ideas.

Earp, Wyatt (URP) Wyatt Earp was a United States marshal and a gunfighter in the WILD WEST.

Edison, Thomas A. Thomas A. Edison was an inventor of the late 1800s and early 1900s who perfected the electric light bulb and the phonograph, an early form of the record player.

Eisenhower, Dwight D. (EYE-zuhn-how-uhr) Dwight D. Eisenhower, nicknamed "Ike," was an American general and the commander of the Allied forces in Europe in WORLD WAR II. He was the president of the United States from 1953 to 1961.

Ellis Island Ellis Island is a small island in New York harbor, near the STATUE OF LIBERTY. In the early 1900s, immigrants (people moving to the United States from other countries) had to stop first at Ellis Island to register before they could enter the country.

FDR *See* ROOSEVELT, FRANKLIN D.

Freedom Riders The Freedom Riders were people, both black and white, who traveled through the southern

Thomas A. Edison. Seated beside his tin-foil phonograph.

states in the 1960s to protest against SEGRE-GATION and racial injustice. They were an important part of the CIVIL RIGHTS MOVEMENT.

Geronimo (juh-RON-uh-moh) Geronimo was an APACHE chieftain who was one of the last Indian warriors to fight against whites.

Glenn, John In 1962, John Glenn was the first American astronaut to orbit the earth.

Great Depression The Great Depression was the worst economic period in American history and began when the stock market collapsed, or crashed, in 1929. Businesses, banks, and factories had to close, leaving many people unemployed. The Depression lasted for nearly ten years.

Hickok, Wild Bill Wild Bill Hickok was a United States marshal in the WILD WEST who was famous for his gunfights with outlaws.

Hoover, J. Edgar J. Edgar Hoover was the head of the FEDERAL BUREAU OF INVESTIGATION (FBI) from the 1920s to the early 1970s.

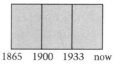

1865   1900   1933   now

I have a dream These words are from a speech given by the Reverend MARTIN LUTHER KING, JR., during the struggle for civil rights in the 1960s. The speech described his dream, which was to see peace and equality among blacks and whites. *See also* CIVIL RIGHTS MOVEMENT.

integration Integration is the act of bringing people, especially of different races, together in schools, neighborhoods, and public places such as restaurants and bus stations that were once segregated. The integration of blacks and whites was one of the goals of the CIVIL RIGHTS MOVEMENT. *Compare* SEGREGATION.

James, Jesse Jesse James was the leader of a gang of outlaws in the WILD WEST. The gang became legendary for its daring robberies of banks and trains.

JFK *See* KENNEDY, JOHN F.

Johnson, Lyndon B. Lyndon B. Johnson became president of the United States in 1963, after JOHN F. KENNEDY was assassinated, and served until 1969. He started the WAR ON POVERTY and increased American participation in the VIETNAM WAR.

Keller, Helen Helen Keller, who was blind and deaf as a child, learned to read and write and use sign language. She graduated from college in the early 1900s and inspired many people by overcoming her handicaps. The play and the movie *The Miracle Worker* are about Helen Keller and the woman who taught her sign language.

Kennedy, John F. John F. Kennedy, also known as JFK, was the president of the United States for only two years. He is remembered for his youth, good looks, and impressive speaking style. He was the first Roman Catholic president and the youngest man ever elected to that office. He encouraged the development of the space program and promised that one day an American would walk on the moon. Kennedy was assassinated in 1963 in Dallas, Texas. *See also* ASK NOT WHAT YOUR COUNTRY CAN DO FOR YOU.

Kentucky Derby The Kentucky Derby is a famous horse race held in Louisville, Kentucky, each spring.

King, Martin Luther, Jr. Martin Luther King, Jr., was a clergyman who led the CIVIL RIGHTS MOVEMENT in the South in the 1960s. He organized marches to protest SEGREGATION and racial injustice and delivered one of the most powerful speeches in American history, in which he told the nation, "I HAVE A DREAM" of peace and racial equality. He urged his followers to use nonviolent means, known as "passive resistance," to call attention to the wrongs suffered by blacks. During various protest activities, civil rights workers were often attacked by the police or angry whites, but the civil rights workers did not fight back. Their courage eventually won support for their cause from many people.

Korean War (kuh-REE-uhn) The Korean War was fought between North Korea and South Korea in the early 1950s. North Korea was supported by the Soviet Union and the People's Republic of China. South Korea was supported by the United Nations, but most of the troops were United States soldiers. A truce, or end to the fighting, was declared, but there is still great tension between the two Koreas.

John F. Kennedy

Martin Luther King, Jr. Delivering his "I have a dream" speech in Washington, D.C., on August 28, 1963.

Ku Klux Klan The Ku Klux Klan was a group of white people in the South who committed acts of terror and violence against blacks after the CIVIL WAR. They wore white sheets and white, pointed hoods to disguise themselves and frighten their victims. Other racist groups calling themselves the Ku Klux Klan were formed in the 1920s. In the 1960s, similar groups opposed the CIVIL RIGHTS MOVEMENT.

Labor Day Labor Day is an American holiday honoring workers and is celebrated on the first Monday in September.

Memorial Day Memorial Day is the holiday observed on the last Monday in May in honor of American soldiers killed in wartime.

Nixon, Richard Richard Nixon was the president of the United States from 1969 to 1974. He was elected to a second term by a large margin, but because of the WATERGATE scandal he became the first president ever to resign from office.

nonviolence Nonviolence, or nonviolent resistance, is a method of protest that was used by members of the CIVIL RIGHTS MOVEMENT in the 1950s and 1960s. To protest against SEGREGATION in public areas such as buses and restaurants, blacks would sit in places meant for whites and whites would sit in places meant for blacks. Even when they were taunted or beaten by people who wanted to maintain segregation, the protesters would not fight back. Some of them were seriously injured in these demonstrations, but their methods succeeded in gaining sympathy for the civil rights movement. Nonviolent methods of protest have also been used to further other political and social causes.

only thing we have to fear is fear itself, the These words were spoken by President FRANKLIN D. ROOSEVELT dur-

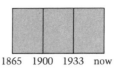

1865 1900 1933 now

ing the GREAT DEPRESSION. He was trying to encourage Americans not to panic during this trying economic crisis.

Pearl Harbor Pearl Harbor is a large American naval base in Hawaii. Early in WORLD WAR II, on December 7, 1941, Japanese planes made a surprise attack on the base, killing many people and destroying ships and planes. President FRANKLIN D. ROOSEVELT called the day of the attack "a day which will live in infamy" and declared that the United States was at war with Japan.

Pearl Harbor. Wreckage of the superdreadnought U.S.S. *Arizona* in Pearl Harbor.

Prohibition (proh-uh-BISH-uhn) Prohibition is the common name for the law passed in the 1920s to prevent, or prohibit, alcoholic drinks such as beer, wine, and liquor from being made or sold. Because alcoholic drinks were made and sold widely despite the law, Prohibition was hard to enforce. As a result, the law was repealed in the 1930s, making alcohol legal again.

105

Reagan, Ronald   Ronald Reagan, a former movie actor and governor of California, was the president of the United States from 1981 to 1989.

In 1984, at the age of seventy-three, Reagan became the oldest person ever to be elected president. ❧

Reconstruction   Reconstruction is the name for the ten years after the CIVIL WAR, when the defeated Southern states were reorganized and admitted back into the UNION.

Robinson, Jackie   Jackie Robinson was the first black man to play major league baseball in the twentieth century. Before he joined the Brooklyn Dodgers, no major league team since the late 1800s had hired black players. Robinson came to represent the struggle of blacks to achieve social equality with whites. When his baseball career ended, he became a businessman and a spokesman for the CIVIL RIGHTS MOVEMENT.

Roosevelt, Eleanor   (ROH-zuh-velt)   Eleanor Roosevelt, the wife of President FRANKLIN D. ROOSEVELT, was a humanitarian, social reformer, political activist, and writer.

Roosevelt, Franklin D.   (ROH-zuh-velt)   Franklin Delano Roosevelt, also known as FDR, was the president of the United States during the GREAT DEPRESSION and WORLD WAR II whose social and economic policies helped to end the Depression. A calm and encouraging leader, he often spoke to the American people over the radio in what became known as fireside chats. He was the only president to be elected to four terms of office. *See also* WORLD WAR II.

Franklin D. Roosevelt

Babe Ruth

Roosevelt, Theodore R. (ROH-zuh-velt) Theodore Roosevelt was the president of the United States in the early 1900s. He was sickly as a child but overcame his ailments to become a robust and physically active rancher, big-game hunter, and outdoorsman. During the SPANISH-AMERICAN WAR, he led a troop of volunteer cavalry soldiers called the Rough Riders. As president, he conducted an aggressive foreign policy, particularly in Latin America. He summed up his policy by saying, "Speak softly, and carry a big stick."

Rose Bowl The Rose Bowl is the oldest of college football's postseason bowl games. It is also the name of the stadium in Pasadena, California, where the game is usually played on New Year's Day.

Ruth, Babe Babe Ruth was a baseball player for the New York Yankees in the 1920s and 1930s. He was the first great home run hitter and is considered by many fans to be the greatest player of all time.

segregation Segregation is the practice of keeping people separated, especially on the basis of race. A segregated school is a school that admits students of only one race. A segregated neighborhood is one where people of only one race live. Segregation is illegal in the United States. *Compare* INTEGRATION.

Sitting Bull Sitting Bull was the Sioux chief of the late 1800s who led his warriors at the Battle of the Little Big Horn, also known as CUSTER'S LAST STAND.

Spanish-American War The Spanish-American War was a brief war between Spain and the United States that was fought in Cuba and in the Philippines at the end of the 1800s. The American victory gave the United States control over Puerto Rico, Guam, Hawaii, and the Philippines.

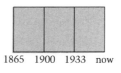

1865 1900 1933 now

Super Bowl The Super Bowl is the game played every January for the championship of the National Football League.

Thorpe, Jim Jim Thorpe, an athlete in the early 1900s, is considered one of the finest all-around athletes of all time. An American Indian by ancestry, he played college and professional football, professional baseball, and won a number of Olympic events in track and field.

Sitting Bull

Truman, Harry S Harry S Truman became the president of the United States when FRANKLIN D. ROOSEVELT died, at the end of WORLD WAR II, and served during the KOREAN WAR, until 1953. Truman was president when the United States dropped atomic bombs on Japan, in 1945. After World War II, he supported programs to aid European and Japanese recovery.

> **W**hen he was born, Truman was given a middle initial that did not stand for anything, so the "S" is often printed without a period after it. ❧

Vietnam War (vee-et-NAHM) The Vietnam War was fought in Southeast Asia between South Vietnam and communist North Vietnam in the 1960s and 1970s. The United States became seriously involved in the war in the early 1960s, hoping to prevent communists from taking over Southeast Asia. From the beginning, some Americans objected to United States participation in the war, and antiwar sentiment grew stronger and more widespread during the 1960s. Conflicts in the United States between supporters and protesters of the war became extremely bitter and sometimes violent. The war ended when North Vietnam conquered South Vietnam in 1975.

War on Poverty The War on Poverty is the name given to the social and economic programs of the 1960s, started by President LYNDON B. JOHNSON, that were designed to end poverty in the United States.

Washington, Booker T. Booker T. Washington was a leader who attempted to improve the situation of black people in the 1800s and early 1900s. He

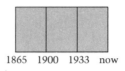

1865   1900   1933   now

founded the Tuskegee Institute, a college dedicated to educating blacks.

Watergate Watergate, the worst political scandal in American history, occurred in the early 1970s during the reelection campaign of President RICHARD NIXON. Its name comes from the Watergate Hotel in Washington, D.C., where five men were caught breaking into the headquarters of the DEMOCRATIC PARTY. It was later discovered that the men were operating under orders from high officials in Nixon's administration, and the president himself was found to be involved in an effort to cover up the crime. Many people believed that Nixon should be impeached, or formally charged with committing crimes while in office, but he resigned from office before he could be brought to trial. He became the first president to resign from the presidency.

Wild West The Wild West is a name given to the states and territories west of the Mississippi River during the late 1800s. The outlaws, gunfighters, sheriffs, and cowboys of the time are depicted in many movies and books.

Wilson, Woodrow Woodrow Wilson was the president of the United States early in the 1900s, when the country entered WORLD WAR I. After the war, he helped found the League of Nations, a peacekeeping organization that the United States did not join. The league proved important as a forerunner of the UNITED NATIONS. *See also* WORLD WAR I.

World Series The World Series is the baseball championship played every October. The winners of the National

Politics and
Economics

olitics concerns the way a society is organized and governed. It pertains both to na-
onal governments and to smaller groups, such as states, cities, and even clubs and
isinesses. There are a number of different political systems, including democracies,
onarchies, and dictatorships. There are also different ideas about how a government
ould operate. Here we focus especially on the American political system.

Economics is the study of how people earn and spend money and make and sell
ds. An economic system is a particular way of producing, distributing, and consum-
g the goods and services of society so that members of that society can prosper. Just
there are different political systems, so, too, there are different economic systems.
vo of the most important ones are capitalism and socialism.

endment   An amendment is a change
de in a law. The first ten amendments to
CONSTITUTION are called the BILL OF
GHTS.

l of Rights   The first ten amendments to
CONSTITUTION, called the Bill of Rights,
ine the rights and freedoms of American
izens in relation to their government. They
cern: (1) freedom of religion, speech, press,
embly, and petition; (2) the right to bear
ns; (3) the right not to quarter soldiers;
protection from unreasonable searches and
zures; (5) the rights of those accused of
nes; (6) the right to a jury trial in criminal
es; (7) civil suits; (8) protection from unrea-
able bail and cruel punishment; (9) other

rights not specifically discussed in the Constitution; and (10) powers not enumerated in
the Constitution and kept by the states or the
people.

budget   A budget is a plan for spending
money. The national budget in the United
States is the yearly plan for how much money
the government will spend on different programs.

capitalism   Capitalism is the economic system under which most economic decisions
are made and ownership retained by individuals rather than the government. For instance,
an individual owner of a business can decide
whether to make a certain product and how

)

Wright brothers. The first flight at Kitty Hawk, North Carolina. Orville i the controls while Wilbur remains on the ground.

League and the American League meet in a best-of-seven series in which the first team to win four games wins the world championship.

World War I World War I began in Europe in 1914. Germany and its allies fought against other countries, led by Britain and France. The United States at first tried to stay neutral; that is, it tried not to take sides. In 1917, however, the United States entered the war on the side of Britain and France. The war ended in 1918 when Germany surrendered. *See also* WORLD WAR I *under "World History Since 1600."*

World War II World War II began in 1939 with the German invasion of Poland. The United States entered the war formally in 1941, after the Japanese attack on PEARL HARBOR. During the war, American workers produced an astonishing number of planes, ships, weapons, and ammunition to

support the Allied forces in Britain, France, and the Soviet also required Americans to and conserve essential suppli line. In Europe, Allied troops ican general DWIGHT D. EISI in France on June 6, 1944, wl D-DAY. During the next year through France, liberated Pa many, and raced toward Berl rendered in May 1945. The ended when American plane bombs on the Japanese citi and Nagasaki. *See also* WOR *"World History Since 1600."*

Wright brothers bur Wright inven when they flew the first m ier-than-air flying machine North Carolina, in the early

The Capitol

much to charge. Capitalism is sometimes called FREE ENTERPRISE. It is often considered the opposite of SOCIALISM.

Capitol, the   The Capitol is the white, domed building on Capitol Hill, in Washington, D.C., where the United States CONGRESS meets.

CIA   The CIA (Central Intelligence Agency) is a government agency that keeps track of information, or "intelligence," regarding other nations. Some people who work for the CIA are spies.

civil rights   In the United States, people have the right to be treated the same regardless of their race, sex, or religion. These rights, which are guaranteed by law, are often called civil rights.

communism   Communism is an economic and political movement started in the 1800s

by KARL MARX. Marx called for a form of SOCIALISM in which all property is owned by the community. Communists believe that workers should take power and control all aspects of social and economic life.

Congress   In the United States, the part of the FEDERAL GOVERNMENT that makes the laws, the legislative branch, is called Congress. (*Legislative* means "lawmaking.") It consists of two groups, or houses: the SENATE and the HOUSE OF REPRESENTATIVES. Members of both houses are elected by the people.

conservative   A conservative is a person who believes that the main purpose of government is to maintain or change gradually the established order and tradition. Conservatives often oppose the viewpoints of LIBERALS. *See also* LIBERAL.

Constitution   The Constitution is the document that established the United States gov-

111

ernment and its system of laws. It describes the different branches of the government and defines the rights to which all Americans are entitled. The Preamble to the Constitution reads:

> We, the people of the United States, in order to form a more perfect Union, establish justice, insure domestic tranquillity, provide for the common defense, promote the general welfare, and secure the blessings of liberty to ourselves and our posterity, do ordain and establish this Constitution for the United States of America.

consumer   A consumer buys goods or uses services.

> **T**hings that people use up and wear out, such as food and clothing, are called consumer goods. ❧

corporation   A corporation is a business owned by a group of people, called shareholders, each of whom has bought shares of the business. *See also* STOCK.

credit   A person who buys something now and agrees to pay for it later is buying it on credit.

debt   A debt is a sum of money that one person owes another. To be in debt is to owe money.

Declaration of Independence   The Declaration of Independence, written mainly by THOMAS JEFFERSON, is the document that declared the United States to be an independent nation. It begins:

> When, in the course of human events, it becomes necessary for one people to dissolve the political bands which have connected them with another and to assume, among the powers of the earth, the separate and equal station to

which the laws of nature and nature's God entitle them, a decent respect to the opinions of mankind requires that they should declare the causes which impel them to the separation.

> We hold these truths to be self-evident; — That all men are created equal; that they are endowed by their Creator with certain unalienable rights; that among these are life, liberty, and the pursuit of happiness.

democracy   Democracy is the form of government in which power is held by the people and granted to their freely elected representatives for the purpose of running the government.

Democratic party   The Democratic party is one of the two main parties in American politics. (A party is a group of people, holding a range of views in common, who work to get its members elected to office.) Members of the Democratic party are called Democrats. The other main party in the United States is the REPUBLICAN PARTY.

deposit   A deposit is a sum of money that is put in a bank.

dictatorship   A government in which all the power is held by one person or a small group of people is called a dictatorship.

discount   A discount is the lowering, or reduction, of a price. If something usually costs $5 but a merchant is now selling it for $4, the buyer benefits from a discount of $1.

down payment   When you buy something for a large amount of money, you sometimes pay only part of the price right away and agree to pay the rest later. The part you pay right away is called a down payment.

e pluribus unum   *E pluribus unum* is a Latin phrase meaning "Out of many, one." It is a motto (special saying) of the United States

E pluribus unum. The Great Seal
of the United States.

because we are one nation made up of many
states.

election   An election is the process of vot-
ing, through which we choose a person for an
elective position. In a national election, we
choose a president.

executive branch   The executive branch is
one of the three main parts, or branches, of
the FEDERAL GOVERNMENT. It is made up of
the PRESIDENT, the vice president, and other
officials. Its function is to carry out laws
passed by the LEGISLATIVE BRANCH (CON-
GRESS).

fascism   Fascism is a system of government
dominated by one strong leader, often called a
dictator.

FBI   The FBI (Federal Bureau of Investigation) is a national law enforcement group
that gathers information and investigates the
breaking of federal laws.

federal government   The United States has
a national, or federal, government, which is
based in Washington, D.C. It helps to govern
the fifty states, each of which has its own
STATE GOVERNMENT.

feminism   Feminism is a political movement that works to achieve equal rights for
women and men.

free enterprise   Free enterprise is another
name for CAPITALISM. In a free enterprise system, most economic decisions are made by
individuals rather than by the government.

freedom of the press   The United States
CONSTITUTION grants freedom of the press,
which means that all Americans may write
what they please and make public what they
think in books, magazines, newspapers, radio,
and television.

freedom of religion   The United States
CONSTITUTION grants freedom of religion,
which means that all Americans are allowed
to practice whatever religion they choose
without interference.

freedom of speech   The United States CON-
STITUTION grants freedom of speech, which
means that all Americans may express their
ideas even if they disagree with and criticize
the government.

governor   In the United States, the head of
each of the fifty states is called the governor.

> **R**epresentatives, or congressmen,
> are elected for two years. Their
> chief officer is called the Speaker
> of the House. ❧

House of Representatives   One of the two
groups, or houses, in the United States CON-
GRESS is the House of Representatives. The
number of representatives, each of whom is
elected for a term of two years, is based on the
number of people who live in each state. *See
also* SENATE.

113

import When one country brings in a product that was made in another country, it is said to import that product. The product itself is also called an import. *Compare* EXPORT.

inflation Inflation is an economic term that means prices are rising. One dollar buys less as a result of inflation.

interest Interest is an extra sum of money you must pay to someone who has lent you money when you pay back the loan. For instance, if you were charged 10% interest on a $500 loan, you would have to pay back $550, the extra $50 (10% of $500) being the interest.

investment An investment is something you pay money for in the hope that it will become more valuable over time. For instance, you could invest in piano lessons because you hope to earn money or gain enjoyment by playing well in the future.

judge A judge rules over a court of law and makes decisions about legal procedures.

judicial branch The judicial branch is one of the three main parts, or branches, of the FEDERAL GOVERNMENT. It is made up of the courts, which explain and apply the laws passed by the LEGISLATIVE BRANCH. *See also* EXECUTIVE BRANCH.

labor union A labor union is a group of workers formed to get its members better pay, better working conditions, and job security.

legislative branch The legislative branch is one of the three main parts, or branches, of the FEDERAL GOVERNMENT. It is responsible for making the laws and is made up of the two houses of CONGRESS. *See also* EXECUTIVE BRANCH; JUDICIAL BRANCH.

liberal A liberal is a person who believes that the main purpose of government is to increase freedom and equality. Liberals often oppose the viewpoints of CONSERVATIVES.

Library of Congress The Library of Congress, in Washington, D.C., is the largest library in the United States. It is run by the federal government.

Lincoln Memorial The Lincoln Memorial is a large monument in Washington, D.C., built in memory of Abraham Lincoln, the president of the United States during the CIVIL WAR. His picture appears on one side of the penny, and the Lincoln Memorial is shown on the other.

The Lincoln Memorial, in Washington, D.C., contains a statue of Lincoln and the texts of his Second Inaugural Address and Gettysburg Address engraved in stone. ✒

---

loan A loan is a sum of money that one person or institution gives another with the expectation of being repaid.

local government Local government usually means city or county government as distinct from STATE GOVERNMENT and FEDERAL GOVERNMENT. A mayor is part of local government.

Marx, Karl Karl Marx was a German writer in the 1800s who believed that CAPITALISM would be destroyed and the workers would come to power. Marxism formed the basis of COMMUNISM. With Friedrich Engels, he wrote two important books, *Das Kapital* (*Capital*) and *The Communist Manifesto*.

monarchy A government that is headed by a king or a queen is called a monarchy. (Kings and queens are not elected by the people. Their power is inherited, that is, passed on to them through their families.)

NASA NASA (the National Aeronautics and Space Administration) is the United

NASA. The National Aeronautics and Space Administration emblem.

The Pentagon. An aerial view.

States government agency that runs the space program.

nationalism   Nationalism is the devotion to the interests and culture of one's nation. People who share a common language, history, and culture often identify themselves as a nation.

Pentagon   The Pentagon is a large, five-sided (pentagonal) building that is the headquarters of the United States armed forces. It is in Arlington, Virginia, across the river from Washington, D.C.

Pledge of Allegiance   The Pledge of Allegiance is a formal promise of loyalty to the United States that is often recited at public events. It says: "I pledge allegiance to the flag of the United States of America and to the Republic for which it stands, one nation, under God, indivisible, with liberty and justice for all."

president   The president is the chief executive of the United States and thus holds the highest elected position in the government. He is the head of the EXECUTIVE BRANCH of the FEDERAL GOVERNMENT and commander-in-chief of the armed forces. In the United States, a presidential election is held every four years. A president may serve no more than two four-year terms.

propaganda   Propaganda is rhetoric, whether spoken, written, or visual, that seeks to persuade people to believe certain political ideas. Propaganda is often sly and dishonest.

republic   A republic is a type of democracy in which power is distributed to officials who are elected by the people.

Republican party   The Republican party is one of the two main parties in American politics. (A party is a group of people, holding a range of views in common, who work to get its members elected to office.) Members of the Republican party are called Republicans. The other main party is the DEMOCRATIC PARTY.

United States senators are elected for a term of six years. Their presiding officer is the vice president. ❧

Senate   One of the two groups, or houses, in the United States CONGRESS is the Senate. Each state is represented by two senators, each of whom is elected for a term of six years. The other group is the HOUSE OF REPRESENTATIVES.

socialism   Under the economic system called socialism, the government runs the economy and tries to spread the wealth so that nobody will be poor. Natural resources are controlled by the government, which also owns the FACTORIES. Socialism is often opposed to CAPITALISM. *See also* COMMUNISM.

state government   State government is controlled by the GOVERNOR. It is distinct from LOCAL GOVERNMENT and the FEDERAL GOVERNMENT.

Statue of Liberty   The Statue of Liberty is the large statue of a lady holding a torch in one hand and a book in the other at the entrance to New York City's harbor. The statue, which represents Liberty (or freedom), was given to the United States by France in the late 1800s.

The Statue of Liberty

Supreme Court. The Supreme Court Building.

stock   Stock is the ownership of a corporation and is divided into parts, or shares. A stock certificate is issued to represent one or more of those shares.

strike   A strike occurs when a group of people stop working because they believe they are being treated unfairly. People often go on strike for higher wages.

Supreme Court   The highest, or most powerful, court in the American judicial system is called the Supreme Court. It can overturn (reject) the decisions of lower courts and has the final say on how our laws are applied. The Supreme Court meets in Washington, D.C.

The base of the Statue of Liberty is inscribed with a poem by Emma Lazarus that includes the lines: "Give me your tired, your poor, / Your huddled masses yearning to breathe free." ❧

Uncle Sam. A World War I army poster.

Uncle Sam Uncle Sam is a symbol of the United States and is shown as a tall old man with a white beard, dressed in clothes that look like parts of the American flag. He is often seen on posters and in newspaper cartoons. (Uncle Sam's initials — U.S. — are the same as those of the United States.)

union A union is an organization of workers. Its leaders represent the workers' interests in bargaining with employers.

Washington Monument The Washington Monument is a narrow, tall shaft of white stone in Washington, D.C. It was built to honor George Washington, the first president of the United States.

White House The White House, in Washington, D.C., is both the home and office of the president of the United States.

John Adams was the first president to live in the White House.

The Washington Monument

The White House

World History
to 1600

This section lists important people and events in world history from the earliest times through the 1500s. We pay particular attention to European history because Europe is so closely related to the United States. In fact, the cultures of Europe and the Americas, taken together, are often referred to as *Western* culture. The cultures of Asia are referred to as *Eastern* culture. In America, we are just beginning to learn more about the cultures of Africa.

Western culture has its roots in the ancient civilizations of Israel, Greece, and Rome. The history and culture of ancient Israel are described in the Bible section. Here we focus on ancient Greece and Rome, which have given us many of our central ideas about politics, law, art, nature, and the meaning of human life. We also include two later periods of European history, the Middle Ages and the Renaissance. In the Middle Ages, Christianity was the major force in European life. The Renaissance (which means "rebirth") was an age when great artists and explorers flourished and when America was discovered by Europeans.

The symbol at the beginning of most of the following entries places the events or persons described in their approximate place in time. See the legend for the span of years indicated by the symbol.

A.D.   A.D. is an abbreviation used with a date to indicate a year after the birth of Jesus. It stands for *anno Domini*, a Latin phrase meaning "in the year of the Lord." Many writers now use the abbreviation c.e., which means "of the common era," instead of a.d. *Compare* b.c.

Alexander the Great   Alexander the Great, one of the greatest military leaders of all time, was a king of ancient Greece who conquered most of western Asia. According to legend, he conquered the whole ancient world and then cried because he had no more worlds to conquer.

Alexander the Great. Portrayed on an ancient coin.

Aztecs. The Aztec Calendar Stone was used in ceremonies to honor the sun god Tonatiuh. Tonatiuh's face can be seen in the center of the calendar.

Athens   Athens is the capital of GREECE. In ancient times, it was a city-state and the first democracy. It was also the home of great artists, poets, playwrights, and philosophers.

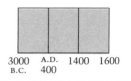

| 3000 B.C. | A.D. 400 | 1400 | 1600 |

Aztecs   The Aztecs were American Indians who once ruled a great empire in Mexico. In the 1500s, the Aztec empire was conquered by the Spanish. *See also* CORTÉS, HERNANDO; MONTEZUMA.

Babylon (BAB-uh-luhn; BAB-uh-lon)   Babylon was a city in the ancient MIDDLE EAST that was known for its great wealth.

B.C.   Events that took place in ancient times often bear the abbreviation B.C., which means "before Christ." Many writers now use the abbreviation B.C.E., which means "before the common era," instead. In these dates, the larger the number, the earlier the year. *Compare* A.D.

Bronze Age   The Bronze Age was the period of history, from about 4000 to about 2000 B.C., when people learned to use metal in making tools and weapons. The most important metal they used was bronze, an alloy of copper and tin. The Bronze Age was followed by the IRON AGE.

Brutus (BROOH-tuhs)   Brutus was a political leader in ancient Rome who is remembered for betraying JULIUS CAESAR. Although Caesar had been a friend, Brutus helped to murder him.

Caesar, Augustus (aw-GUS-tuhs SEE-zuhr)   Augustus Caesar was the first ruler of the ROMAN EMPIRE. The month of August is named after him. *See also* CAESAR, JULIUS.

Caesar, Julius (JOOHL-yuhs SEE-zuhr)   Julius Caesar was a Roman general who became the ruler of Rome. He was

119

Christopher Columbus. Presenting New World treasures to King Ferdinand and Queen Isabella of Spain.

killed by a group of Romans who were unhappy with his command. Among the murderers was Caesar's friend BRUTUS. Caesar's family continued to reign through the days of the Roman Empire. *See also* AUGUSTUS CAESAR; ROMAN EMPIRE.

Charlemagne (SHAR-luh-mayn) Charlemagne, also known as Charles the Great, was the king of France and the emperor of several other countries during the MIDDLE AGES.

The legends of King Arthur and his knights portray the age of chivalry. The idea of behaving "like a gentleman" is based on the knight's code of conduct. 🐝

China China, one of the principal civilizations of Asia, has had a continuous history from ancient times to the present.

chivalry Chivalry was the code of behavior by which the KNIGHTS of the European MIDDLE AGES were expected to live. A chivalrous knight fought fairly and bravely in battle and treated women with special courtesy.

civilization A civilization is a large and complex culture with systems of transportation and communication. It is run by an organized government that makes and keeps the laws. A civilization often has its own written language, religion, literature, and art. There are large buildings, and at least some of the people live in cities. (The word *civilization* is derived from the Latin word for "city.") Some of the world's first great civilizations were those of EGYPT, INDIA, and CHINA. The civilizations of ancient GREECE and ROME were especially important in the development of Western CULTURE.

Cleopatra   (KLEE-uh-PAT-ruh) Cleopatra was a famous queen of ancient EGYPT who fell in love with the Roman general Marc Anthony.

Columbus, Christopher Christopher Columbus was an Italian explorer who discovered America in 1492, when he was searching for a new route to the Indies. His three ships were the *Niña*, the *Pinta*, and the *Santa Maria*. *See also* FERDINAND AND ISABELLA.

Cortés, Hernando (kawr-TEZ) Cortés was a Spanish explorer who conquered the Aztec Empire in the 1500s. *See also* MONTEZUMA.

Crusades   During the European MIDDLE AGES, the HOLY LAND (the area that is now Israel) was ruled by MOSLEMS. Many Christians in Europe believed that this region, where Jesus lived and died, should be governed by Christians. Christian armies from all over Europe tried to conquer the Holy Land but eventually had to withdraw.

> **F**rom the Crusades we now have the term "a crusade," meaning a strong effort for an idea or cause. 🐦

culture   The culture of a particular group is its total way of life. It includes all the things the group as a whole thinks, believes, and does. To study a group's culture is to study its art, literature, religion, philosophy, sports, clothing, politics, customs, and habits. We may speak of the culture of a country (American culture), the culture of a region of the

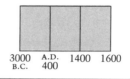

3000 B.C.   A.D. 400   1400   1600

world (Southeast Asian culture), or the culture of a racial group (black culture). A culture that is especially large and complex is called a CIVILIZATION.

Egypt   Egypt, a country in northeastern Africa, is the home of one of the world's oldest civilizations. The ancient Egyptians built great monuments, such as the PYRAMIDS and the SPHINX. Many preserved bodies of ancient Egyptians, called mummies, can still be seen in museums. The Egyptians used a system of picture writing called HIEROGLYPHICS. *See also* PHARAOH.

Elizabeth I   Elizabeth I was a queen of England in the 1500s. During her reign, WILLIAM SHAKESPEARE gained fame as a playwright and the SPANISH ARMADA was defeated. Her time on the throne is called the Elizabethan period.

Ferdinand and Isabella (IZ-uh-BEL-uh) King Ferdinand and Queen Isabella were the rulers of Spain in the late 1400s who sponsored CHRISTOPHER COLUMBUS's voyage to America.

feudalism   Feudalism was the political system of Europe during the MIDDLE AGES. Under this system, rulers granted land to certain people under their authority called VASSALS. In return, the vassals promised to support their rulers in time of war. Those who owned land were called nobles. The poor people who lived and worked on the land were called SERFS.

Greece   Greece is a country in southeastern Europe. One of the earliest civilizations appeared in ancient Greece and lasted from about 3000 to about 300 B.C. Its high point was in Athens from 700 to 300 B.C. The first great poets, artists, playwrights, and philosophers of Europe lived in Greece during this period. Among them were poets like HOMER, playwrights like Sophocles, and philosophers like PLATO and ARISTOTLE. Ancient Greece was divided into city-states (cities that ruled themselves as if they were separate countries). The two most important city-states were ATHENS, the first DEMOCRACY, and SPARTA. Later, when the Romans conquered Greece, they took over much of Greek culture, including the myths described in the mythology section of this dictionary. The influence of ancient Greece can still be felt in the literature, art, philosophy, and political ideas of Europe and America.

guild A guild was an organization of workers during the MIDDLE AGES and RENAISSANCE in Europe. Each guild was made up of individuals who participated in the same craft, profession, or business. Guilds set standards of quality and tried to ensure that their members were paid a fair price for their work.

Some of the important guilds in Europe in the 1400s were those for judges, bankers, doctors, wool and silk manufacturers, shoe makers, stone and wood carvers, innkeepers, carpenters, armorers, and bakers. ❧

Hannibal Hannibal was a general from the ancient city of Carthage, in northern Africa. When Carthage went to war with Rome, Hannibal set off to invade Italy. He led his army and a large number of elephants across the tall mountains called

The word *hieroglyphics* comes from a Greek term meaning "holy writing," because the ancient Egyptians believed that Thoth, the god of learning, had invented writing. ❧

Hieroglyphics. From the tomb of Hesire.

the ALPS, one of the most notable accomplishments in military history.

hieroglyphics Hieroglyphics are a type of writing used in ancient EGYPT and elsewhere. This system uses designs rather than letters to stand for language.

Huns The Huns were a warlike people from Asia who fought the Romans in the last days of the ROMAN EMPIRE.

I came, I saw, I conquered JULIUS CAESAR was a general of ancient Rome. After one of his military victories, he told the Roman government, "I came, I saw, I conquered."

Ice Ages The Ice Ages describe the time that GLACIERS covered much of North America and Europe. This period lasted until about 40,000 B.C.

Incas The Incas were a group of American Indians who ruled an empire in western South America and built great cities high in the Andes Mountains. They were conquered by the Spanish in the 1500s.

India India, one of the chief civilizations of Asia, has had a continuous history from ancient times to the present. The ancient Indian culture is often called the Indus Valley civilization because it flourished in the valley of the Indus River.

Iron Age The Iron Age was the period of history following the BRONZE AGE when iron was the most important metal used in tools, weapons, and machines. The Iron Age began around 2000 B.C. and has continued into modern times.

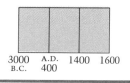

3000 B.C.　A.D. 400　1400　1600

Joan of Arc Joan of Arc was a young French girl in the Middle Ages who became one of the national heroines of France. She lived during a period when France and England were at war and England occupied much of France. Joan heard voices that she believed were those of God and certain Christian saints; the voices inspired her to lead the French in battle. She was eventually captured by the English, tried for witchcraft, and burned at the stake. Later, she was named a saint of the ROMAN CATHOLIC CHURCH.

Incas. Ruins of Machu Picchu, near Cuzco, Peru.

Knight. Knights at a jousting tournament.

knight In the European MIDDLE AGES, a knight was a soldier of the noble class trained as a horseman. He sometimes wore armor, metal protection, over his body. A knight pledged loyalty to a particular ruler, who gave him land in return. Knights were expected to follow the ideals of CHIVALRY.

Magellan, Ferdinand (muh-JEL-uhn) Ferdinand Magellan was a Portuguese explorer of the 1500s who led the first group of ships that sailed around the world. Magellan himself died on the voyage, but some of his sailors were able to complete the journey.

Magna Carta The Magna Carta was the great charter of CIVIL RIGHTS granted by the English king to his nobles in the MIDDLE AGES. It is one source of American ideals of liberty.

Middle Ages The period of European history between the fall of Rome and the RENAISSANCE, from about 500 to about 1500, is called the Middle Ages. During this time, the Christian church had an especially strong influence on all aspects of European life. FEUDALISM was the dominant political system. The first half of the Middle Ages is sometimes called the Dark Ages. *See also* ROMAN EMPIRE.

The Middle Ages, sometimes referred to as medieval times, were when the great European cathedrals were built. ❧

Montezuma (MON-tuh-ZOOH-muh) Montezuma was the ruler of the AZTEC Empire when it was conquered by the Spanish in the 1500s. *See also* CORTÉS, HERNANDO.

Norman Conquest   In 1066, England was conquered by an army of Normans (people from Normandy, in northern France) at the Battle of Hastings, in southern England. After the Norman Conquest, French language and culture became a part of English life. *See also* WILLIAM THE CONQUEROR.

pharaoh (FAIR-oh)   In ancient EGYPT, the ruler was called the pharaoh.

Polo, Marco   Marco Polo was an Italian explorer during the MIDDLE AGES. He traveled as far as China and later returned to tell the Europeans about his travels in Asia.

> **M**arco Polo wrote about a number of things known to the people of Asia that Europeans had never heard of, such as paper money, coal, and the fireproof material called asbestos. ❧

Pyramids   The Pyramids are huge stone monuments in Egypt. Each one has four triangular sides, which come to a point at the top, and a square base. They were built in ancient times as tombs for the Egyptian PHARAOHS.

Reformation, the   In the 1500s, many Roman Catholics rebelled against the authority of the church and broke away to set up new churches, which became known as Protestant churches. This rebellion is called the Reformation because it began as an effort to reform Christianity. After the Reformation, much of northern Europe became

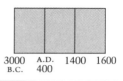

3000   A.D.   1400   1600
B.C.   400

Protestant while most of southern Europe remained Catholic.

> **T**he Renaissance was a time of brilliant new discoveries. Now we use the word *renaissance* (from a French word meaning "rebirth") to refer to a time of blossoming in any area. ❧

Renaissance (REN-i-SANS)   The period of European history from about 1400 to about 1600 is called the Renaissance and marks the end of the MIDDLE AGES. The Renaissance was a time of great achievements in art and literature when artists such as LEONARDO DA VINCI and MICHELANGELO and writers such as Cervantes and SHAKESPEARE were active. The Renaissance was also the great age of exploration, when CHRISTOPHER COLUMBUS discovered the New World.

Roman Empire   In ancient times, Rome (which today is the capital of Italy) was the center of a great empire. At the height of its power, the Roman Empire included Italy, Greece, France, Britain, Spain, and parts of North Africa and the eastern Mediterranean. The Romans were remarkable soldiers, engineers, and lawmakers. Their empire was connected by a huge network of roads, many of which can still be seen in Europe. The Roman Empire also left its mark on the languages of Europe, for Italian, French, and Spanish all come from Latin, the language of the Romans. English, too, has many Latin words. The Roman Empire lasted from just before the birth of Jesus to about

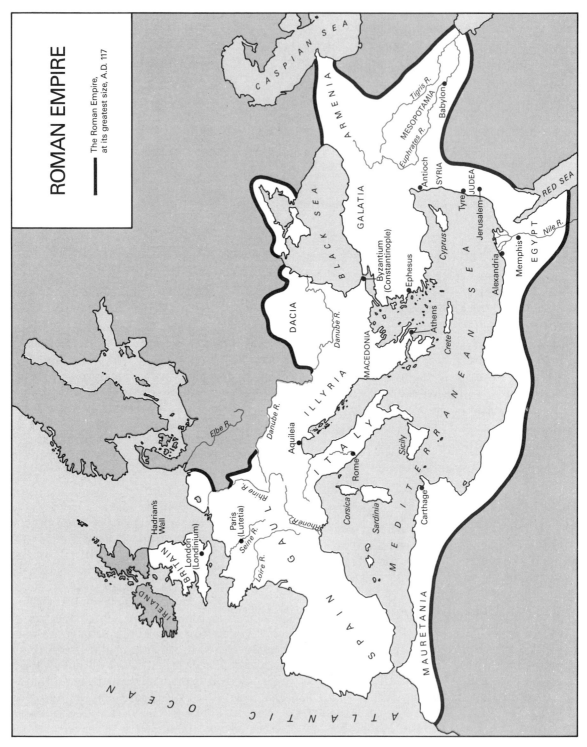

ROMAN EMPIRE

—— The Roman Empire,
at its greatest size, A.D. 117

CASPIAN SEA

ARMENIA

Tigris R.

MESOPOTAMIA

Euphrates R.

Babylon

Antioch

SYRIA

JUDEA

RED SEA

GALATIA

BLACK SEA

Byzantium
(Constantinople)

Ephesus

Cyprus

Tyre

Jerusalem

Alexandria

Memphis

EGYPT

Nile R.

DACIA

Danube R.

Athens

MACEDONIA

Crete

ILLYRIA

MEDITERRANEAN SEA

Danube R.

Elbe R.

Aquileia

ITALY

Rome

Sicily

Corsica

Sardinia

Carthage

Rhine R.

GAUL

Hadrian's
Wall

Paris
(Lutetia)

Rhône R.

London
(Londinium)

BRITAIN

Seine R.

Loire R.

IRELAND

SPAIN

MAURETANIA

ATLANTIC OCEAN

Sphinx. Late-nineteenth-century photograph of the Great Sphinx in Giza, Egypt.

A.D. 500. *See also* CAESAR, AUGUSTUS; CAESAR, JULIUS.

Rome *See* ROMAN EMPIRE.

serf Under the feudal system of the MIDDLE AGES, the land was farmed by poor people who were called serfs. The serfs were under the complete control of the nobles who owned the land. *See also* FEUDALISM.

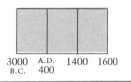

| 3000 B.C. | A.D. 400 | 1400 | 1600 |

Spanish Armada The Spanish Armada was a huge fleet of ships that the king of Spain sent to attack England in the 1500s. The Armada was destroyed by the English ships. *See also* ELIZABETH I.

Sparta Sparta was one of the two most important city-states of ancient Greece. The Spartans were known as a warlike, disciplined people. *See also* ATHENS.

Sphinx The Sphinx is an enormous stone statue built by the ancient Egyptians. It has the head of a man and the body of a lion.

Stone Age The Stone Age was the earliest period of human history. During this time, before people learned how to shape metal, all tools were made of stone. *See also* BRONZE AGE; IRON AGE.

Stonehenge Stonehenge is a circle of huge stones standing upright on an open plain in England. The stones were set

Stonehenge

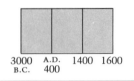

3000 A.D. 1400 1600
B.C. 400

Archaeologists now know that the Vikings traveled to North America around the year 1000, almost five hundred years before Christopher Columbus. ❧

---

in place in ancient times, but no one knows who put them there or what precisely they were used for.

vassal   In the feudal system, a KNIGHT who swore loyalty to a particular ruler became the vassal, or follower, of that ruler. *See also* FEUDALISM.

Vikings   The Vikings were sea-going warriors from Scandinavia who were famous for their skill as sailors. During the MIDDLE AGES, they repeatedly raided the coasts of Europe, attacking and looting towns.

William the Conqueror   William the Conqueror was the leader of the Normans, who conquered England in 1066. *See also* NORMAN CONQUEST.

World History Since 1600

Here we describe important people and events in the last four hundred years or so. This period has seen three world-shaking revolutions, when the American, French, and Russian peoples overthrew their governments. These years have also seen two world wars and the rise of dictators such as Hitler and Stalin. In this period, the expansion of science and technology has enabled people to live in increasing comfort, to conquer disease, and to venture as far as the moon. The spread of technology has brought problems, however, especially that of pollution. In the first part of this period, the nations of Europe were dominant. Today, the nations of Asia, Africa, and Latin America have gained their independence from European rule and are playing a growing role in shaping world events.

The symbol at the beginning of most of the following entries places the events or persons described in their approximate place in time. See the legend for the span of years indicated by the symbol.

apartheid (uh-PAHRT-heyet) In the nation of South Africa, a white minority rules over a black majority. The government enforces a policy of segregation of the races known as apartheid. This policy, which helps to keep blacks powerless, has been condemned by most of the countries in the world.

Bastille (bas-TEEL) The Bastille was a large prison in Paris, France. At the beginning of the FRENCH REVOLUTION, in the late 1700s, it was attacked and taken over by the revolutionaries. The day of the attack, July 14, is now a national holiday in France called Bastille Day.

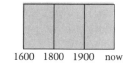

1600 1800 1900 now

Berlin Wall East Germany built the Berlin Wall in the 1960s to prevent citizens of East Berlin from escaping to West Berlin, a part of West Germany that it surrounded. The wall was torn down in 1989 during the peaceful popular uprising that led to the 1990 reunification of Germany. *See also* GERMANY.

129

Winston Churchill

Castro, Fidel Fidel Castro, a communist, is the dictator of Cuba.

Churchill, Winston Winston Churchill, as prime minister of Great Britain during WORLD WAR II, inspired the British people to stand up to HITLER.

Cold War Between World War II and the 1980s, a state of tension and military rivalry existed between the Soviet Union and the United States. This was called the Cold War, because there was no "hot" war, with actual fighting. But because each country believed that the other threatened its existence, both stockpiled thousands of nuclear weapons, a number being reduced slowly through disarmament talks and treaties.

colonialism A colony is a settlement established in a distant land that maintains social and economic ties with the country of origin. Colonialism usually means governing colonies to benefit not the colonized land and people but the colonizing country and people. In unpopulated or sparsely populated areas, such as the Americas, colonized by the British, French, Spanish, and Portuguese in the 1500s and 1600s, colonies can lead to the creation of new nations. In more populated areas, such as the parts of Asia and Africa colonized by the British, French, Belgians, Dutch, and Germans in the 1700s and 1800s, colonies are often absorbed or rejected by the local people, who establish or reestablish their own nations.

concentration camp A concentration camp is a kind of prison used by governments to confine large groups of people for political reasons. During World War II, millions of people died in concentration camps run by the NAZIS. *See also* HITLER, ADOLF; HOLOCAUST.

Cook, Captain James Captain James Cook, an English explorer of the 1700s, discovered the Hawaiian Islands.

D-Day During WORLD WAR II, a huge army of American and English troops landed on the coast of Normandy in France to fight the Germans, who had taken control of most of Europe. This invasion was the turning point of the war and the beginning of Germany's defeat. The day of the landing, June 6, 1944, is known as D-Day.

De Gaulle, Charles (di-GOHL) Charles De Gaulle was a French president in the mid-1900s. During World War II, he led the French Resistance, those people who defied Germany's occupation of France.

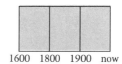

Anne Frank

Frank, Anne   Anne Frank, a Dutch Jewish girl, spent two years hiding from the NAZIS in Amsterdam during WORLD WAR II. She was eventually captured and sent to a CONCENTRATION CAMP, where she died. Her diary from her time in Amsterdam was found and published and is now a famous book, *Anne Frank: The Diary of a Young Girl.* *See also* HOLOCAUST.

French Revolution   In 1789, the French people revolted against their government. The revolution began with the storming of the BASTILLE, a prison. The king was overthrown and executed and France was declared a republic, but the struggle for freedom lasted several years and included the period known as the Reign of Terror. The revolutionary government was eventually overthrown by NAPOLEON, who made himself ruler of France. *See also* MARIE ANTOINETTE.

Gandhi, Mohandas   (GAHN-dee) Mohandas Gandhi was the greatest political and spiritual leader of modern India. Using nonviolent methods, he led India to independence from British rule.

French Revolution. The storming of the Bastille on July 14, 1789.

Mohandas Gandhi. The Indian leader, frequently shown spinning to symbolize his plan for India's economic self-sufficiency. Photograph by Margaret Bourke-White.

George III George III was the king of England during the American Revolution.

Hiroshima During World War II, American forces dropped an atomic bomb on the Japanese city of Hiroshima — the first time a nuclear device had been used as a weapon in wartime.

Hitler, Adolf Adolf Hitler was the leader of the Nazi movement. The NAZIS called him Der Führer (the Leader). After he became dictator of Germany, Hitler started WORLD WAR II in 1939 by invading neighboring countries, because he believed that Germany was destined to rule Europe. He hated the Jewish people and spread this hatred among his followers. Millions of Jews and other groups of people were murdered in CONCENTRATION CAMPS in a program of death and suffering that is known as the HOLOCAUST.

Holocaust During World War II, the NAZIS murdered more than six million Jews and other people whom Hitler considered inferior. This mass murder has become known as the Holocaust. *See also* HITLER, ADOLF; NAZIS.

Many children worked in factories in the 1700s, and by the early 1800s, Great Britain and other countries had to pass laws to keep the supervisors from making the children work too hard for too many hours. ⁊

Industrial Revolution Before the 1700s, most people in Europe lived and worked on farms. In the 1700s and 1800s,

Adolf Hitler

many new machines were invented, and they produced goods on a scale that had never been known before. Factories were built to house the machines. People moved from the country to find work in the factories, and industrial towns sprang up. Along with the machines came new methods of transportation, such as the railroad. Together, all these changes brought about by the rise of industry are called the Industrial Revolution. It had both good and bad effects on people's lives. More goods were available than ever before. Better means of transportation and communication were invented. On the other hand, most factory workers were poor, and factory towns were dirty and polluted.

Iron Curtain The term "Iron Curtain," first used by the British prime minister Winston Churchill, refers to an imaginary dividing line between the independent nations of Western Europe and the nations of Eastern Europe that came under the communist domination of the Soviet Union after World War II. The Eastern European countries once said to be "behind the Iron Curtain" began to regain their autonomy in the 1980s. *See also* COMMUNISM.

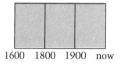

1600 1800 1900 now

Mao Zedong

Jolly Roger The Jolly Roger is a flag that shows a white skull and crossbones against a black background. It was once flown by pirate ships, when pirates were active in the 1600s and 1700s.

KGB The KGB is the secret police force in the Soviet Union.

Kidd, Captain Captain Kidd was a famous pirate of the 1600s.

Korean War The Korean War was fought in the early 1950s. The United States helped South Korea defend itself against an invasion from communist North Korea.

Lenin, V. I. V. I. Lenin was the leader of the communist group that seized power during the RUSSIAN REVOLUTION and became the first political leader of the Soviet Union.

Louis XIV Louis XIV, known as the Sun King, was a king of France during the 1600s, when France was the most important country in Europe. He is famous because of the absolute power he held over his people and for his support of the arts.

Louis XIV is often quoted as having said, "L'état, c'est moi" ("I am the state"), meaning that he did not consider anyone else to have a say in how France should be run. ❧

Mao Zedong (mowd-zuh-DOONG) Mao Zedong, also spelled Mao Tse-tung, was the first leader of mainland (communist) China after he led the communists to victory in the late 1940s. He became a very powerful dictator and controlled every aspect of his people's lives.

Marie Antoinette (muh-REE an-twuh-NET) Marie Antoinette was the queen of France at the time of the FRENCH REVOLUTION. She and the king, Louis XVI, were executed by the revolutionaries.

Mussolini, Benito (mooh-suh-LEE-nee) Benito Mussolini was the political leader of Italy during WORLD WAR II.

Napoleon (nuh-POH-lee-uhn) Napoleon Bonaparte was a general and the emperor of France in the early 1800s. He conquered much of Europe before being defeated by the British at the Battle of Waterloo.

133

NATO (North Atlantic Treaty Organization)   NATO is a group of democratic countries, mainly in Europe, that joined the United States to defend each other against aggression from the Soviet Union and its allies.

Nazis (NAHT-seez)   The Nazis were members of the political party that ruled Germany before and during WORLD WAR II. They hated Jews and other groups of people and believed that Germans were superior to all other peoples and should rule the world. Their leader was ADOLF HITLER, whose policies led to the HOLOCAUST.

Nightingale, Florence   Florence Nightingale was an English nurse of the 1800s. She became famous for her work tending wounded soldiers and helped establish the modern profession of nursing.

Pearl Harbor   On December 7, 1941, the Japanese attacked the United States naval base at Pearl Harbor, Hawaii. After the attack, the United States declared war on Japan, which led to direct American participation in WORLD WAR II in Europe as well as in Asia.

Russian Revolution   In 1917 and 1918, the Russian people overthrew their government. The Bolsheviks, a communist group, came to power and created the Union of Soviet Socialist Republics (USSR), which is also called the Soviet Union. *See also* LENIN, V. I.

slave trade   In the 1500s, Europeans, with the help of Africans, began to bring people from Africa to work as slaves on the farms and plantations of North and South America. The slave trade did not end in America and Europe until the 1800s, when many European countries passed laws against slavery.

Napoleon

Florence Nightingale

1600 1800 1900 now

Joseph Stalin

Stalin, Joseph (STAH-lin) Joseph Stalin was the leader of the Soviet Union in the early and middle 1900s, including WORLD WAR II. Notorious for his cruelty, he caused the deaths of millions of his people.

Teresa, Mother Mother Teresa, a Roman Catholic nun who lives in India, won the Nobel Peace Prize in 1979 for helping unfortunate and poor people.

Titanic The *Titanic* was an ocean liner that struck an iceberg and sank during its maiden (first) voyage, from England to New York, in April 1912. The ship, a luxury liner, had been considered unsinkable.

The *Titanic*

United Nations. Emblem of
the United Nations.

United Nations   The United Nations, or U.N., is an organization that was formed after World War II to promote world peace. Almost all of the nations of the world belong to the United Nations and send representatives to its headquarters in New York City.

Victoria, Queen   Queen Victoria was the ruler of Great Britain during the later 1800s and gave her name to that time, which is now known as the Victorian period. During her lengthy reign, Great Britain became the world's most powerful nation.

Vietnam War   The Vietnam War, between North and South Vietnam, lasted from the 1950s to 1975. Because North Vietnam was a communist country, the United States sent troops to help the South Vietnamese government. The war ended with the defeat of the South Vietnamese. *See also* VIETNAM WAR *under "American History Since 1865."*

Warsaw Pact   The Warsaw Pact is an alliance of communist nations in Eastern Europe that was organized by the Soviet Union after WORLD WAR II as a response to NATO.

Queen Victoria

Waterloo   Waterloo is the village in Belgium where NAPOLEON was finally defeated at the Battle of Waterloo in 1815. People who are defeated are said to have "met their Waterloo."

World War I   World War I was fought in Europe between 1914 and 1918. Great Britain, Russia, and France joined forces against Germany and Austria-Hungary. (Austria-Hungary was an empire made up of a number of eastern European countries.) In 1917, the United States entered the war on the side of Great Britain and its allies. World War I was the largest and bloodiest war that had ever been fought in Europe. It was especially shocking because of the use of destructive devices such as airplanes, poison gas, and machine guns. Much of the fighting took place in trenches (special holes dug by the soldiers). The war ended with the defeat of Germany and Austria-Hungary. *See also* WORLD WAR I *under "American History Since 1865."*

W orld War I was known as the Great War, or the World War, until World War II. ❧

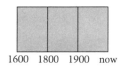

1600 1800 1900 now

World War II World War II was fought in Europe and Asia between 1939 and 1945. On one side were the Axis powers (Germany, Italy, and Japan), and on the other side were the Allies (including the United States, Great Britain, the Soviet Union, and China). The war began when Germany and Japan invaded neighboring countries. The turning point of the war in Europe came when Allied troops landed in France on D-DAY, June 6, 1944. Germany surrendered early in 1945. Japan gave up several months later, after the United States dropped atomic bombs on the Japanese cities of HIROSHIMA and Nagasaki. *See also* DE GAULLE, CHARLES; HITLER, ADOLF; PEARL HARBOR; STALIN, JOSEPH. *See also* WORLD WAR II *under "American History Since 1865."*

United States Geography

Geography is the study of the surface of the earth, its division into regions, and the different characteristics of those regions. This section of the dictionary focuses on the United States. It lists and locates the fifty states and some of the country's territories, the major natural formations, such as mountain ranges and rivers, the different regions of the country, and some of the major cities.

The symbol at the beginning of most entries indicates the region of the United States in which the state, city, or physical feature is found.

Adirondack Mountains (ad-uh-RON-dack) The Adirondacks are a mountain range in northeastern New York state.

Alabama Alabama is a state in the South.

Alaska Alaska, which is north and west of Canada, is the largest state. *See map on page 140.*

Allegheny Mountains (al-uh-GAY-nee) The Alleghenies are a mountain range extending from northern Pennsylvania to southwestern Virginia.

Annapolis (uh-NAP-uh-lis) Annapolis is the capital of Maryland and the site of the United States Naval Academy.

Appalachian Mountains (AP-uh-LAY-chee-uhn) The Appalachians are a mountain chain that extends almost the entire length of the East Coast, from Quebec, Canada, to Alabama.

The Appalachian Trail is the world's longest continuous hiking path; it runs through part of the Appalachian Mountains.

Arizona Arizona is a state in the Southwest.

Arkansas (AHR-kuhn-saw) Arkansas is a state in the South.

138

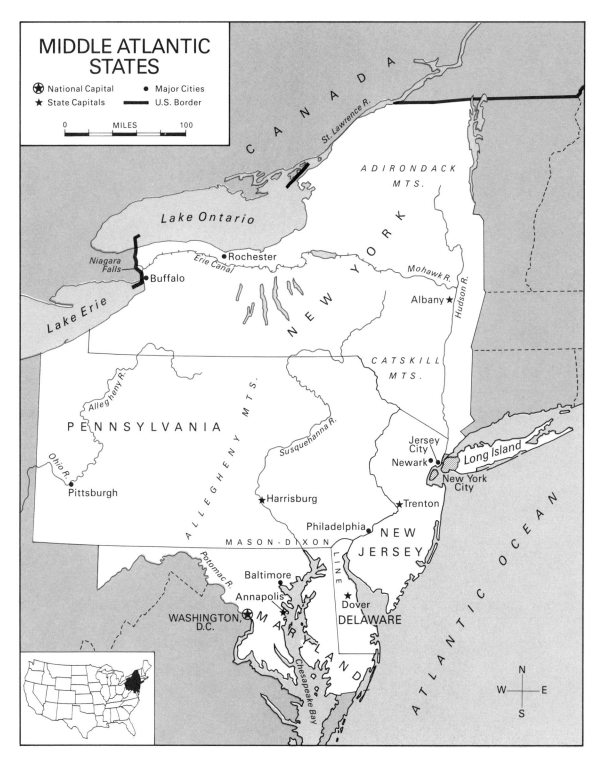

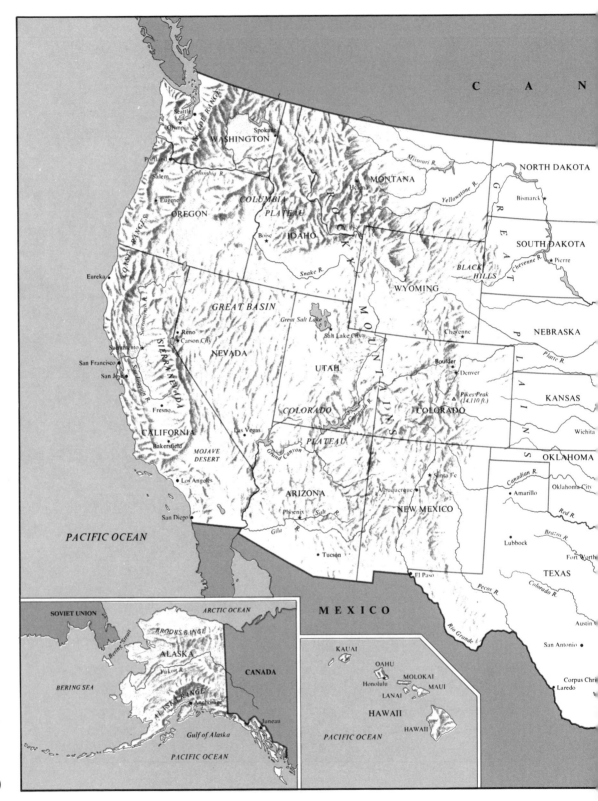

CANADA

NORTH DAKOTA
Bismarck ★

SOUTH DAKOTA
Pierre ★

WASHINGTON
Seattle
Olympia
Portland
Salem
Eugene
OREGON

Spokane

MONTANA
Helena

Missouri R.

Yellowstone R.

CASCADE RANGE

COLUMBIA PLATEAU

COLUMBIA R.

Boise
IDAHO

Snake R.

ROCKY

GREAT PLAINS

Cheyenne R.

BLACK HILLS

WYOMING

Chrome

NEBRASKA

Platte R.

KANSAS

Wichita

Eureka

COAST RANGES

GREAT BASIN

Great Salt Lake

Salt Lake City

Reno
Carson City

NEVADA

UTAH

Boulder
Denver

Sacramento R.

Sacramento
San Francisco
San Jose

SIERRA NEVADA

San Joaquin R.

Fresno

Las Vegas

COLORADO

Colorado R.

Pikes Peak
△ (14,110 ft.)

COLORADO

MOUNTAINS

OKLAHOMA

CALIFORNIA
Bakersfield

MOJAVE DESERT

PLATEAU

Santa Fe

Canadian R.

Oklahoma City

Los Angeles

ARIZONA

Grand Canyon

Albuquerque

Amarillo

Red R.

San Diego

Phoenix
Salt R.

Gila R.

Tucson

NEW MEXICO

Lubbock

Brazos R.

Fort Worth

TEXAS

Austin

PACIFIC OCEAN

El Paso

Pecos R.

Colorado R.

San Antonio

Corpus Chri
Laredo

MEXICO

Rio Grande

SOVIET UNION

ARCTIC OCEAN

BROOKS RANGE

ALASKA

Bering Strait

Yukon R.

CANADA

KAUAI

OAHU
Honolulu

MOLOKAI
MAUI

BERING SEA

ALASKA RANGE

Anchorage

LANAI

Juneau

HAWAII

PACIFIC OCEAN

Gulf of Alaska

HAWAII

PACIFIC OCEAN

140

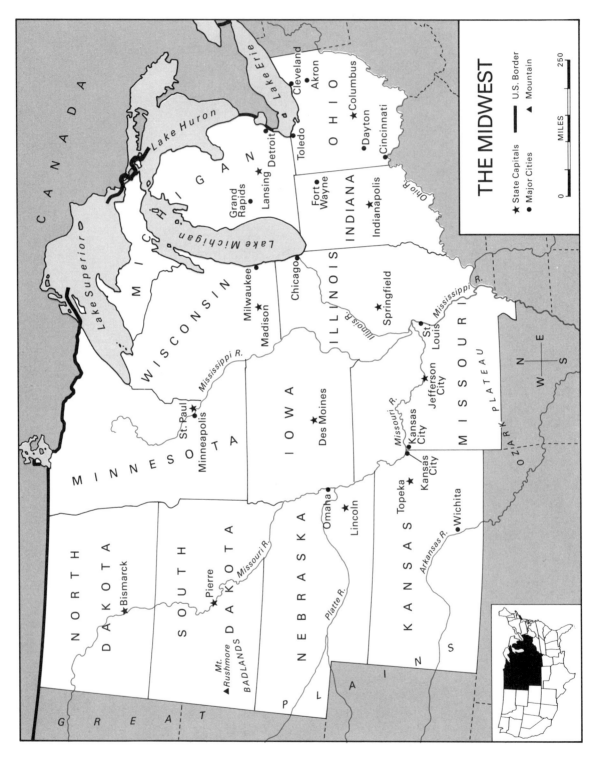

THE MIDWEST

★ State Capitals U.S. Border
● Major Cities ▲ Mountain

250
MILES
0

CANADA

Lake Superior

Lake Huron

Lake Erie

Cleveland ● Akron
OHIO
Columbus ★
Dayton ● Cincinnati ●
Toledo ●

MICHIGAN
Grand Rapids ● Lansing ★ Detroit ●

Lake Michigan

Fort Wayne ●
INDIANA
Indianapolis ★
Ohio R.

WISCONSIN
Milwaukee ●
Madison ★

Chicago ●

ILLINOIS
Springfield ★

Illinois R.

Mississippi R.

Mississippi R.

St. Louis ●
Jefferson City ★
Kansas City ●
MISSOURI
Missouri R.
OZARK PLATEAU

N
W — E
S

MINNESOTA
St. Paul ★
Minneapolis ●

IOWA
Des Moines ★

Kansas City ●
Topeka ★
Kansas City

NORTH DAKOTA
Bismarck ★

SOUTH DAKOTA
Pierre ★
Missouri R.
Mt. Rushmore ▲
BADLANDS

NEBRASKA
Omaha ●
Lincoln ★

Platte R.

KANSAS
Wichita ●
Arkansas R.

G R E A T   P L A I N S

142

Atlanta   Atlanta is the capital of Georgia and the state's most populous city. It is one of the major cities of the South.

Badlands   The Badlands, in South Dakota, is an area of barren hills and gullies caused by erosion.

Blue Ridge Mountains   The Blue Ridge Mountains, part of the Appalachian mountain chain, are mostly in Virginia and North Carolina.

Boston   Boston is the capital of Massachusetts and the largest city in New England.

Brooklyn   Brooklyn is a part, or borough, of New York City. The BROOKLYN BRIDGE, between MANHATTAN and Brooklyn, is a famous structure.

Thousands of settlers rushed to California after gold was discovered there in 1848. ❧

California   California, on the Pacific coast, is the most populous state. Two of its most important cities are Los Angeles and San Francisco.

Cape Canaveral   (kuh-NAV-uhr-uhl)   Cape Canaveral, in Florida, is the site of the John F. Kennedy Space Center, where the space program launches rockets. (A cape is an area of land that extends out into the water.)

Cape Cod   Cape Cod is a resort area on the Atlantic Ocean in southeastern Massachusetts. (A cape is an area of land that extends out into the water.)

Charleston   Charleston, South Carolina, is an old seacoast city. Another city named Charleston is the capital of West Virginia.

Chesapeake Bay   A bay is part of a larger body of water and extends into the land. The Chesapeake Bay is in the Atlantic Ocean, bordered by Maryland and Virginia.

Chicago   (shi-KAH-goh)   Chicago, Illinois, is a major midwestern city and the country's third most populous city. On the shores of Lake Michigan, it is nicknamed the Windy City because of the strong winds that blow off the lake.

Colorado   Colorado is one of the Rocky Mountain states.

Colorado River   The Colorado River, in the Southwest, is one of the country's longest rivers.

Columbia River   The Columbia River is in the Pacific Northwest.

Connecticut   (kuh-NET-i-kuht)   Connecticut is one of the New England states and was one of the original thirteen.

Dallas   Dallas is a large city in Texas and a major city in the Southwest.

Death Valley, at 280 feet below sea level, is the lowest point in North America. ❧

Death Valley   Death Valley is a desert valley in eastern California that is so named because of its harsh climate. In summer, it is one of the hottest places in the United States.

The Grand Canyon

 **Delaware** Delaware is one of the Middle Atlantic states and was one of the original thirteen.

 **Denver** Denver is the capital of Colorado and its largest city. It is the major city of the Rocky Mountain region.

 **Detroit** (di-TROIT) Detroit, in Michigan, is called the Motor City because it is the center of automobile manufacturing in the country.

District of Columbia *See* Washington, D.C.

 **East Coast** The East Coast is the name for the part of the country on the Atlantic Ocean.

 **Erie Canal** (EER-ee) The Erie Canal was a canal in New York state that connected the Atlantic Ocean to the Great Lakes. It was a major transportation and shipping route in the 1800s, in the days before the railroad and automobile, when freight was carried on boats.

 **Everglades** The Everglades is a large, marshy region in southern Florida famous for its wildlife, including alligators.

 **Far West** The Far West is the part of the country west of the Rocky Mountains, on the Pacific Ocean.

 **Florida** Florida, a state in the South, is the southernmost state on the East Coast.

Florida Keys   The Florida Keys are a long chain of islands off the southern tip of Florida.

Georgia (JAWR-juh) Georgia is a southern state on the East Coast, just north of Florida, and was one of the original thirteen.

Grand Canyon   The Grand Canyon is a deep, wide canyon in Arizona formed by the Colorado River. It is known for its spectacular scenery.

Great Lakes   The Great Lakes are a group of five lakes in the north-central part of the United States along the Canadian border: Lake Superior, Lake Michigan, Lake Huron, Lake Erie, and Lake Ontario. They are the largest group of freshwater lakes in the world.

Great Plains   The Great Plains is the vast, flat area of prairie, or grassland, that extends through parts of the Midwest, the West, and the Southwest. The prairie has very rich soil and grows vast quantities of corn and wheat.

Great Salt Lake   The Great Salt Lake is a large saltwater lake in Utah.

Great Smoky Mountains   The Great Smokies are the part of the Appalachian Mountains along the Tennessee–North Carolina border.

T he Smokies are named for the smokelike haze that hangs over them. ❧

Gulf of Mexico   The Gulf of Mexico is the part of the Atlantic Ocean bordered by the southern coast of the United States and the eastern coast of Mexico. (A gulf is a large body of ocean that is partly enclosed by land.) *See maps on pages 141, 153.*

Hawaii (huh-WAH-ee)   Hawaii, the only state in the Pacific Ocean, is a group of tropical islands far to the southwest of the United States mainland. *See map on page 140.*

H awaii is the fiftieth state. Its islands are famous for their spectacular beauty and for their many volcanoes, some of which are active. ❧

Hollywood   Hollywood, the traditional center of the movie industry, is part of Los Angeles, California.

Honolulu (HON-uh-LOOH-looh)   Honolulu is the capital of Hawaii. *See map on page 140.*

Houston (HYOOH-stuhn)   Houston is the largest city in Texas and one of the major cities of the Southwest.

Hudson River   The Hudson is a river in New York state. It flows to the Atlantic Ocean past the west side of Manhattan Island.

Idaho (EYE-duh-HOH)   Idaho is one of the Rocky Mountain states, famous for its potatoes.

Illinois (IL-uh-NOI)   Illinois is a state in the Midwest noted for its largest city, Chicago, and for being where ABRAHAM LINCOLN, as a young man, started his career.

Indiana (IN-dee-AN-uh)   Indiana is a state in the Midwest.

Indianapolis   Indianapolis is the capital of Indiana and its largest city.

Iowa (EYE-uh-wuh)   Iowa is a state in the Midwest.

Kansas (KAN-zuhs)   Kansas is a state in the Midwest.

Kansas City (KAN-zuhs)   Kansas City is a major midwestern city in Missouri; a smaller part of the city lies in Kansas.

Kentucky   Kentucky is a state in the South, the birthplace of ABRAHAM LINCOLN.

Lake Erie   Lake Erie is one of the Great Lakes north of Ohio.

Lake Huron (HYOOR-uhn)   Lake Huron, one of the Great Lakes, is northeast of Michigan.

Lake Michigan (MISH-i-guhn)   Lake Michigan is one of the Great Lakes, bordered by Michigan to the east and Wisconsin to the west.

Lake Ontario   Lake Ontario, one of the Great Lakes, is north of New York state.

Lake Superior   Lake Superior, the largest Great Lake, is north of Michigan.

> Lake Superior is the largest freshwater lake in the world. 🍂

Las Vegas   Las Vegas is a city in Nevada famous for its entertainment and gambling casinos.

Long Island   Long Island is an island east of New York City that contains part of the city and many of its suburbs. The eastern end of the island is also known as a resort area.

Los Angeles (laws-AN-juh-luhs)   Los Angeles, in southern California, is the second most populous city in the United States (after New York City).

Louisiana (looh-EE-zee-AN-uh)   Louisiana is a state in the South.

Maine   Maine, one of the New England states, is the northernmost state on the East Coast.

Manhattan   Manhattan is an island and the part of New York City noted for its skyscrapers, theaters, and financial district, known as Wall Street.

> In the 1600s, Manhattan Island was bought from the Indians by Dutch settlers for $24 worth of trinkets. 🍂

Maryland (MER-uh-luhnd)   Maryland is one of the Middle Atlantic states and was one of the original thirteen.

Massachusetts (MAS-uh-CHOOH-sits)   Massachusetts is a state in New England and was one of the original thirteen.

Miami (meye-AM-ee)   Miami is the largest city in Florida. Miami Beach, just east across Biscayne Bay, is a famous resort town.

Michigan (MISH-i-guhn)   Michigan is a state in the Midwest. Detroit is its largest city.

Middle Atlantic states   The Middle Atlantic states, Pennsylvania, New York, New Jersey, Delaware, and Maryland, are on the east coast. All but Pennsylvania touch the Atlantic Ocean, although Philadelphia is connected with the Atlantic

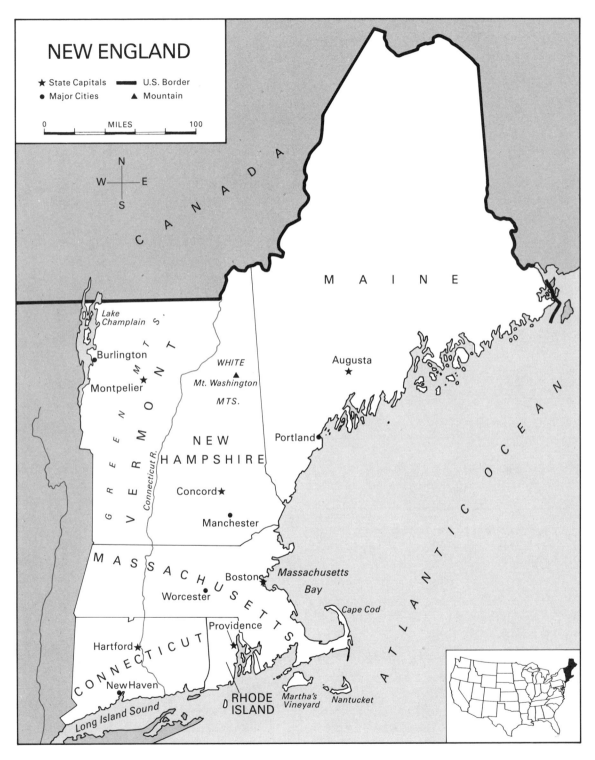

NEW ENGLAND

★ State Capitals   ▬ U.S. Border
● Major Cities   ▲ Mountain

0   MILES   100

N
W—E
S

C A N A D A

M A I N E

Lake Champlain

● Burlington

G R E E N   M T S.

V E R M O N T

Montpelier ★

Connecticut R.

WHITE
▲ *Mt. Washington*
MTS.

N E W
H A M P S H I R E

Augusta ★

Portland ●

Concord ★

● Manchester

M A S S A C H U S E T T S

Boston ★   *Massachusetts Bay*

● Worcester

Cape Cod

A T L A N T I C   O C E A N

Providence ★

Hartford ★

C O N N E C T I C U T

New Haven ●

R H O D E
I S L A N D

Martha's Vineyard   *Nantucket*

Long Island Sound

by the Delaware River. This region is the most densely populated area in the country.

Middle West   *See* MIDWEST, THE.

Midwest, the   The Midwest, or Middle West, is the vast, flat area in the northern middle section of the United States. Mainly on the Great Plains, it has some of the richest farmland in the world. The midwestern states are North Dakota, South Dakota, Nebraska, Kansas, Minnesota, Wisconsin, Iowa, Missouri, Illinois, Indiana, Michigan, and Ohio.

Minnesota   (MIN-i-SOH-tuh) Minnesota is a state in the Midwest.

Mississippi   Mississippi is a state in the South.

Mississippi River   The Mississippi, in the center of the country, is the longest river in the United States. It runs from Minnesota in the north to Louisiana in the south and empties into the Gulf of Mexico.

The Mississippi is an important shipping channel. ❧

Missouri   (muh-ZOOR-uh; muh-ZOOR-ee)   Missouri is a state in the Midwest.

Missouri River   (muh-ZOOR-uh; muh-ZOOR-ee)   The Missouri is a large river in the West and Midwest and flows into the Mississippi River.

Mojave Desert   (moh-HAH-vee) The Mojave Desert is in southern California.

Montana   (mon-TAN-uh)   Montana is one of the Rocky Mountain states.

Mount Rushmore. From left to right: George Washington, Thomas Jefferson, Theodore Roosevelt, and Abraham Lincoln.

Mount McKinley   Mount McKinley, in Alaska, is the highest mountain in the United States.

Mount Rainier   (ray-NEER; ruh-NEER)   Mount Rainier is a high mountain in the state of Washington.

Mount Rushmore   Mount Rushmore is a high cliff in the Black Hills of South Dakota where the faces of four American presidents (GEORGE WASHINGTON, THOMAS JEFFERSON, ABRAHAM LINCOLN, and THEODORE ROOSEVELT) are carved. Each face is about sixty feet tall.

Mount Saint Helens   Mount Saint Helens is an active volcano in the state of Washington.

Nashville   Nashville is the capital of Tennessee and the center of the country music industry.

148

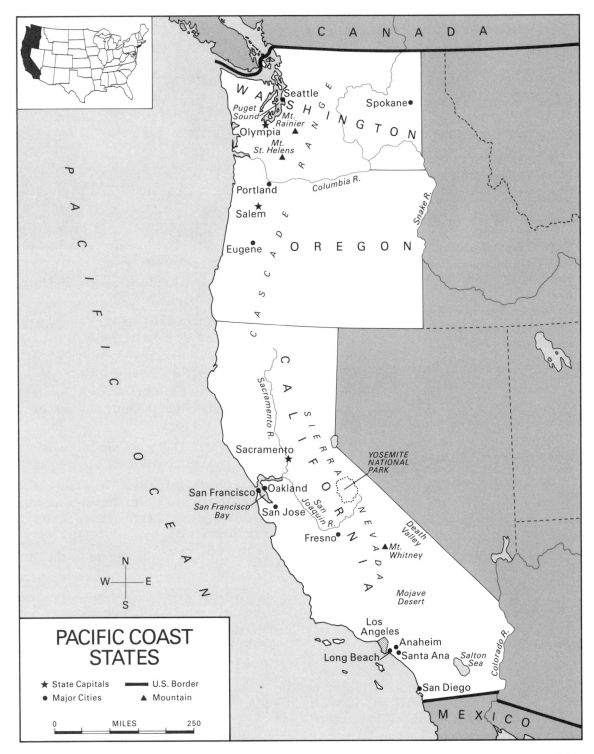

PACIFIC COAST STATES

★ State Capitals ━━ U.S. Border
● Major Cities ▲ Mountain

0   MILES   250

149

Nebraska Nebraska is a state in the Midwest.

 Nevada (nuh-VAD-uh) Nevada is one of the Rocky Mountain states. Its best-known city is Las Vegas.

Many of the events that led up to the American Revolution took place in New England. ❧

 New England New England is the northeastern region of the United States. It is a hilly and forested area, with many picturesque small towns. The New England states are Maine, New Hampshire, Vermont, Massachusetts, Connecticut, and Rhode Island.

 New Hampshire New Hampshire is a state in New England and was one of the original thirteen.

 New Jersey New Jersey is one of the Middle Atlantic states and was one of the original thirteen.

 New Mexico New Mexico is a state in the Southwest.

 New Orleans (AWR-lee-uhnz; AW-luhnz; aw-LEENZ) New Orleans is a port city in Louisiana, near the mouth of the Mississippi River, known for a yearly festival called Mardi Gras.

 New York New York is a Middle Atlantic state and was one of the original thirteen.

 New York City New York City, a port city on the Atlantic Ocean, is the most populous city in the United States. It has been an important business and cultural center since the 1800s and is now considered

Niagara Falls

the fashion capital and commercial and financial center of the country.

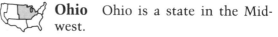 **Niagara Falls** (neye-AG-ruh; neye-AG-uh-ruh) Niagara Falls is a pair of spectacular waterfalls in western New York state on the Canadian border.

North Carolina North Carolina is a state in the South and was one of the original thirteen.

North Dakota North Dakota is a state in the Midwest.

Northeast, the The Northeast is the region of the United States that includes NEW ENGLAND and the MIDDLE ATLANTIC STATES.

Ohio Ohio is a state in the Midwest.

Ohio River The Ohio River flows along the southern borders of Ohio, Indiana, and Illinois before joining the Mississippi River.

Oklahoma Oklahoma is a state in the Southwest, north of Texas.

Oregon (AWR-i-guhn) Oregon is one of the Pacific Coast states, north of California.

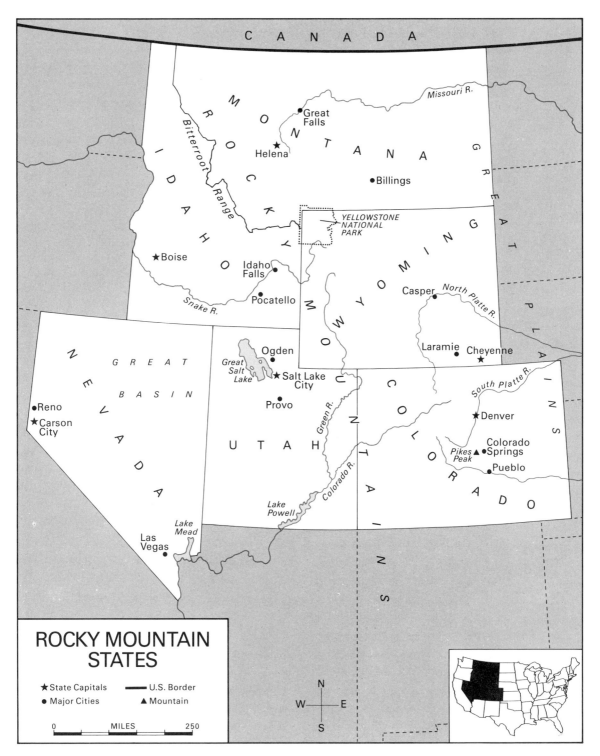

CANADA

MONTANA

Missouri R.

● Great Falls

★ Helena

● Billings

ROCKY

Bitterroot Range

I D A H O

YELLOWSTONE NATIONAL PARK

★ Boise

Idaho Falls ●

Snake R.

● Pocatello

WYOMING

Casper ●

North Platte R.

MOUNTAINS

GREAT PLAINS

Laramie ●

Cheyenne ★

NEVADA

GREAT BASIN

Ogden ●

Great Salt Lake

★ Salt Lake City

● Provo

U T A H

Green R.

South Platte R.

★ Denver

COLORADO

● Reno

★ Carson City

Colorado R.

Pikes Peak ▲

Colorado ● Springs

● Pueblo

Lake Powell

Las Vegas ●

Lake Mead

MOUNTAINS

ROCKY MOUNTAIN STATES

★ State Capitals ━━━ U.S. Border
● Major Cities ▲ Mountain

0   MILES   250

N
W E
S

151

Pacific coast states   The Pacific coast states, on the west coast along the Pacific Ocean, are Washington, Oregon, and California. They are known for their scenic mountains and shoreline.

Pacific Northwest   The Pacific Northwest is a name for the northwestern part of the United States. It includes Washington, Oregon, and northern California.

Panama Canal   *See* PANAMA CANAL *under "World Geography."*

Pennsylvania   (PEN-suhl-VAYN-yuh)   Pennsylvania is one of the Middle Atlantic states and was one of the original thirteen.

P ennsylvania is named for William Penn, a Quaker who settled the area when he was granted the land by the king of England. ❧

Philadelphia   (fil-uh-DEL-fee-uh)   Philadelphia is the largest city in Pennsylvania. Noted for its historical sites, it was the capital of the United States for a short time in the late 1700s.

Pikes Peak   Pikes Peak is a mountain in Colorado.

T he song "America the Beautiful" was inspired by a view from Pikes Peak. ❧

Pittsburgh   Pittsburgh is an industrial city in western Pennsylvania known for its steel mills.

Portland   Portland is the largest city in Oregon and a major city in the Pacific Northwest.

Potomac River   (puh-TOH-muhk)   The Potomac River flows along the southwestern border of Washington, D.C., the nation's capital.

Puerto Rico   (pawr-tuh-REE-koh; pwer-tuh-REE-koh)   Puerto Rico, an island southeast of Florida, in the Caribbean Sea, is a commonwealth of the United States. Its people are United States citizens, although they may not vote in national elections. *See map on page 176.*

Rhode Island   Rhode Island is a state in New England and was one of the original thirteen.

Rio Grande (REE-oh-GRAND, REE-oh-GRAND-ee)   The Rio Grande (Spanish for "Big River") is a river in the Southwest. It flows along the southern border of Texas and divides the United States from Mexico.

Rocky Mountains   The Rocky Mountains, in the West and Southwest, run from Alaska in the north, through Canada, and south to Mexico.

Rocky Mountain states   The Rocky Mountain states are the landlocked states in the western part of the country: Idaho, Montana, Wyoming, Nevada, Colorado, and Utah. They are known for their spectacular mountains and wilderness areas.

St. Lawrence River   The St. Lawrence is a river in eastern Canada that connects the Atlantic Ocean to the Great Lakes. Part of it borders New York state.

St. Lawrence Seaway   The St. Lawrence Seaway is a system of dams and canals in eastern Canada and along the New York state border that was built by American and Canadian engineers. The seaway makes it possible for ships to transport goods along the St. Lawrence River from the Atlantic Ocean to the Great Lakes.

WASHINGTON, D.C.

WEST VIRGINIA
Charleston ★

Ohio R.

A L L E G H E N Y   M T S.

Potomac R.

Shenandoah Valley

Richmond ★

VIRGINIA

Norfolk
Virginia Beach

Chesapeake Bay

Louisville ●
Frankfort ★
Lexington ●

Ohio R.

KENTUCKY

Cumberland Gap

Nashville ★
Knoxville ●

NORTH CAROLINA
★ Raleigh

T E N N E S S E E

A P P A L A

B L U E   R I D G E   M T S.

Great Smoky Mts.

Fort Smith ●
Arkansas R.

A R K A N S A S

Memphis ●
Chattanooga ●

Charlotte ●

Little Rock ★

SOUTH CAROLINA
★ Columbia

Mississippi R.

Tennessee R.

Birmingham ●

Atlanta ★

Savannah R.

Charleston ●

Shreveport ●

MISSISSIPPI

ALABAMA

GEORGIA

Jackson ★

Red R.

Montgomery ★

Alabama R.

Savannah ●

Baton Rouge ★

L O U I S I A N A

Mobile ●

F

★ Tallahassee

Jacksonville ●

New Orleans

G U L F   O F   M E X I C O

Cape Canaveral

Tampa ●

L
O
R
I
D
A

Lake Okeechobee

St. Petersburg ●

Everglades

Miami ●

Florida Keys

A T L A N T I C   O C E A N

THE SOUTH

⊛ National Capital
★ State Capitals
● Major Cities

N
W   E
S

0   MILES   250

153

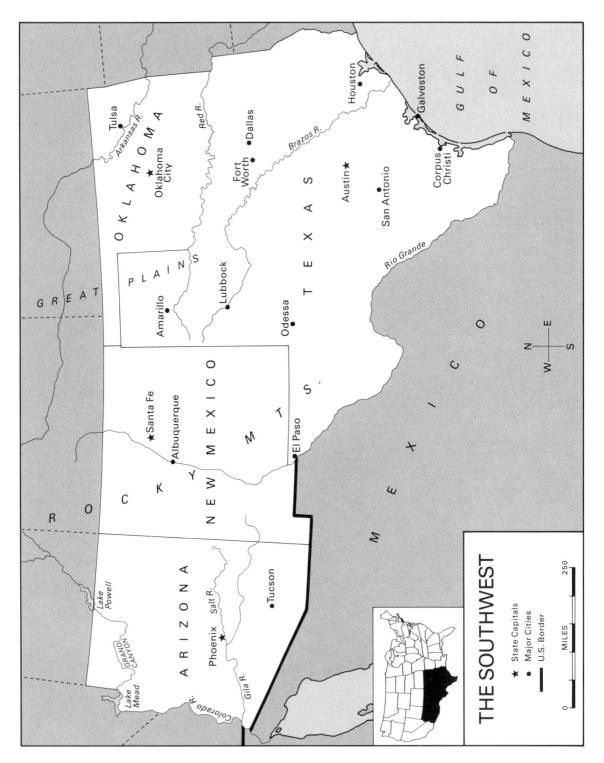

THE SOUTHWEST

State Capitals ★
Major Cities ●
U.S. Border ▬

MILES
0   250

St. Louis (saynt-LOOH-uhs) St. Louis is a major midwestern city in Missouri on the Mississippi River.

St. Louis was called the Gateway to the West in the 1800s because it served as a starting place for wagon trains. 🐂

Salt Lake City Salt Lake City is the capital of Utah and is the center of the Church of Jesus Christ of Latter-day Saints, called the Mormon Church.

San Andreas Fault The San Andreas Fault, in California, is where parts of the earth's surface rub each other and cause earthquakes.

San Francisco (fruhn-SIS-koh) San Francisco is the largest city in northern California and is known for the Golden Gate Bridge.

Seattle (see-AT-l) Seattle is the largest city in Washington and a major city in the Pacific Northwest.

Shenandoah Valley (shen-uhn-DOH-uh) The Shenandoah, in Virginia, is noted for its scenic beauty and its importance as a site of military action in the CIVIL WAR.

Mount Whitney, at 14,280 feet the highest peak in the United States (outside Alaska), is in the Sierra Nevada range. 🐂

Sierra Nevada (see-ER-uh nuh-VAH-duh) The Sierra Nevada is a mountain range in eastern California.

South, the The South is made up of the states in the southeastern region of the country: Arkansas, Louisiana, Kentucky, Tennessee, West Virginia, Virginia, North Carolina, South Carolina, Mississippi, Alabama, Georgia, and Florida.

South Carolina South Carolina is a state in the South that was one of the original thirteen.

South Dakota South Dakota is a state in the Midwest.

Southwest, the The Southwest is the region of the country known for its magnificent desert scenery and oil, gas, and mineral deposits. The southwestern states are Arizona, New Mexico, Oklahoma, and Texas.

Tennessee Tennessee is a state in the South.

Texas Texas is a state in the Southwest and, after Alaska, the biggest state.

Times Square Times Square is a section of Manhattan, in New York City, where people gather every year to celebrate New Year's Eve.

Utah (YOOH-taw) Utah is one of the Rocky Mountain states.

Vermont Vermont is a state in New England, known for its maple syrup.

Virgin Islands The Virgin Islands are resort areas in the Caribbean Sea. Some of the islands belong to the United States; others belong to the British commonwealth.

Virginia (vuhr-JIN-yuh) Virginia is a state in the South that was one of the original thirteen.

Washington Washington is a state in the Pacific Northwest, north of Oregon.

155

Washington, D.C. Washington, D.C., the capital of the United States, is on the Potomac River between Maryland and Virginia. The initials D.C. stand for District of Columbia, which is a federal district established in the 1800s by acts of Congress.

The headquarters of the three major branches of the United States government are in Washington, D.C.: the Capitol, the Supreme Court, and the White House. 🌢

West Coast The West Coast is the name for the part of the United States on the Pacific Ocean.

West Point West Point is a small town on the Hudson River in New York state where the United States Military Academy is located. The school is often referred to as West Point.

West Virginia (vuhr-JIN-yuh) West Virginia is a state in the South.

Wisconsin Wisconsin is a state in the Midwest, known for its dairy products.

Wyoming (weye-OH-ming) Wyoming is one of the Rocky Mountain states.

Yellowstone National Park Yellowstone, in the Rocky Mountains, was the first national park in the United States. It is famous for its spectacular scenery, wildlife, and geysers, including Old Faithful.

Yosemite National Park (yoh-SEM-uh-tee) Yosemite National Park, in eastern California, is noted for its views and waterfalls, including Yosemite Falls, the highest waterfall in North America.

World Geography

Geography is the study of the surface of the earth. Physical geography concerns physical features such as mountains, continents, and oceans. Political geography concerns countries and cities. Few people can name all the nations of the world, but most educated people recognize the names of most countries and have a general idea of where they are. You probably could not name the countries of eastern Africa, but if you came across Kenya in your reading, you should be able to know it is a country in Africa.

Listed below are the continents, countries, important cities, bodies of water, and major land formations of the world as well as the chief mountains and deserts. The symbols at the beginning of most of the following entries represent the continent on which the country, city, or physical feature is located. For bodies of water and islands, page numbers refer you to a map. In many countries, the name of the official language is related to the name of the country; for example, Polish (Poland) and French (France). In some cases where that is not so, we indicate the most frequently spoken language or languages of the country.

Acapulco   (AK-uh-POOL-koh) Acapulco is a resort city in Mexico on the Pacific Ocean.

Aconcagua Mountain   Aconcagua, in Argentina, is the highest peak in the Andes. It is the highest mountain in South America and the highest in the world outside Asia.

Aegean Sea (i-JEE-uhn)   The Aegean Sea is the northeastern part of the Mediterranean Sea between Greece and Turkey. Many of the famous Greek islands are found there. *See map on page 169.*

Afghanistan   (af-GAN-i-STAN) Afghanistan is a mountainous country in southern Asia between the Soviet Union and Pakistan.

Africa   Africa is the second largest continent (after Asia). It is bordered on the north by the Mediterranean Sea, on the east by the Indian Ocean, and on the west by the Atlantic Ocean. Many tribal and European languages are spoken.

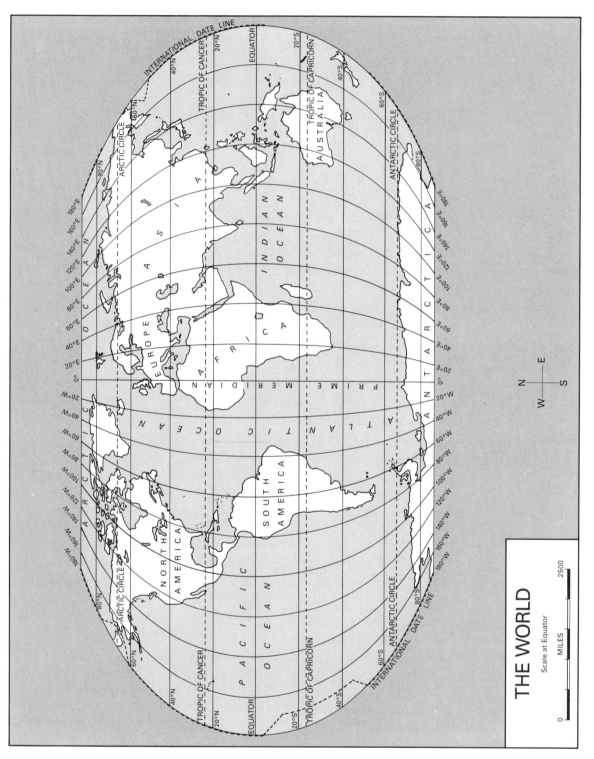

THE WORLD

Scale at Equator

MILES

0   2500

Albania (al-BAY-nee-uh)   Albania, a country in southeastern Europe, is south of Yugoslavia and north of Greece.

 Algeria (al-JEER-ee-uh)   Algeria is an Arabic-speaking country in northern Africa on the Mediterranean Sea between Morocco and Libya.

Alps   The Alps are a range of high mountains that cover parts of Germany, France, Italy, Switzerland, and Austria.

The Amazon River is named after the mythological female warriors called Amazons. ❧

Amazon River (AM-uh-ZON)   The Amazon is the longest river in South America. After the Nile, it is the longest river in the world and carries more water than any other river. Most of its length runs west to east in northern Brazil.

Amsterdam   Amsterdam is the capital of the Netherlands and is noted for its many canals.

Andes (AN-deez)   The Andes are a mountain range along the western coast of South America, on the Pacific Ocean.

Angola (ang-GOH-luh)   Angola is a Bantu- and Portuguese-speaking country in southwestern Africa on the Atlantic Ocean.

Antarctic Circle (ant-AHRK-tik; ant-AHR-tik)   The Antarctic Circle is an imaginary latitude line around the earth about 1600 miles from the South Pole and parallel to the equator. South of this line is the polar

region of Antarctica, where it stays cold all year, much colder than in the Arctic Circle. *See map on page 158.*

Antarctica (ant-AHRK-ti-kuh)   Antarctica is the continent at the South Pole. Most of it is covered with ice. *See map on page 158.*

 Arabia (uh-RAY-bee-uh)   Arabia is a large, oil-rich peninsula in southwestern Asia that is bounded on the east by the Persian Gulf, on the south by the Indian Ocean, and on the west by the Red Sea. *See also* SAUDI ARABIA.

Arctic Circle (AHRK-tik; AHR-tik)   The Arctic Circle is an imaginary latitude line around the earth about 1600 miles from the North Pole and parallel to the equator. North of this line is the polar region of the Arctic, where it stays cold all year. *See map on page 158.*

Arctic Ocean   The Arctic Ocean surrounds the North Pole. *See map on page 158.*

The Arctic Ocean is the world's smallest ocean. It is mostly covered by solid ice, ice floes, and icebergs. ❧

Argentina (AHR-juhn-TEE-nuh)   Argentina is a Spanish-speaking country in southern South America that extends all the way to the tip of the continent on the Atlantic side. Its capital and

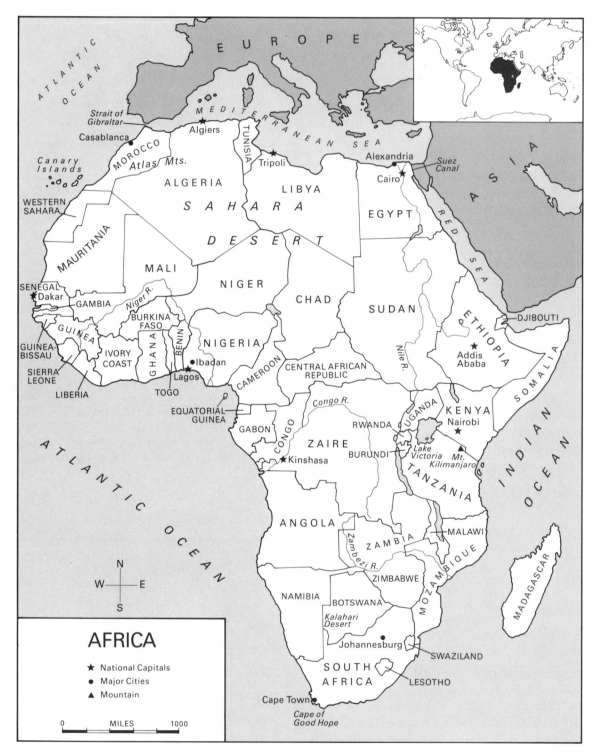

AFRICA

★ National Capitals
● Major Cities
▲ Mountain

0 — MILES — 1000

160

most populous city is Buenos Aires. To the west is Chile. In Spanish, *argentina* means "of silver," a metal that has been mined there.

 Asia (AY-zhuh) Asia is the world's largest continent and is populated by more than half of the world's people. It is bordered on the east by the Pacific Ocean, on the south by the Indian Ocean, and on the west by Europe. Because Europe and Asia are connected, they are sometimes referred to as Eurasia.

Athens Athens is the capital of Greece and the site of the PAR-THENON.

Atlantic Ocean The Atlantic Ocean, the second largest ocean in the world, extends from the Arctic Ocean to Antarctica. It is east of North and South America and west of Europe and Africa. *See map on page 158.*

atlas An atlas is a book of maps.

Australia (aw-STRAYL-yuh) Australia, the smallest continent, is bordered on the east by the southern Pacific Ocean and on the west by the Indian Ocean. Its main language is English. Australia is the only country on the continent. Its most populous city is Sydney.

Australia is known for its unusual animals and plants, such as the koala, kangaroo, platypus, and the giant eucalyptus. ❧

Austria (AW-stree-uh) Austria is a German-speaking mountainous country in the Alps of southeastern Europe, east of Switzerland. Its most populous city and capital is Vienna.

axis The earth's axis is the imaginary line around which it spins. It lies between the North and South poles and goes through the center of the earth.

Bahamas The Bahamas is an English-speaking country in the Atlantic Ocean, southeast of Florida, that is made up of hundreds of islands. *See map on page 176.*

Balkan Mountains The Balkan Mountains are a mountain range in southeastern Europe.

Balkans, the The countries in the region of the Balkan Mountains on the Balkan Peninsula are known as the Balkan countries, or the Balkans: Albania, Bulgaria, and parts of Greece, Romania, Turkey, and Yugoslavia.

Baltic Sea The Baltic Sea, in northern Europe, is bordered by the Scandinavian countries on the west and the Soviet Union on the east. *See map on page 168.*

 Bangkok (BANG-kok) Bangkok is the capital of Thailand and its principal port and commercial center.

Beijing (BAY-JING) Beijing (or Peking) is the capital of China, known for its grand palaces and temples.

 Beirut (bay-ROOHT) Beirut is the capital of Lebanon.

Belfast Belfast is the capital of Northern Ireland, which is part of the United Kingdom.

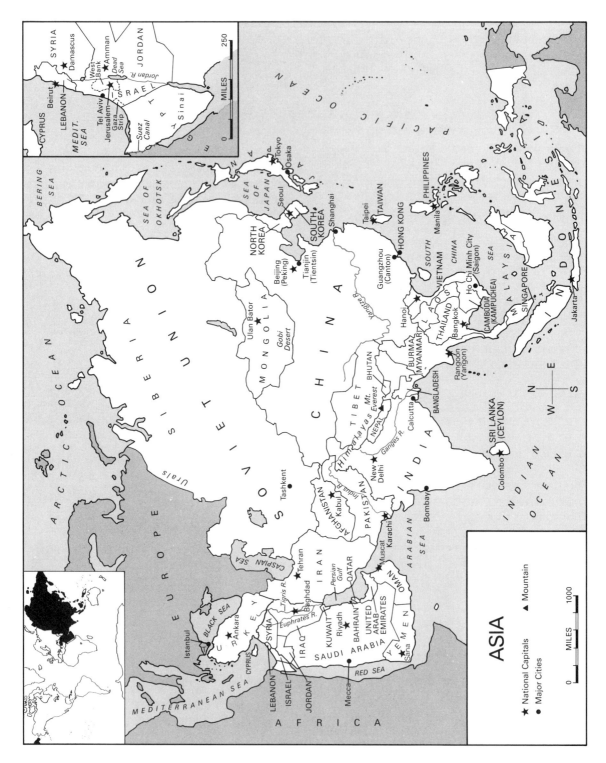

ASIA

★ National Capitals　▲ Mountain
● Major Cities

Inset map (upper left):

SYRIA
Damascus
CYPRUS
Beirut
LEBANON
MEDIT. SEA
Tel Aviv
Jerusalem
Gaza Strip
West Bank
Dead Sea
Amman
JORDAN
ISRAEL
Jordan R.
Suez Canal
Sinai
EGYPT
MILES
250
0

Main map labels:

BERING SEA
SEA OF OKHOTSK
ARCTIC OCEAN
SIBERIA
S O V I E T   U N I O N
EUROPE
Urals
SEA OF JAPAN
Tokyo
Osaka
Seoul
NORTH KOREA
SOUTH KOREA
Shanghai
PACIFIC OCEAN
Taipei
TAIWAN
HONG KONG
PHILIPPINES
Manila
MONGOLIA
Ulan Bator
Gobi Desert
Beijing (Peking)
Tianjin (Tientsin)
C H I N A
Guangzhou (Canton)
SOUTH CHINA SEA
CHINA
VIETNAM
Ho Chi Minh City (Saigon)
Hanoi
LAOS
MALAYSIA
CAMBODIA (KAMPUCHEA)
SINGAPORE
I N D O N E S I A
Jakarta
Yangtze R.
TIBET
BHUTAN
Mt. Everest
Himalayas
NEPAL
New Delhi
Calcutta
BANGLADESH
BURMA (MYANMAR)
Rangoon (Yangon)
THAILAND
Bangkok
Ganges R.
I N D I A
SRI LANKA (CEYLON)
Colombo
Bombay
Tashkent
AFGHANISTAN
Kabul
PAKISTAN
Indus R.
Karachi
ARABIAN SEA
INDIAN OCEAN
N E W S
CASPIAN SEA
Tehran
I R A N
Persian Gulf
QATAR
Muscat
OMAN
UNITED ARAB EMIRATES
YEMEN
Sana
BLACK SEA
Istanbul
Ankara
T U R K E Y
CYPRUS
SYRIA
LEBANON
ISRAEL
JORDAN
Tigris R.
Baghdad
Euphrates R.
IRAQ
KUWAIT
Riyadh
BAHRAIN
SAUDI ARABIA
Mecca
RED SEA
MEDITERRANEAN SEA
A F R I C A

MILES
1000
0

162

Belgium (BEL-juhm) Belgium is a French- and Dutch-speaking country in western Europe that is north of France and south of the Netherlands. Its capital is Brussels.

Belgium is the headquarters of NATO (the North Atlantic Treaty Organization). ❧

 Belgrade Belgrade, on the Danube River, is the capital of Yugoslavia and its largest city.

Bering Sea (BEER-ing) The Bering Sea is the part of the Pacific Ocean between Alaska and the Soviet Union. *See maps on pages 162, 176.*

Berlin Berlin is the capital of Germany. Divided after World War II into East Berlin, the capital of East Germany, and West Berlin, a part of West Germany, it was reunified along with Germany in 1990. *See also* BERLIN WALL *and* GERMANY.

Bermuda (buhr-MYOOH-duh) Bermuda is an English-speaking group of islands in the Atlantic Ocean, about 600 miles east of the United States. It is a British colony. *See map on page 176.*

Black Sea The Black Sea lies between Europe and Asia and is almost completely enclosed by land except for a narrow connection to the Aegean Sea. *See maps on pages 162, 169.*

Bolivia (buh-LIV-ee-uh) Bolivia is a Spanish-speaking country in western South America and is named for Simón Bolívar, a South American revolutionary leader and statesman.

 Bonn (BON) Bonn, a city on the Rhine River, was the capital of West Germany.

Brazil (bruh-ZIL) Brazil, in eastern South America, is the largest country on the continent. Its two most populous cities are São Paulo, then Rio de Janeiro. The capital is the planned, twentieth-century city of Brasília. Brazil's official language is Portuguese.

Britain *See* UNITED KINGDOM.

British Columbia British Columbia is a province in western Canada, on the Pacific Ocean.

 British Isles The British Isles are English-speaking islands in western Europe comprising the United Kingdom and the Republic of Ireland. There are two main islands. One holds England, Scotland, and Wales; the other, Northern Ireland and the Republic of Ireland.

Brussels Brussels is the capital of Belgium and the headquarters of NATO.

Budapest (BOOH-duh-PEST) Budapest is the capital of Hungary. It combines two older towns, Buda and Pest, which faced each other across the Danube.

Buenos Aires (BWAY-nuhs-EYER-iz) Buenos Aires is the capital of Argentina and one of the most populous cities in South America.

Bulgaria Bulgaria is a Balkan country in southeastern Europe, south of Romania.

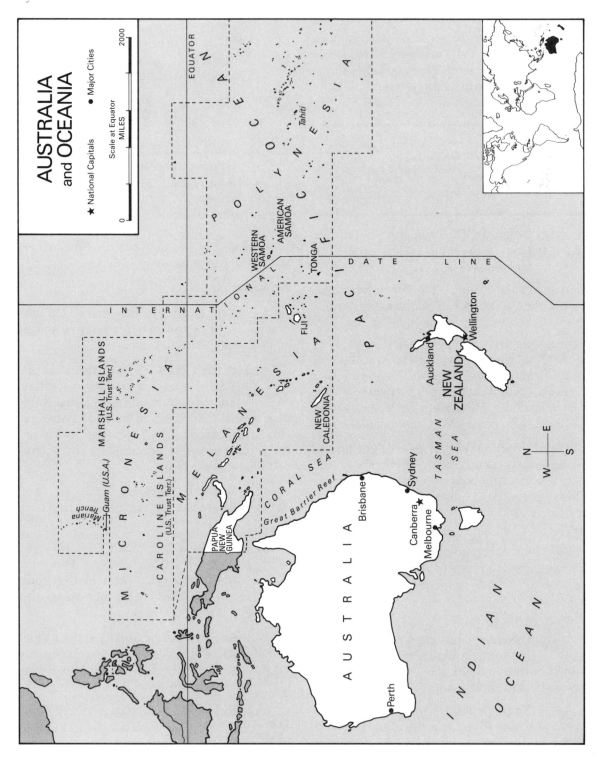

AUSTRALIA and OCEANIA

★ National Capitals ● Major Cities

Scale at Equator
MILES

0   2000

EQUATOR

O C E A N I A

P O L Y N E S I A

Tahiti

WESTERN SAMOA

AMERICAN SAMOA

TONGA

INTERNATIONAL

DATE LINE

FIJI

M E L A N E S I A

MICRONESIA

MARSHALL ISLANDS
(U.S. Trust Terr.)

Guam (U.S.A.)

Mariana Trench

CAROLINE ISLANDS
(U.S. Trust Terr.)

P A C I F I C

NEW CALEDONIA

CORAL SEA

Great Barrier Reef

PAPUA NEW GUINEA

Wellington

Auckland

NEW ZEALAND

TASMAN SEA

Brisbane

Sydney

Canberra ★

Melbourne

A U S T R A L I A

Perth

INDIAN OCEAN

N
W — E
S

164

Burma   Burma is a country in Southeast Asia, south of China. It is also known as Myanmar.

 Cairo (KEYE-roh)   Cairo is the capital of Egypt and the most populous city in Africa.

 Calcutta   Calcutta is a city in eastern India and the most populous in the nation.

Cambodia   (kam-BOH-dee-uh) Cambodia is a country in Southeast Asia, south of Thailand. It is also known as Kampuchea.

Canada   Canada, the country north of the United States, is the world's second largest country (after the Soviet Union). Its capital is Ottawa, in the province of Ontario. Its most populous cities are Toronto, Montreal, and Vancouver. Its main provinces are Nova Scotia, Quebec, Ontario, and British Columbia. The languages of Canada are English and, in the province of Quebec, French.

Caracas (kuh-RAH-kuhs)   Caracas is the capital and most populous city of Venezuela.

Caribbean Sea (KAR-uh-BEE-uhn; kuh-RIB-ee-uhn)   The Caribbean Sea is the part of the Atlantic Ocean bordered by Central America, South America, and the West Indies. It is also called simply the Caribbean. *See maps on pages 176, 180.*

 Caspian Sea   The Caspian Sea is the largest body of water in the world that is completely surrounded by land, making it really a huge salt water lake. It lies between the Soviet Union and Iran.

 Central America   Central America is the name for the narrow strip of land between Mexico and South America. It is sometimes considered part of

South America because its people speak Spanish and are culturally related to the people of South America. Geographically, however, it is considered part of North America. The countries of Central America are Belize, Guatemala, El Salvador, Honduras, Nicaragua, Costa Rica, and Panama.

Ceylon   *See* SRI LANKA.

Chang   *See* YANGTZE.

Chile (CHIL-ee)   Chile is a Spanish-speaking country on the western slopes of the Andes in southwestern South America. Long and narrow, it goes along the Pacific Coast to the southern tip of South America. Its capital and most populous city is Santiago.

China   China, in eastern Asia, has the largest population of any country in the world. Officially, it is called the People's Republic of China. Its capital is Beijing (Peking).

China is the third largest country in area in the world (after the Soviet Union and Canada) and the largest in population. ❧

Colombia   Colombia is a Spanish-speaking country in northern South America, east of Panama. It is named for CHRISTOPHER COLUMBUS.

165

Congo   *See* ZAIRE.

 Congo River   The Congo, in central Africa, is the second longest river in Africa (after the Nile).

 Copenhagen   (KOH-puhn-HAY-guhn)   Copenhagen is the capital of Denmark and its most populous city.

 Costa Rica   (KOS-tuh-REE-kuh)   Costa Rica is a Spanish-speaking country in Central America, west of Panama. Its name means "rich coast" in Spanish.

Cuba (KYOOH-buh)   Cuba is a Spanish-speaking island country between the Caribbean Sea and the Atlantic Ocean, south of Florida. Its most populous city is Havana. *See map on page 176.*

Cyprus (SEYE-pruhs)   Cyprus is a Greek- and Turkish-speaking island country in the Mediterranean Sea, south of Turkey. Its name comes from the Greek word for copper, which was mined there in ancient times. *See map on page 162.*

 Czechoslovakia   (chek-uh-sloh-VAH-kee-uh) Czechoslovakia is a country in east-central Europe, east of Germany. Its capital is Prague.

Danube River (DAN-yoohb)   The Danube is the second longest river in Europe (after the Volga). It forms part of the border between several countries, including Czechoslovakia, Hungary, Romania, and Bulgaria.

Dead Sea   The Dead Sea is a salt lake between Israel and Jordan in southwestern Asia, in what is commonly called the Middle East. Its surface is the lowest point on the surface of the earth. It is called dead because its water is too salty for fish to survive.

 Delhi (DEL-ee)   Delhi is a region in India as well as a populous city in this region. *See also* NEW DELHI.

Denmark   Denmark is a Scandinavian country in northern Europe between the North and the Baltic seas. Its capital is Copenhagen.

Dominican Republic (duh-MIN-i-kuhn)   The Dominican Republic is a Spanish-speaking country in the West Indies. It is the eastern part of the same island, east of Cuba, that contains Haiti. *See map on page 176.*

Dublin   Dublin is the capital of the Republic of Ireland and the birthplace of several famous writers, such as James Joyce and W. B. Yeats.

East Asia   The region of the world called the Far East is more appropriately known as East Asia. It is only "far" from the western point of view. *See also* FAR EAST.

East Germany   *See* GERMANY *and* BERLIN.

Ecuador   Ecuador is a Spanish-speaking country in northwestern South America. It lies on the equator, with its west coast on the Pacific Ocean.

Edinburgh   (ED-n-buh-ruh)   Edinburgh is the capital of Scotland, where an arts festival takes place each summer.

The oldest biblical scrolls in existence have been found near the Dead Sea. Some of them are called the Dead Sea Scrolls. ❧

Egypt (EE-jipt)   Egypt is an Arabic-speaking country in northeastern Africa, near the region known as the Middle East. It is the home of a great, ancient civilization, which was ruled by the pharaohs. The Nile River flows through it, and the Pyramids and the Sphinx are found there. Its capital is Cairo.

El Salvador (SAL-vuh-DAWR)   El Salvador is a country in Central America. Its capital is San Salvador. In Spanish, *salvador* means Savior, a term for Jesus.

England   England is a country in northwestern Europe. Along with Scotland, Northern Ireland, and Wales, it is part of the United Kingdom. England is on an island, called Great Britain, with Scotland and Wales.

English Channel   The English Channel is a very narrow part of the Atlantic Ocean that separates England and France. Strong athletes have swum across the English Channel.

equator   The equator is the imaginary line that circles the middle of the earth between the two poles and divides it into two halves, the Northern and Southern Hemispheres. It is the zero line of latitude. *See map on page 158.*

 Ethiopia   (EE-thee-OH-pee-uh) Ethiopia is a mountainous country in eastern Africa, whose main product is coffee.

Eurasia   *See* ASIA; EUROPE.

 Europe (YOOR-uhp)   Europe is the continent west of Asia. It is bordered on the north by the Arctic Ocean, on the south by the Mediterranean Sea, and on the west by the Atlantic Ocean. Because Europe and Asia are connected, they are sometimes referred to as Eurasia.

 Far East   The Far East is a name used popularly in the Western world to refer to the countries of eastern Asia: China, Japan, North Korea, South Korea, and Taiwan. The term sometimes includes the countries of Southeast Asia as well.

Federal Republic of Germany   The official name of Germany and, formerly, of West Germany. *See* GERMANY.

 Finland   Finland is a Scandinavian country in northern Europe between Sweden and the Soviet Union. Its capital is Helsinki.

France   France is a large country in western Europe and the second most populous country on the European continent (after Germany). Its capital is Paris.

Ganges River (GAN-jeez)   The Ganges is a river in India that is sacred to members of the Hindu religion. *See also* HINDUISM.

Geneva (juh-NEE-vuh)   Geneva is a city in Switzerland where many international conferences are held.

German Democratic Republic   The official name of the area formerly called East Germany. *See* GERMANY.

167

FINLAND

elsinki

Tallinn

ESTONIA

Riga

LATVIA

THUANIA

Vilnius

●Minsk

●Kiev

SOVIET UNION

●Leningrad

Gorky

★
Moscow

Volga R.

U R A L S

A S I A

CASPIAN SEA

ROMANIA

Bucharest
★

Danube R.

M t s .

★Sofia

BULGARIA

Istanbul

BLACK SEA

TURKEY

A S I A

GREECE

AEGEAN SEA

Athens

Crete

S E A

A N

N
W · E
S

EUROPE

★ National Capitals ▲ Mountain

● Major Cities

0   MILES   500

169

Germany Germany is a country in central Europe bordered on the west by the Netherlands, Belgium, and France; on the east by Poland and Czechoslovakia; on the north by Denmark; and on the south by Switzerland and Austria. Its capital is Berlin. Originally unified in the late 1800s, Germany was divided after World War II into communist East Germany and democratic West Germany and was not reunified until 1990.

Ghana (GAH-nuh) Ghana is a country in western Africa. Its main export is raw chocolate. Its official language is English.

Gibraltar (ji-BRAWL-tuhr) Gibraltar is a peninsula in southern Spain overlooking a narrow sea lane between the Atlantic Ocean and the Mediterranean Sea. It is often called the Rock of Gibraltar.

Gobi Desert (GOH-bee) The Gobi Desert is in Mongolia. Dinosaur eggs have been found there.

Great Britain Great Britain is the island in northwestern Europe containing England, Scotland, and Wales. *See also* UNITED KINGDOM.

Greece Greece is a Balkan country in southern Europe, on the Mediterranean Sea, the site of a great ancient civilization.

Greenland Greenland is the world's largest island that is not a continent. It is in the northern Atlantic Ocean and is part of Denmark. *See map on page 176.*

Greenwich *See* LONGITUDE; PRIME MERIDIAN.

Guam (GWAHM) Guam, an island in Micronesia, is a territory of the United States. *See map on page 164.*

 Guatemala (GWAH-tuh-MAH-luh) Guatemala is a Spanish-speaking country in Central America.

Gulf of Mexico The Gulf of Mexico is the part of the Atlantic Ocean bordered by the southern coast of the United States and the eastern coast of Mexico. (A gulf is a large body of ocean that is partly enclosed by land.) *See map on page 176.*

Haiti (HAY-tee) Haiti is a French- and Creole-speaking country in the West Indies. It is the western part of the same island, east of Cuba, that contains the Dominican Republic. *See map on page 176.*

Havana (huh-VAN-uh) Havana is the capital of Cuba, known for its cigars. *See map on page 176.*

Helsinki (HEL-sing-kee) Helsinki is the capital of Finland.

hemisphere A hemisphere is one half of the planet Earth. *Hemi* means "half" and *sphere* means "a round ball or globe." The earth can be divided into the Northern and Southern hemispheres. The Northern Hemisphere is the half of the globe north of the equator; the Southern Hemisphere is the half of the globe south of the equator. The earth can also be divided into the Eastern and Western hemispheres. The Eastern Hemisphere is the part of the world east of zero longitude and contains Africa, Asia, Australia, and Europe. The Western Hemisphere is the part west of zero longitude and contains North America and South America.

 Himalayas (him-uh-LAY-uhz; huh-MAHL-yuhz) The Himalayas are a mountain range in south-central

170

Asia. The highest mountains in the world are found there, including the very highest, Mount Everest.

Hindu and Buddhist monks are known to make pilgrimages (religious journeys) to holy places in the Himalayas, the highest mountain range in the world. ❧

Holland   *See* NETHERLANDS, THE.

 Honduras (hon-DOOR-uhs)   Honduras is a Spanish-speaking country in Central America.

 Hong Kong   Hong Kong is a British crown colony in eastern Asia, which will become part of China in 1997. Most of Hong Kong is on an island in the South China Sea off the southeastern coast of China.

 Hudson Bay   Hudson Bay is a sea in northeastern Canada that is almost completely surrounded by land. It connects with the Atlantic Ocean.

 Hungary   Hungary is a country in east-central Europe. Its capital is Budapest.

Iceland   Iceland is an island country in northwestern Europe in the north Atlantic Ocean, north of England and west of Norway. *See map on page 168.*

India   India is the second most populous country in the world (after China). Numerous languages are spoken there, but Hindi and English are its official languages. Its capital is New Delhi.

Indian Ocean   The Indian Ocean, the third largest ocean in the world, lies between the Atlantic and the Pacific oceans. It is south of

Asia, east of Africa, and west of Australia. *See map on page 158.*

Indochina   Indochina is the name of a region in Southeast Asia that contains Burma, Thailand, Laos, Cambodia (Kampuchea), Vietnam, and parts of Malaysia.

Indonesia (IN-duh-NEE-zhuh)   Indonesia is a country in Southeast Asia made up of a string of islands.

international date line   The international date line, the 180th meridian, is the longitude line where, by international agreement, a day begins and ends. If it is 3:00 P.M. on March 21 east of the line, it is 3:00 P.M. on March 22 west of the line! *See also* LONGITUDE; MERIDIAN. *See maps on pages 158, 164.*

Iran (i-RAN)   Iran is a Persian-speaking country in southwestern Asia, in what is called the Middle East, west of Afghanistan and south of the Soviet Union. Its capital is Tehran.

The area that is now Iraq was the site of the ancient Mesopotamian empire. ❧

Iraq (i-RAK)   Iraq is an Arabic-speaking country in southwestern Asia, in what is called the Middle East, west of Iran and east of Syria.

Ireland   *See* NORTHERN IRELAND; REPUBLIC OF IRELAND.

Israel (IZ-ree-uhl)   Israel is a Hebrew-speaking country at the eastern end of the Mediterranean Sea, in southwestern Asia, in what is called the Middle East. It is in a region also known as Palestine. Its capital and most populous city is Jerusalem.

Istanbul (IS-tan-BOOHL)   The most populous city in Turkey, Istanbul is located mostly in the European section of the country and is known for its beautiful domes and towers. In the past, the city was called Constantinople and, before that, Byzantium. *See maps on pages 162, 169.*

 Italy   Italy is a country in southern Europe. On a map, it looks like a boot jutting out into the sea. It was the center of the ancient Roman civilization and the home of many great artists. Its capital is Rome.

Jamaica (juh-MAY-kuh)   Jamaica is an English-speaking island country in the West Indies. It is south of Cuba, in the Caribbean Sea. *See map on page 176.*

Japan   Japan is a country made up of islands in eastern Asia, east of Korea and the Soviet Union. Its capital is Tokyo, which is one of the most populous cities in the world.

Jerusalem (juh-ROOH-suh-luhm)   Jerusalem is the capital of Israel and a holy city for Christians, Jews, and Moslems.

Jordan   Jordan is an Arabic-speaking country in southwestern Asia, east of Israel, in what is called the Middle East.

Jordan River   The Jordan is a river in southwestern Asia, in what is called the Middle East. It is in Israel and Jordan and is sacred to Christians.

Kenya (KEN-yuh)   Kenya is a Swahili- and English-speaking country in eastern Africa, south of Ethiopia. Its capital is Nairobi.

Important archaeological discoveries have been made in Kenya, such as the remains of the world's earliest known humans. ✒

Kilimanjaro (kil-uh-muhn-JAHR-oh)   Kilimanjaro, in Tanzania, is the highest mountain in Africa.

Korea   *See* NORTH KOREA; SOUTH KOREA.

Kuwait (kooh-WAYT)   Kuwait is a small, oil-rich, Arabic-speaking country in southwestern Asia, in what is called the Middle East. It is south of Iraq and north of Saudi Arabia on the Arabian Peninsula.

Lake Victoria   Lake Victoria, in central Africa, is the second largest freshwater lake in the world (after Lake Superior). It is a source of the Nile River.

 Laos (LAH-ohs; lah-AWS)   Laos, a country in Southeast Asia, lies south of China and west of Vietnam.

Latin America   Latin America is a name for the Spanish- and Portuguese-speaking countries of North and South America, including Mexico and the countries of Central and South America. The name Latin America arose because both the Spanish and Portuguese languages developed from Latin, an ancient language. Central America and Mexico are culturally related to South America, though geographically they are part of North America. *See maps on pages 176, 180.*

latitude   Latitude is a way of measuring, in degrees, the distance north and south of the

EQUATOR. Lines of latitude are imaginary lines around the earth that are parallel to the equator and run east and west. A place on the earth can be located on a map by marking the place where its line of latitude and its line of LONGITUDE cross each other.

 Lebanon (LEB-uh-nuhn) Lebanon is an Arabic-speaking country in southwestern Asia, in what is called the Middle East. It lies at the eastern end of the Mediterranean Sea, north of Israel.

 Libya (LIB-ee-uh) Libya is an Arabic-speaking country in northern Africa that lies west of Egypt on the Mediterranean Sea.

 Lisbon (LIZ-buhn) Lisbon is the capital of Portugal and its most populous city.

Loire River (LWAHR) The Loire is the longest river in France.

 London London is the capital of England and of the United Kingdom. One of the most populous cities of Europe, it is the site of Big Ben and Buckingham Palace. It is on the Thames River.

longitude Longitude is a way of measuring, in degrees, the distance east and west of the PRIME MERIDIAN. The prime meridian is an imaginary line that runs from the North Pole to the South Pole through the city of Greenwich, England, and is zero degrees longitude. Lines of longitude run north and south through the two poles, where they come together. They are farthest apart at the EQUATOR. A place on the earth can be found on a map by marking the spot where its line of longitude and its line of LATITUDE cross each other.

 Madagascar (MAD-uh-GAS-kuhr) Madagascar is an island country in the Indian Ocean, off the southeastern coast of Africa.

 Madrid (muh-DRID) Madrid, the capital of Spain and its most populous city, is the home of the Prado museum.

Magellan, Strait of *See* STRAIT OF MAGELLAN.

Malaysia (muh-LAY-zhuh) Malaysia is a country in Southeast Asia and lies south of Thailand.

Manila (muh-NIL-uh) Manila is the most populous city of the Philippines. *See map on page 162.*

map A map is a simplified picture that usually depicts areas on the surface of the earth.

map scale A map scale is the relation between distances on the earth and distances on a map.

Matterhorn The Matterhorn is a mountain in the European Alps between Switzerland and Italy. It is famous for its distinctive, pointed peak.

Mediterranean Sea (MED-i-tuh-RAY-nee-uhn) The Mediterranean Sea is bordered by southern Europe, Asia, and northern Africa. It is the largest inland sea in the world and connects with the Atlantic Ocean through the narrow Strait of Gibraltar. *See maps on pages 162, 168–169.*

Mercator projection (muhr-KAY-tuhr) A Mercator projection is a kind of map that is made by drawing the land masses of the globe on a flat surface. The Mercator projection is easier to look at than a globe because all the major continents can appear on the same map. However, this kind of map makes the northern and southern land masses appear larger than they really are.

meridian   A meridian is a line of LONGITUDE.

 Mexico   Mexico, the country directly south of the United States, borders California, Arizona, New Mexico, and Texas. Its capital is Mexico City, one of the largest cities in the world. In ancient times, Mexico was the home of the Mayan and the Aztec civilizations. Its language is Spanish.

Mexico City   Mexico City is the capital and most populous city of Mexico. It is also the most populous city in North America.

Micronesia (MEYE-kroh-NEE-zhuh)   Micronesia is a group of many islands in the western Pacific Ocean. Its name means "small islands." *See map on page 164.*

The Middle East was the site of ancient civilizations, such as Egypt, Babylonia, and Phoenicia, and the birthplace of Judaism, Christianity, and Islam. ✥

Middle East   The Middle East is a name used popularly in the Western world to refer to certain countries of western Asia and the northeastern part of Africa. It is called middle because, from the western point of view, it lies between the Western world and the "Far East." The region includes the African countries of Egypt and Libya and the Asian countries of Iran, Iraq, Israel, Jordan, Kuwait, Lebanon, Syria, Saudi Arabia, and other countries of the Arabian peninsula. Turkey and Cyprus are sometimes considered part of this region. It is also sometimes called the Near East.

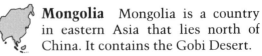 **Mongolia**   Mongolia is a country in eastern Asia that lies north of China. It contains the Gobi Desert.

Mont Blanc   Mont Blanc, in the Alps, is the highest mountain in western Europe.

Montreal (MON-tree-AWL)   Montreal is the second most populous city in Canada. It is in the province of Quebec, where the principal language is French.

Morocco (muh-ROK-oh)   Morocco is an Arabic-speaking country in the northwestern corner of Africa, west of Algeria, on the Atlantic Ocean and the Mediterranean Sea.

Moscow   Moscow, the capital and the most populous city of the Soviet Union, is the site of the KREMLIN.

Mount Everest   Mount Everest, in the Himalayas of central Asia, is the highest mountain in the world.

Munich (MYOOH-nik)   Munich, a city in southern Germany and the capital of the state of Bavaria, is the most populous city in that region of the country.

Nairobi (neye-ROH-bee)   Nairobi is the capital and most populous city of Kenya.

Netherlands, the   The Netherlands (sometimes called Holland) is a Dutch-speaking country in western Europe, north of Belgium across the sea from England. Its name means "Low Countries" because much of the country is below sea level. Its capital is Amsterdam.

New Delhi (DEL-ee) New Delhi, the administrative section of the old city of Delhi, is the capital of India.

New Zealand (ZEE-luhnd) New Zealand is an English-speaking island country in the southern Pacific Ocean, southeast of Australia. It includes two islands, South Island and North Island. *See map on page 164.*

 Newfoundland (NOOH-fuhn-luhnd) Newfoundland is a province in eastern Canada, on the Atlantic coast.

 Nicaragua (NIK-uh-RAH-gwuh) Nicaragua is a Spanish-speaking country in Central America, north of Costa Rica.

Nigeria (neye-JEER-ee-uh) Nigeria is an English-speaking country in central west Africa.

> **T**he Nile River valley in Egypt is the site of one of the first great civilizations. ❧

 Nile River The Nile is the longest river in the world. It is in Africa, mainly in Egypt, and empties into the Mediterranean Sea.

North America North America is the northern continent with the Atlantic Ocean on its east and the Pacific Ocean on its west. It includes Canada, the United States, Mexico, and the countries of Central America.

North Korea (kuh-REE-uh) North Korea is a country in eastern Asia, east of China and west of Japan.

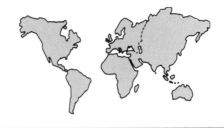

North Pole The North Pole, in the Arctic, is the northernmost point on the earth.

North Sea The North Sea is the part of the Atlantic Ocean between Great Britain and continental Europe.

Northern Ireland Northern Ireland is the part of Ireland that is included in the United Kingdom. *See also* REPUBLIC OF IRELAND.

Norway Norway is a Scandinavian country in northern Europe, west of Sweden, known for its fjords. Its capital is Oslo.

Nova Scotia (NOH-vuh-SKOH-shuh) Nova Scotia is a province in eastern Canada, on the Atlantic coast. Its name means "New Scotland" in Latin.

Oceania (OH-shee-AN-ee-uh) Oceania is a name for the thousands of islands in the central and southern Pacific Ocean. *See map on page 164.*

> **O**ceania is sometimes referred to as the South Seas. ❧

 Ontario (on-TAIR-ee-OH) Ontario is a province of Canada north of the Great Lakes. It includes Toronto, the country's most populous city, and Ottawa, the Canadian capital.

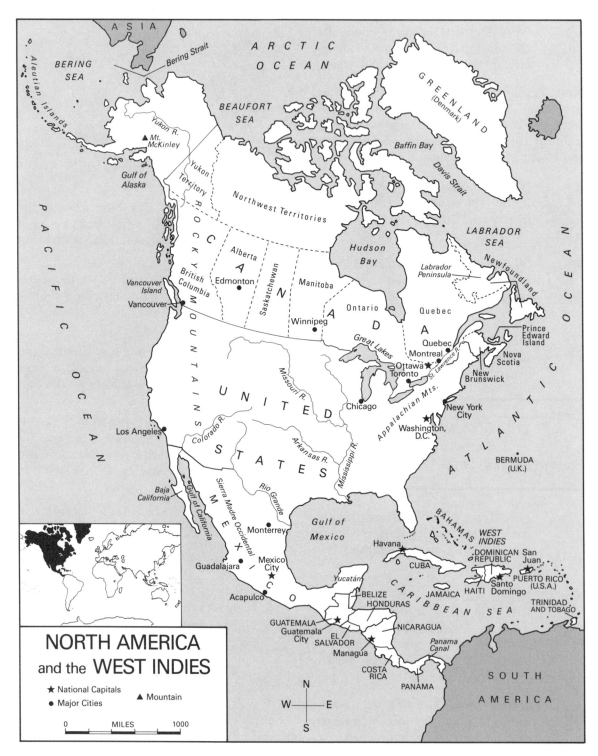

ASIA

ARCTIC OCEAN

BERING SEA

Bering Strait

BEAUFORT SEA

GREENLAND (Denmark)

Baffin Bay

Aleutian Islands

Yukon R.

▲ Mt. McKinley

Gulf of Alaska

Yukon Territory

Northwest Territories

Davis Strait

LABRADOR SEA

PACIFIC OCEAN

R O C K Y

Alberta

C A N A D A

Saskatchewan

Manitoba

Hudson Bay

Labrador Peninsula

Newfoundland

British Columbia

Edmonton

Ontario

Quebec

Vancouver Island

Vancouver

Winnipeg

Great Lakes

Quebec

Prince Edward Island

M O U N T A I N S

Missouri R.

U N I T E D

Montreal

Ottawa ★

Toronto

St. Lawrence R.

Nova Scotia

New Brunswick

ATLANTIC OCEAN

Chicago

Appalachian Mts.

New York City

Los Angeles

Colorado R.

S T A T E S

Arkansas R.

Mississippi R.

Washington, D.C. ★

Baja California

Gulf of California

Sierra Madre Occidental

Río Grande

Gulf of Mexico

BERMUDA (U.K.)

BAHAMAS

WEST INDIES

Monterrey

M E X I C O

Havana

CUBA

DOMINICAN REPUBLIC

San Juan

Guadalajara

Mexico City

Yucatán

JAMAICA

HAITI

Santo Domingo

PUERTO RICO (U.S.A.)

Acapulco

BELIZE

HONDURAS

C A R I B B E A N   S E A

TRINIDAD AND TOBAGO

GUATEMALA

Guatemala City

NICARAGUA

EL SALVADOR

Managua

Panama Canal

COSTA RICA

PANAMA

SOUTH AMERICA

NORTH AMERICA and the WEST INDIES

★ National Capitals   ▲ Mountain

● Major Cities

N
W E
S

0   MILES   1000

Orient, the The Orient is a name used popularly in the Western world to refer to the countries of eastern Asia. It means "the East," from the Latin word for the rising sun, because the sun rises in the east.

A word that is sometimes opposed to Orient is *Occident,* meaning "the West." ❧

 Oslo (OZ-loh) Oslo is the capital and most populous city of Norway and is located on a fjord.

 Ottawa (OT-uh-wuh) Ottawa, in the province of Ontario, is the capital of Canada.

Pacific Ocean The Pacific is the largest ocean in the world, extending from the Arctic Ocean to Antarctica. It is west of North and South America and east of Asia and Australia. *See map on page 158.*

 Pakistan Pakistan is an Urdu- and English-speaking country in southern Asia that lies northwest of India.

Palestine Palestine is a region in southwestern Asia, on the Mediterranean Sea, that comprises parts of Israel, Jordan, and Egypt. It is often referred to as the Holy Land.

Panama Panama is the Spanish-speaking Central American country that borders South America. At its narrowest point is the Panama Canal, which allows ships to move between the Atlantic and Pacific oceans without going around the southern tip of South America.

Panama Canal The Panama Canal, in the Central American country of Panama, was

built by American engineers in the early 1900s. Ships use the Panama Canal to sail between the Atlantic and the Pacific oceans, avoiding the lengthy journey around the tip of South America. *See map on page 176.*

Papua New Guinea (PAP-yooh-uh-NOOH-GIN-ee) Papua New Guinea is an English-speaking tropical country in the western Pacific Ocean north of Australia. *See map on page 164.*

Paraguay (PAR-uh-GWAY) Paraguay is a Spanish-speaking country in central South America, north of Argentina.

Paris Paris is the capital of France, on the Seine River. It is the site of the Eiffel Tower.

Paris is an international cultural center as well as a center of fashion and design. ❧

Peking *See* BEIJING.

Persian Gulf (PUR-zhuhn) The Persian Gulf is an inlet of the Indian Ocean, between Iran to the north and Saudi Arabia to the south. It is bordered by several other Arab countries as well.

Peru (puh-ROOH) Peru is a Spanish-speaking country in western South America on the Pacific Ocean, south of Ecuador. It was the home of the old civilization of the Incas.

Philippines (FIL-uh-PEENZ)   The Philippines is a Filipino- and English-speaking country made up of a group of islands in the southwestern Pacific Ocean. Its most populous city is Manila. *See map on page 162.*

 Poland   Poland is a country in central Europe, between Germany on the west and the Soviet Union on the east. Its capital is Warsaw.

pole   A pole is an imaginary point at each end of the earth's AXIS. *See also* NORTH POLE; SOUTH POLE.

Polynesia (POL-uh-NEE-zhuh)   Polynesia is a group of thousands of islands in the central and southern Pacific Ocean. Its name means "many islands." Hawaii is in Polynesia. *See map on page 164.*

 Portugal (PAWR-chuh-guhl)   Portugal is a country in southwestern Europe on the Atlantic Ocean, west of Spain. Its capital is Lisbon.

 Prague (prahg)   Prague is the capital of Czechoslovakia and its most populous city.

prime meridian   The prime meridian is an imaginary line that runs from the North to the South Pole through the city of Greenwich, England. The prime meridian is the first meridian (*prime* means "first") because all the others are numbered from it. *See map on page 158. See also* LONGITUDE.

 Pyrenees (PEER-uh-neez)   The Pyrenees are a mountain range in Europe between France and Spain.

 Quebec (kwi-BEK)   Quebec is a province in eastern Canada. Most of the people in Quebec have French ancestors, and the principal language is French.

Red Sea   The Red Sea is a long, narrow part of the Indian Ocean between Saudi Arabia and Africa. It is joined to the Mediterranean Sea by the Suez Canal in Egypt. *See map on page 162.*

Republic of Ireland   The Republic of Ireland is an English-speaking country in northern Europe. Its capital is Dublin. *See also* NORTHERN IRELAND.

Rhine River (REYEN)   The Rhine is a major river in central Europe and carries more boat traffic than any other river in the world.

Rhodesia   *See* ZIMBABWE.

Rhone River (ROHN)   The Rhone is a river in southern Europe that empties into the Mediterranean Sea in southern France.

Rio de Janeiro (REE-oh-day-zhuh-NAIR-oh)   Rio de Janeiro is a populous city in Brazil. It is sometimes called simply Rio.

Rio is famous for its yearly carnival, featuring parades of people with spectacular costumes. 🙾

Rock of Gibraltar   *See* GIBRALTAR.

Romania (roh-MAY-nee-uh)   Romania (or Rumania) is a Balkan country in southeastern Europe, east of Hungary and south of the Soviet Union.

Rome   Rome is the capital of Italy and is known for its ancient ruins and the Vatican. The Tiber River flows through Rome.

Rumania   *See* ROMANIA.

Russia   Russia is the largest republic in the Union of Soviet Socialist Republics (USSR), or the Soviet Union. The whole USSR is often called Russia. *See also* UNION OF SOVIET SOCIALIST REPUBLICS.

 Sahara   The Sahara is the largest desert in the world. It lies in northern Africa.

St. Lawrence River   *See* ST. LAWRENCE RIVER *under "United States Geography."*

Samoa   Samoa is a group of islands in Polynesia. *See map on page 164.*

 São Paulo (SOUN-POW-looh)   São Paulo, Brazil, is the most populous city in South America and one of the largest cities in the world.

 Mecca, the holy city of the Moslems, is in Saudi Arabia. 🐫

 Saudi Arabia (SOU-dee-uh-RAY-bee-uh)   Saudi Arabia is an oil-rich, Arabic-speaking country in southwestern Asia, in what is called the Middle East.

 Scandinavia (SKAN-duh-NAY-vee-uh)   Scandinavia is the name of a group of neighboring countries of northern Europe: Denmark, Finland, Iceland, Norway, and Sweden.

Scotland   Scotland is an English-speaking region north of England on the island of Great Britain. It is part of the United Kingdom.

Seine (SEN)   The Seine is a river in France that flows through Paris and eventually empties into the Atlantic Ocean at the English Channel.

 Shanghai (shang-HEYE)   Shanghai is the most populous city in China and one of the largest in the world.

Siberia (seye-BEER-ee-uh)   Siberia is a large northern region in the eastern, or Asian, part of the Soviet Union.

Sicily (SIS-uh-lee)   Sicily is the largest island in the Mediterranean Sea. Part of Italy, it is off the southern tip of Italy's "boot."

Singapore   Singapore is an island country in Southeast Asia, between Malaysia and Indonesia.

 South Africa   South Africa is the country at the southern tip of Africa and famous for its production of gold and diamonds. Several Bantu languages are spoken there, but its official languages are English and Afrikaans, a dialect of Dutch.

South America   South America is a continent in the Southern Hemisphere with the Atlantic Ocean on its east and the Pacific Ocean on its west. Its main languages are Spanish and Portuguese.

South Korea (kuh-REE-uh)   South Korea is a country on a peninsula in eastern Asia, south of North Korea and west of Japan.

South Pole   The South Pole, in Antarctica, is the southernmost point on the earth.

CARIBBEAN SEA

N. AMER.

★ Caracas
VENEZUELA

GUYANA

SURINAME

FRENCH
GUIANA

Medellín

★ Bogotá

COLOMBIA

★ Quito
ECUADOR
Guayaquil

Amazon R.

A
N
D
E
S

BRAZIL

Lima
★ PERU

La Paz
★

BOLIVIA

★ Brasília

PARAGUAY

Paraná R.

São Paulo

Rio de
Janeiro

Asunción
★

Paraná R.

URUGUAY

Aconcagua
▲

Valparaíso

Santiago

CHILE

A
R
G
E
N
T
I
N
A

A
N
D
E
S

Buenos
Aires

Montevideo

Patagonia

P
A
C
I
F
I
C

O
C
E
A
N

A
T
L
A
N
T
I
C

O
C
E
A
N

Falkland Islands
(U.K.)

Strait of
Magellan

Tierra
del Fuego

Cape Horn

N
W   E
S

SOUTH AMERICA

★ National Capitals
● Major Cities
▲ Mountain

0   MILES   1000

South Seas   The South Seas is a name for the southern part of the Pacific Ocean, which contains many of the Polynesian islands, including Samoa and Tahiti.

Southeast Asia   Southeast Asia is a name that refers to the countries that lie southeast of China: Burma, Thailand, Laos, Cambodia (Kampuchea), Vietnam, Malaysia, Singapore, Indonesia, and the Philippines.

Soviet Union   The Soviet Union is another name for the Union of Soviet Socialist Republics (USSR), or Russia. *See also* UNION OF SOVIET SOCIALIST REPUBLICS. *See maps on pages 162, 169.*

Bullfighting is a popular spectator sport in Spain. ❧

Spain   Spain is a country in southwestern Europe, east of Portugal and south of France, at the western end of the Mediterranean Sea. Its capital is Madrid.

Sri Lanka (sree-LAHNG-kuh)   Sri Lanka is an island country off the southeastern coast of India that is noted for its tea. It used to be called Ceylon.

Stockholm   Stockholm is the capital of Sweden and where the Nobel Prizes are awarded each year.

Strait of Magellan (muh-JEL-uhn)   The Strait of Magellan is a channel just north of the southern tip of South America that joins the Atlantic and Pacific oceans. *See map on page 180. See also* MAGELLAN, FERDINAND.

Sudan (soo-DAN)   The Sudan is an Arabic-speaking country in eastern Africa, south of Egypt.

Suez Canal (sooh-EZ)   The Suez Canal, in Egypt, connects the Mediterranean Sea and the Red Sea. Ships use it to travel from the Mediterranean Sea to the Indian Ocean, avoiding the lengthy journey around the African continent.

Sweden (SWEED-n)   Sweden is a Scandinavian country in northern Europe, east of Norway.

Switzerland   Switzerland is a small country in central Europe that lies in the Alps. Its most populous city is Zurich, and its official languages are French, German, Italian, and Romansh.

Switzerland is known for its neutrality, that is, its refusal to take sides in any arguments between other countries. ❧

Sydney (SID-nee)   Sydney is the most populous city in Australia.

Syria (SEER-ee-uh)   Syria is an Arabic-speaking country in southwestern Asia, in what is called the Middle East. It lies at the eastern end of the Mediterranean Sea, north of Lebanon and west of Iraq.

Tahiti (tuh-HEE-tee)   Tahiti is an island in Polynesia, famous for its beauty. *See map on page 164.*

Taiwan (TEYE-WAHN) Taiwan, also called the Republic of China, is a Chinese-speaking island country in the Pacific Ocean in eastern Asia, east of China. It was once named Formosa and was part of China. *See map on page 162.*

 Tanzania (tan-zuh-NEE-uh) Tanzania is a Swahili- and English-speaking country in eastern Africa, south of Kenya, on the Indian Ocean.

Tehran (te-RAHN) Tehran is the capital of Iran.

Tel Aviv (TEL-uh-VEEV) Tel Aviv is a large city in Israel.

Thailand (TEYE-land) Thailand is a country in Southeast Asia. Part of Indochina, it lies south of Burma and Laos and north of Cambodia (Kampuchea) and Malaysia. Its capital is Bangkok.

Thailand was formerly called Siam (from which we get Siamese cats). ❧

 Thames (TEMZ) The Thames is a river in England that flows through London.

Tiber River The Tiber is a river in Italy that flows through Rome.

 Tibet (ti-BET) Tibet is a region in the Himalayas in southwest China.

Tokyo (TOH-kee-OH) Tokyo is the capital and most populous city of Japan. It is also one of the largest cities in the world. *See map on page 162.*

Toronto (tuh-RON-toh) Toronto is the most populous city in Canada as well as the capital of the province of Ontario.

Tropic of Cancer The Tropic of Cancer is an imaginary line around the earth in the Northern Hemisphere. It is about 1600 miles north of and parallel to the equator and marks the northern boundary of the tropical regions, where it stays hot all year. *See map on page 158.*

Tropic of Capricorn The Tropic of Capricorn is an imaginary line around the earth in the Southern Hemisphere. It is about 1600 miles south of and parallel to the equator and marks the southern boundary of the tropical regions, where it stays hot all year. *See map on page 158.*

 Turkey Turkey is a country between the Black Sea and the Mediterranean Sea, lying mostly in southwestern Asia and partly in southeastern Europe. It is part of a region that historically, since ancient times, was called Asia Minor. Its capital is Ankara, and its most populous city is Istanbul.

Uganda (yooh-GAN-duh) Uganda is a country in eastern Africa, west of Kenya.

Union of Soviet Socialist Republics (USSR) The Union of Soviet Socialist Republics, also known as the Soviet Union and popularly as Russia, has the largest land area of any country in the world. The eastern two-thirds of the Soviet Union is in Asia; the western third is in Europe. Its capital is Moscow, and Russian is its language. *See maps on pages 162, 169.*

United Kingdom (U.K.) The United Kingdom is an English-speaking country in northwestern Europe made up of England, Scotland, Wales, and Northern Ireland, which are united under one government, based in London. Great Britain is officially the name of the island that contains England, Scotland, and Wales, but sometimes Great Britain, or simply Britain, is used to refer to the United Kingdom as a whole.

Ural Mountains (YOOR-uhl) The Urals are a mountain range in the Soviet Union that divide Europe and Asia. The largest cities in the country, Moscow and Leningrad, are west of the Urals. *See maps on pages 162, 169.*

 Uruguay (YOOR-uh-GWEYE) Uruguay is a Spanish-speaking country on the Atlantic Ocean, on the east coast of South America. It lies south of Brazil and north of Argentina.

Vancouver (van-KOOH-vuhr) Vancouver, British Columbia, is the third most populous city in Canada.

Vatican City In Rome, Vatican City is the seat of the Roman Catholic Church and the home of the pope.

Venezuela (VEN-uh-ZWAY-luh) Venezuela is a Spanish-speaking country in northern South America. It is at the northern tip of the continent on the Caribbean Sea.

Venice (VEN-is) Venice, a city in northern Italy, is built on islands in the Adriatic Sea. The islands are connected largely by canals, and people and goods are carried by boats, most notably the traditional long, black gondolas.

Victoria *See* LAKE VICTORIA.

Vienna (vee-EN-uh) Vienna is the capital and most populous city of Austria.

Vietnam (VEE-et-NAHM) Vietnam is a country in Southeast Asia. It lies south of China. Its capital is Hanoi.

Volga The Volga, in the Soviet Union, is the longest river in Europe.

 Wales (waylz) Wales is a region west of England on the island of Great Britain. It is part of the United Kingdom.

Warsaw Warsaw is the capital of Poland and its most populous city.

West Germany *See* GERMANY.

West Indies The West Indies are the group of islands east and south of Florida and north of South America that lie between the Atlantic Ocean and the Caribbean Sea. They were discovered by Columbus in 1492. Among the islands are the Bahamas, Cuba, Jamaica, and Puerto Rico. *See map on page 176.*

Yangtze River (YANG-see) The Yangtze, in China, is the longest river in Asia. The Chinese call it the Chang.

183

Yucatán (yooh-kuh-TAN) The Yucatán is a region in southern Mexico that was the home of the ancient Mayan civilization. It is also a peninsula that includes parts of Guatemala and Honduras.

Yugoslavia (YOOH-goh-SLAH-vee-uh) Yugoslavia is a Balkan country in southern Europe, across the Adriatic Sea (an arm of the Mediterranean) from Italy.

Yukon Territory (YOOH-KON) The Yukon Territory is in northwestern Canada, east of Alaska.

Thousands of people rushed to the Yukon Territory in the 1890s, when gold was discovered in the Klondike mining district. ❧

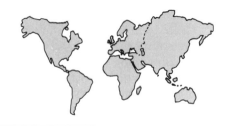

 Zaire (zeye-EER) Zaire is a French- and Swahili-speaking country in central Africa that used to be called the Belgian Congo.

 Zimbabwe (zim-BAHB-way) Zimbabwe is a country in southern Africa that used to be called Rhodesia. English is its official language.

Zurich (ZOOR-ik) Zurich is the largest city in Switzerland.

Mathematics

Mathematics is a way of thinking that often uses numbers and symbols instead of words. A typical statement in mathematics is $2 + 2 = 4$ (two plus two equals four). Most statements in mathematics can be expressed as equations, although many scientists in different fields use advanced mathematics. For example, an astronomer uses mathematical equations to discover how far certain stars are from the earth or from each other. Almost everyone uses basic arithmetic — like addition and subtraction — in everyday life. When we shop, we use numbers to compare prices. In sports, we use numbers to compare players or teams. For example, calculating a batting average is a mathematical operation.

Here we define the basic mathematical terms and operations that most people find useful. Knowing them is especially helpful if you want to learn more advanced scientific and mathematical ideas.

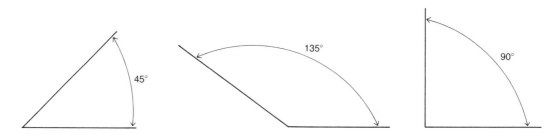

Angle. From left to right: Acute angle, obtuse angle, and right angle.

acute angle An acute angle is an ANGLE that measures less than a RIGHT ANGLE, that is, less than 90 DEGREES (90°).

addition Addition is one of the four basic operations of ARITHMETIC (along with SUBTRACTION, MULTIPLICATION, and DIVISION). Its symbol is the plus sign: +. To add two numbers means to combine them to get a total number, which is called the SUM. For example, the sum of 7 and 5 is 12; $7 + 5 = 12$ (seven plus five equals twelve).

angle An angle is created when two lines meet at the same POINT. The resulting angle is always measured in DEGREES. *See also* ACUTE ANGLE; ARC; OBTUSE ANGLE; RIGHT ANGLE.

arc An arc is a part of the CIRCUMFERENCE of a CIRCLE and is measured in DEGREES. Any ANGLE can form an arc on the CIRCUMFERENCE when the two lines of the angle are RADII of the circle. A full circle has 360 degrees.

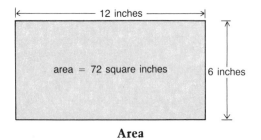

Area

area Area is the amount of surface contained by a figure, such as a RECTANGLE, a SQUARE, or a CIRCLE. Area is measured in units such as the square inch, which is an area the size of a square with sides 1 inch long. Some common units of area are:

square inch (abbreviated as sq in or in²)
1 square foot (sq ft or ft²) = 144 square inches
1 square yard (sq yd or yd²) = 9 square feet
1 acre = 4840 square yards
1 square mile (sq mi or mi²) = 640 acres

Area can also be measured using the METRIC SYSTEM:

square centimeter (sq cm or cm²)
1 square meter (sq m or m²) = 10,000 square centimeters
1 square kilometer (sq km or km²) = 1,000,000 square meters

arithmetic Arithmetic is a kind of mathematics that studies how to solve problems with numbers and no VARIABLES in them. The four basic operations of arithmetic are ADDITION, SUBTRACTION, MULTIPLICATION, and DIVISION.

average The average of a set of numbers is found by adding them together and dividing the SUM by the number of separate numbers in the set. Thus, the average of 5, 6, and 4 is 5, because the sum of 5, 6, and 4 is 15 and there are 3 numbers in the set: 15 ÷ 3 = 5 (fifteen divided by three equals five). An average is one way to describe a set of numbers. For example, to find out the average height of the people in your class, you would measure each person, add up all the heights, and divide the sum by the number of people. The answer would be the average height of the people in your class. Compare MEAN.

bar graph A bar graph is a kind of chart used to compare DATA. For example, if you know the average life span of different animals and want to present the information in a way that is easy to see at a glance, you can make a bar graph.

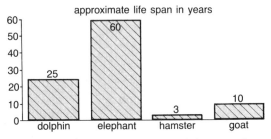

Bar graph. The approximate life span of several animals, shown in years.

braces Braces { } are symbols that indicate a SET. *Compare* PARENTHESES.

calculator A calculator is a machine that solves mathematical problems. It can perform a variety of operations, including ADDITION, SUBTRACTION, MULTIPLICATION, and DIVISION.

cardinal number A cardinal number, such as 1, 5, or 75, indicates the quantity but not the order of things. A cardinal number is not followed by *th*. *Compare* ORDINAL NUMBER.

chord A chord is a straight line joining two POINTS on the same curve or CIRCLE.

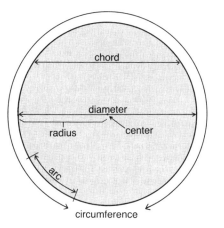

Circle. A circle and its parts.

circle   A circle is a round, closed figure. All the POINTS on its CIRCUMFERENCE (boundary) are the same distance from the center.

circumference   The circumference is the edge or boundary of a circle.

common denominator   A common denominator is a MULTIPLE shared by the DENOMINATORS of two or more FRACTIONS. For example, 6 is a common denominator of the fractions ½ (or ³⁄₆) and ⅓ (or ²⁄₆) because 6 is a multiple of both 2 and 3. In order to add or subtract fractions, you must find their LOWEST COMMON DENOMINATOR. For example, ½ + ⅓ = ³⁄₆ (or ½) + ²⁄₆ (or ⅓) = ⁵⁄₆.

compute   To compute is to solve problems that use numbers. ADDITION, SUBTRACTION, MULTIPLICATION, and DIVISION all involve computation. *See also* COMPUTER.

cone   A cone is a three-dimensional figure that rises from a circular base to a single POINT (called an apex) at its top.

congruent   Congruent figures are identical in size and shape. A triangle that is congruent with another triangle will occupy the same amount of space.

coordinates   The two numbers that define the position of a POINT on a LINE GRAPH are called coordinates. One number represents vertical distance from the zero point, the other horizontal distance. The coordinates define the point where the vertical and horizontal lines cross. *See also* ORDERED PAIR.

cube   *In geometry*, a cube is a three-dimensional figure that has six square faces. A pair of dice are cubes. *In multiplication*, when you cube a number, you multiply the number by itself three times. This is sometimes called raising the number to its third power. The operation of cubing is indicated by the use of an EXPONENT: $2^3 = 2 \times 2 \times 2$. In the expression 2^3, the exponent is 3 and is always so placed halfway above the line.

cylinder   A cylinder is a rounded, three-dimensional figure that has a flat, circular face at each end, such as a rolling pin or a hockey puck.

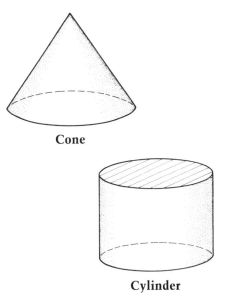

Cone

Cylinder

data   Data are facts that have been collected but not interpreted. For instance, to find out how long the average cat lives, you would have to collect data on the life spans of many cats.

decimal A decimal is a FRACTION written according to the decimal number system. (*Decimal* means "based on the number 10.") Decimals, which are sometimes called decimal fractions, are expressed using a DECIMAL POINT and the PLACE VALUES tenths, hundredths, thousandths, and so on. The fraction ½ is the decimal .5 or ⁵/₁₀; the fraction ¼ is 0.25 or ²⁵/₁₀₀. In a decimal, each place value to the right of the decimal point has ¹/₁₀ (one-tenth) the value of the place immediately to its left. The numbers on a hand calculator appear in decimals.

decimal point A decimal point looks like a period [.] and is used to mark the PLACE VALUE in a number that contains a value lower than 1. For example, in the number 3.45 (or 3⁴⁵/₁₀₀), the decimal point tells you that the 3 is in the *ones* place, the 4 is in the *tenths* place, and the 5 is in the *hundredths* place. If the decimal point was moved and the number was written as 34.5 (34⁵/₁₀), the 3 would be in the *tens* place, the 4 in the *ones* place, and the 5 in the *tenths* place.

degree A degree is a unit of measurement for ANGLES and ARCS and is indicated by a small circle: [°]. We often write 90 degrees as 90°. A circle measures 360 degrees; a right angle measures 90 degrees.

denominator A denominator is the bottom number of a FRACTION and indicates the number of parts needed to make a whole unit. In the fraction ⅔, the denominator is 3 (³/₃ = 1). *See also* NUMERATOR.

diagonal In a four-sided plane (flat) figure, a diagonal is a straight line from one corner of the figure to the opposite corner.

diameter The diameter of a CIRCLE is a straight line across the circle through its center. *See also* CIRCUMFERENCE; RADIUS.

difference The difference between two numbers is the answer you get when you sub-

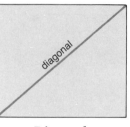

Diagonal

tract the smaller from the larger. The difference between 7 and 4 is 3, because 7 − 4 = 3. *See also* SUBTRACTION.

digit A digit is a single number from 0 to 9 that occupies one place. A number such as 1368 is a four-digit number because it uses four digits in four places. The number 1000 is also a four-digit number, even though three of the digits are the same number. The number 5 is a single-digit number; 45 is a two-digit number. The value of a digit depends on its PLACE VALUE with respect to the decimal point.

dimension Dimension is the indication of how far something extends in space. A line has one dimension: LENGTH. A SQUARE has two dimensions: length and width. (Two-dimensional objects are PLANE, or flat, like drawings on paper.) Real objects (and the objects that are called SOLIDS in mathematics) have three dimensions: length, width, and height, such as a CUBE. *See also* GEOMETRY.

dividend A dividend is a number that is to be divided. In the expression 16 ÷ 2 = 8 (or ₂√16 or ¹⁶/₂ = 8), 16 is the dividend. *See also* DIVISOR.

division Division is one of the four basic operations of ARITHMETIC (along with MULTIPLICATION, ADDITION, and SUBTRACTION). Its symbol is ÷, which means "divided by." To divide is to determine how many times one quantity is contained in another. Therefore, to divide is to determine how many times you have to subtract a number to reach zero. For

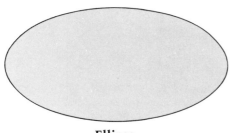

Ellipse

example, $6 \div 3 = 2$ because you subtract 3 from 6 two times to reach zero. This problem may also be represented as $6/2 = 3$. When you divide a larger number by a smaller number, you get a whole number $(8 \div 2 = 4)$ or a mixed number $(8 \div 3 = 2\ 2/3)$. When you divide a smaller number by a larger number, you get a fraction $(3 \div 8 = 3/8)$. *See also* DIVIDEND; DIVISOR; QUOTIENT; REMAINDER.

divisor   A divisor is the number that divides the DIVIDEND. In the expression $20 \div 4 = 5$, 4 is the divisor. *See also* REMAINDER; QUOTIENT.

ellipse   An ellipse is a closed, oval, plane (flat) figure that is not as round as a circle. The ORBITS of the PLANETS are ellipses.

equation   An equation is a statement that two different numbers or mathematical expressions are equal to each other. For example, $3 + 12 = 15$ is an equation. Equations use the equals sign: $=$.

equilateral triangle   An equilateral triangle is a TRIANGLE that has three sides of equal LENGTH and three angles of equal size. Because the angles of a triangle always add up to 180 degrees, each angle of an equilateral triangle is 60 degrees.

estimate   An estimate is a rough guess at a number. If someone asks how long it will take you to read a story and you say, "About 30 minutes," you have made an estimate. Estimates can help you solve problems. If you add

9.26 and 4.21, you can estimate that the answer will be around 13, because $9 + 4 = 13$.

even number   An even number is a number that can be divided by 2 without leaving a REMAINDER. The numbers 2, 4, 6, 8, 10, and so on, can be divided evenly by 2 and are thus even numbers. *Compare* ODD NUMBER.

exponent   An exponent is the small number to the right and above the main number that shows how many times the number is to be multiplied by itself. For instance, in the expression 2^3, 3 is the exponent, or the number of times that 2 is to be multiplied by itself. Thus, $2^3 = 2 \times 2 \times 2 = 8$. The expression 2^3 is read aloud as "two to the power of three," "two to the third," or "two exponent three." *See also* POWER.

factor   In MULTIPLICATION, a factor is a number that is being multiplied. In the expression $3 \times 9 = 27$, the factors are 3 and 9.

formula   A formula is a general mathematical expression that can be applied in particular cases. For example, to calculate the AREA (a) of a SQUARE, you multiply the LENGTH of one side (s) of the square by itself. Thus, the formula for the area of a square is $a = s^2$. No matter how large the square is, if you multiply the length of one side by itself, you will get its area. A formula is usually written as an EQUATION. *Compare* VARIABLE.

fraction   A fraction is a number that expresses a part of a whole. In the fraction $2/3$, 3 is the DENOMINATOR, which is the number of equal parts that make the whole. The number 2 is the NUMERATOR, which is the number of parts you are talking about. If you have two apples to divide among three people, each person would get a fraction of an apple, or $2/3$ (two-thirds) of an apple. Fractions are sometimes expressed as DECIMALS: $4/10 = 0.4$. Sometimes numbers greater than 1 are called

189

fractions when they are written as fractions. For example, ³⁄₂ (or 1½) is sometimes called a fraction.

geometry   Geometry is the mathematical study of shapes (such as TRIANGLES), three-dimensional figures or SOLIDS (such as CUBES and CYLINDERS), and positions in space (such as POINTS).

hexagon   A hexagon is a plane (flat) figure with six straight sides.

horizontal   A horizontal line is PARALLEL to the earth's surface or the bottom of a page; it goes across rather than up and down. *Compare* VERTICAL.

hypotenuse   The hypotenuse is the longest side of a RIGHT TRIANGLE and is opposite the RIGHT ANGLE.

infinity   Infinity refers to a set of numbers that goes on without end, for example: 1, 2, 3, 4, and so on. The symbol for infinity is ∞.

integer   Integers are the set of numbers that includes zero and the negative numbers but not fractions. The set of integers includes 0, 1, 2, 3, and so on; it also includes −1, −2, −3, and so on. *See also* WHOLE NUMBER.

intersect   In geometry, two figures are said to intersect when they cross each other. The POINTS where they cross are their intersections. The place where two roads cross is also called an intersection.

isosceles triangle   An isosceles triangle has two straight sides of EQUAL LENGTH and two angles of EQUAL size.

length   Length is the straight-line distance from one point to another. Some common units for measuring length are:

inch (in)
1 foot (ft) = 12 inches
1 yard (yd) = 3 feet
1 mile (mi) = 5280 feet

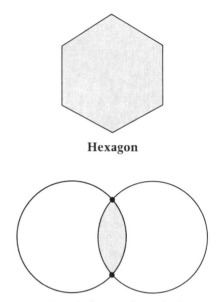

Hexagon

Intersect. Dots indicate where the lines intersect; shading accentuates the intersecting area.

Length can also be measured using the METRIC SYSTEM:

1 millimeter (mm) = 0.1 centimeter
1 centimeter (cm) = 0.39 inch
1 meter (m) = 100 centimeters or 39 inches
1 kilometer (km) = 1000 m or 0.6 mile

line   In geometry, a line is something that has LENGTH but no width. It has only one dimension (its length) and extends infinitely in both directions. On a plane (flat) surface, a straight LINE SEGMENT is the shortest distance between two points. A line is labeled with letters and may be written: line AB or (simply) $\overleftrightarrow{AB}$.

line graph   A line graph is a chart that shows DATA clearly and simply. For example, if you want to show how the cost of milk has changed over the last twenty years, you can use a line graph.

line segment   A line segment is part of a LINE. In theory, a line can go on forever. Therefore, when we draw a line, we are really draw-

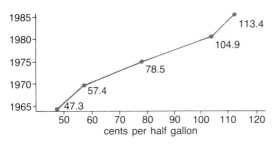

Line graph. Showing the rising cost of a half gallon of milk over twenty years.

ing a part of a line, or a line segment. A line segment is labeled line segment AB or (simply) $\overleftrightarrow{AB}$.

lowest common denominator   The lowest common denominator is the lowest MULTIPLE shared by the DENOMINATORS of two FRACTIONS. For example, 6 is the lowest common denominator of ½ (or ³⁄₆) and ⅓ (or ²⁄₆). To add ½ and ⅓, you must use their lowest common denominator: ½ + ⅓ = ³⁄₆ + ²⁄₆ = ⁵⁄₆.

lowest terms   A FRACTION is in lowest terms when its NUMERATOR and DENOMINATOR cannot both be divided evenly by any whole number greater than 1. The fraction ⁴⁄₈ is not in lowest terms because its numerator (4) and its denominator (8) can each be divided by 4, yielding ½, which is in lowest terms because no number except one can divide both numerator (1) and denominator (2). Finding lowest terms is also known as *reducing* or *simplifying* the fraction.

mean   A mean is the same as an AVERAGE and is found by adding a set of amounts and dividing their sum by the number of different amounts in the set. The mean of 8 + 4 + 3 is the sum (15) divided by the number of items (3): 15 ÷ 3 = 5, which is the mean.

median   When a set of numbers is arranged in order from the least to the greatest, the median is the middle number. In the set 1, 3,

5, 7, 9, the median is 5. For an even number of items, the median is midway between the two middle numbers. The median divides the DATA into two equal parts. *Compare* MEAN.

multiple   A multiple is a quantity into which another quantity can be divided with zero REMAINDER. The numbers 4 and 8 are multiples of 2. A DIVIDEND is a multiple of a DIVISOR if there is zero remainder.

multiplication   Multiplication is one of the four basic operations of ARITHMETIC (along with DIVISION, ADDITION, and SUBTRACTION). Its symbol is the "times" sign: ×. Multiplication is like addition because you add the same number a certain number of times. For example, 2 × 3 = 3 + 3; 5 × 6 = 6 + 6 + 6 + 6 + 6; 5 × 6 also equals 5 + 5 + 5 + 5 + 5 + 5. When you multiply numbers, you get their PRODUCT. The product of 2 and 3 is 6 because 2 × 3 = 6.

negative number   A negative number is less than ZERO (0) and is written with a minus sign in front of it: −3. A negative number often stands for a measurement that is below a certain reference point. For instance, in the CENTIGRADE temperature scale, a temperature of −24°C is 24 degrees below zero, or the freezing point of water.

numeral   A numeral is a symbol that stands for a number. The numeral 4 stands for the number four. In the past, people used different symbols for numbers from the ones we use now. For example, the ancient Romans wrote the number three as III. ROMAN NUMERALS are sometimes used today, but today we usually use symbols called Arabic numerals, so called because they were first taught to Europeans by Arabs. The Arabic numerals are: 1, 2, 3, 4, 5, 6, 7, 8, 9, and 0.

numerator   A numerator is the top part of a FRACTION and the number that is divided by the DENOMINATOR. Therefore, a numerator is

191

a DIVIDEND and a denominator is a DIVISOR. In the fraction ⅔, the numerator is 2.

obtuse angle   An obtuse angle is an ANGLE greater than 90 DEGREES (90°) and less than 180 degrees (180°).

octagon   An octagon is a plane (flat) figure with eight straight sides.

odd number   An odd number is a number that cannot be divided evenly by two. The numbers 1, 3, 5, 7, 9, 11, and so on, are odd numbers. *Compare* EVEN NUMBER.

opposite number   Any two numbers whose sum is ZERO are opposite numbers to each other. Thus, 3 and −3 are opposite numbers because −3 + 3 = 0. The opposite number of −5 is 5. Zero's opposite number is itself, because 0 + 0 = 0. *See also* NEGATIVE NUMBER.

ordered pair   An ordered pair is a pair of numbers that represents a position on a LINE GRAPH. For example, (8,3) is an ordered pair because 8 tells you how far the POINT is to the right of 0 and 3 tells you how far the point is above 0. These numbers are sometimes called COORDINATES.

ordinal number   An ordinal number indicates the order of a thing in a series: first (1st), second (2nd), third (3rd), twenty-fifth (25th), and so on. After 3rd, ordinal numbers use the *th* ending. *Compare* CARDINAL NUMBER.

Parallel. Line segment AB is parallel to line segment CD.

parallel   Parallel lines are lines that never meet. They extend in the same direction and always remain the same distance from each other, like railroad tracks.

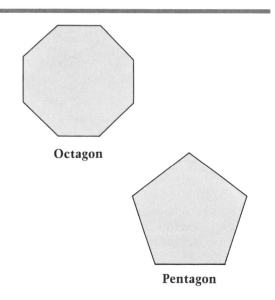

Octagon

Pentagon

parallelogram   A parallelogram is a plane (flat) figure with four straight sides. The sides opposite each other are PARALLEL and the same LENGTH. SQUARES, RECTANGLES, and RHOMBUSES are all parallelograms.

parentheses   Parentheses ( ) are used in mathematics to show that the operation inside the parentheses should be treated as a single quantity. In the equation 2 × (3 + 2) = 10, the digits (3 + 2) should be treated as a single quantity, which is 5. *Compare* BRACES.

pentagon   A pentagon is a plane (flat) figure with five straight sides.

percent   Percent is a way of expressing a number as a FRACTION of 100. (*Percent* means "by hundreds.") The symbol for percent is %. To express the number ½ as a percentage, you change it to a fraction of 100. Thus, ½ = ⁵⁰⁄₁₀₀, which as a percentage is written as 50%. To express 2 as a percentage, you would calculate that 2 = ²⁰⁰⁄₁₀₀, or 200%. Similarly, ⅓ = 33⅓%, because ⅓ of 100 = 33⅓. The fraction ¼ = ²⁵⁄₁₀₀, or 25%.

perimeter   Perimeter is the distance around the edge of a multisided figure. For example, if each of the four sides of a SQUARE measures 2 inches, its perimeter is 8 inches.

perpendicular　Two straight lines are perpendicular when they form a RIGHT ANGLE (an angle that measures 90 DEGREES).

pi　Pi is the RATIO of the CIRCUMFERENCE of a CIRCLE to its DIAMETER. *Pi* is the name of a Greek letter that is written as the symbol π. The actual number is approximately 3.14159 and is used in many calculations.

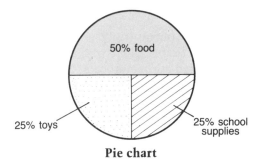

Pie chart

pie chart　A pie chart, or graph, is a way to represent percentages or FRACTIONS. A pie chart is also called a CIRCLE graph because it is circular. This pie chart shows that Mike spends ½ (50%) of his money on food, ¼ (25%) on school supplies, and the remaining ¼ (25%) on toys.

place value　Each DIGIT is given a place value, depending on where it is in a number with more than one digit. In the number 7324, 4 is in the *ones* place; it equals 4 × 1. The number 2 is in the *tens* place; it equals 2 × 10. The number 3 is in the *hundreds* place; it equals 3 × 100. The number 7 is in the *thousands* place; it equals 7 × 1000. Higher place values are ten thousands, hundred thousands, millions, billions, and so on. Lower place values are ten-thousandths, hundred-thousandths, and so on. *See also* DECIMAL POINT.

plane　In GEOMETRY, a plane is a flat area. One-dimensional figures, such as LINES, and two-dimensional figures, such as RECTANGLES, exist in planes. Anything three-dimensional, such as a CUBE or a CONE, exists in space, not in a plane. *See also* DIMENSION.

point　In GEOMETRY, a point represents a position but has no size. A point is represented by a small dot, like the period at the end of this sentence.

polygon　A polygon is a many-sided PLANE figure, such as a PENTAGON or an OCTAGON. (*Poly* means "many" in Greek.)

positive number　A positive number is a number greater than 0.

power　In mathematics, power refers to the number of times a number is to be multiplied by itself. For instance, 2 to the power of 3 (or 2^3) equals 2 × 2 × 2. The symbol that shows to what power a number is raised is called an EXPONENT. In the expression 2^3, the exponent is 3.

prime number　A prime number is a number that cannot be divided evenly by any number except itself and 1. The number 4 is not a prime number because it can be divided evenly by 1, 2, and 4. But 3 is a prime number because it can only be divided evenly by 1 and 3. *See also* FACTOR.

probability　Probability is the chance that a particular thing will happen. For instance, the probability of a coin landing heads up is ½ (1 out of 2, or 50%), because it is one of two possible outcomes.

product　A product is the result of MULTIPLICATION. For example, 6 is the product of 2 and 3 because 2 × 3 = 6. *See also* MULTIPLE.

proportion　A proportion is a RATIO or a comparison of ratios and can be expressed as a FRACTION. For example, ½ is the proportion 1 to 2. It can be compared with the proportion 5 to 10, or ⁵/₁₀. These proportions (or ratios or fractions) are all the same, since they can all be reduced to ½.

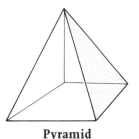

Pyramid

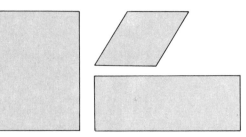

Quadrilateral. Left: Square. Right, top to bottom: Rhombus and rectangle.

pyramid A pyramid is a three-dimensional figure whose base is a POLYGON and whose sides are TRIANGLES that come to a point at the top. *See also* PYRAMIDS *under "World History to 1600."*

quadrilateral A quadrilateral is a plane (flat) figure with four straight sides. RECTANGLES, SQUARES, and RHOMBUSES are quadrilaterals.

quotient A quotient is the result of DIVISION. For example, when 10 is divided by 2, the quotient is 5, because 10 ÷ 2 = 5. This problem may also be represented as $^{10}/_2 = 5$ or $2\overline{)10}^{\,5}$.

radii *See* RADIUS.

radius The radius of a CIRCLE is the length of a straight LINE drawn from the center to the CIRCUMFERENCE. The radius is half the DIAMETER. The plural of radius is RADII.

rate A rate is a way of comparing two different kinds of quantities. Rates use RATIOS. If Bill walked 8 miles in 2 hours, you can find his rate of speed by dividing the number of miles he walked by the number of hours he walked. The rate is $^8/_2$ miles per hour, or 4 miles per hour.

ratio A ratio is a way of comparing two numbers by dividing one by the other. For example, the ratio of 2 to 3 is $^2/_3$. The ratio of 6 to 3 is $^6/_3$, or 2. If there are 15 boys and 10 girls in your class, the ratio of boys to girls is 15 to 10.

In LOWEST TERMS, $^{15}/_{10}$ is $^3/_2$; the ratio of boys to girls is 3 to 2.

reciprocal If you multiply one number by another and get 1 for an answer, the numbers being multiplied are reciprocals. The reciprocal of 2 is $^1/_2$, because $2 \times ^1/_2 = 1$. To get the reciprocal of a FRACTION, you simply flip it over, switching the positions of the NUMERATOR and the DENOMINATOR. Thus, the reciprocal of $^2/_3$ is $^3/_2$, because $^2/_3 \times ^3/_2 = ^6/_6 = 1$. (A fraction whose numerator and denominator are equal, such as $^6/_6$, will always equal 1. Such a fraction is its own reciprocal.)

rectangle A rectangle is a plane (flat) figure with four straight sides that form four RIGHT ANGLES. The sides opposite each other are PARALLEL and of equal LENGTH.

remainder The remainder is the number left over when one number is divided by another. For example, when you divide 9 by 2, you get a QUOTIENT of 4 with a remainder of 1.

repeating decimal A repeating decimal is a DECIMAL with a DIGIT or pattern of digits that repeats itself forever to INFINITY. The numbers 9.14141414 and 1.33333 are repeating decimals. The answers to some division problems are repeating decimals; for example, 28 divided by 3 gives an answer of 9.333333.

rhombus A rhombus is a PARALLELOGRAM that has four straight sides of the same LENGTH but no RIGHT ANGLES. A diamond shape is a rhombus.

right angle   A right angle is an ANGLE that measures 90 DEGREES (90°) and is formed when two PERPENDICULAR lines meet.

right triangle   A right triangle is a TRIANGLE in which two sides meet to form a RIGHT ANGLE.

Roman numerals   Roman numerals are the numbers used by the ancient Romans, which resemble the letters of our alphabet. Some common Roman numerals are:

I = 1	VI = 6	XI = 11
II = 2	VII = 7	L = 50
III = 3	VIII = 8	C = 100
IV = 4	IX = 9	D = 500
V = 5	X = 10	M = 1000

rounding   Rounding is something you do to a number when it does not need to be exact. In many cases, an approximate number (one that is almost exact) is enough. For example, 68,823 people attended a football game. If you were talking to a friend, you would probably round the number up to the nearest thousand and say that about 69,000 people were at the game. Numbers with decimals are often rounded to the next highest whole number when the decimal is .5 or greater or to the same whole number when the decimal is less than .5. For example, 5.63 would be rounded to 6.00; 5.44 to 5.00. *See also* PLACE VALUE.

scale   A scale is a RATIO that shows the size relationship between a diagram and the real thing it represents. For instance, on a map, the scale might be 1 inch = 10 miles. This means that 1 inch on the map represents 10 miles on the land.

scalene triangle   A scalene triangle is a TRIANGLE that has no sides of the same LENGTH or ANGLES of equal measure.

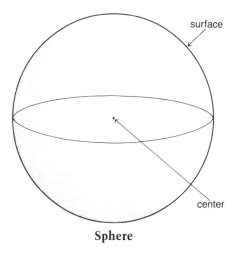

Sphere

set   A set is a group of things with a common property and is indicated by BRACES: { }. For instance, a set of fruits is {oranges, pears, apples}. A set of odd numbers is {−3, −1, 1, 3}.

solid   In GEOMETRY, a solid is a three-dimensional figure such as a CUBE, a CONE, or a PYRAMID.

sphere   A sphere is a three-dimensional round figure, such as a basketball. Every point on a sphere is the same distance from its center.

square   *In geometry*, a square is a RECTANGLE with four straight sides of equal LENGTH. Each side meets with another side to form a RIGHT ANGLE. *In arithmetic*, to square a number is to multiply it by itself once. For example, 3 squared (3^2) is 3×3, which equals 9. The operation of squaring is indicated by using the EXPONENT 2, as in the expression 3^2.

square root   The square root of any number is the number that, when SQUARED (multiplied by itself once), gives the original number as a product. The symbol for square root is $\sqrt{}$. The square root of 4 ($\sqrt{4}$) is 2 because 2 squared (2^2 or 2×2) equals 4. The square root of 9 ($\sqrt{9}$) is 3 because 3^2 equals 9. *See* SQUARE, *as it is used in arithmetic*.

subtraction Subtraction is one of the four basic operations of ARITHMETIC (along with ADDITION, MULTIPLICATION, and DIVISION). It is the opposite of addition, because instead of adding one number to another, you take one number away from another. The symbol for subtraction is the minus sign: −. When you subtract one number from another you find the DIFFERENCE between them. The difference between 12 and 5 is 7; 12 − 5 = 7.

sum A sum is the answer to an ADDITION problem. For example, 8 is the sum of 5 and 3 because 5 + 3 = 8. *Compare* DIFFERENCE.

surface area The surface area of a figure is the measure of its surface expressed in square units, such as square inches or square miles. *See also* AREA.

symmetry If a figure can be divided into two parts that are mirror images of each other, the figure has symmetry or is symmetrical. For example, regular figures such as CIRCLES and SQUARES are symmetrical.

trapezoid A trapezoid is a plane (flat) figure with four straight sides. Only two of the sides are PARALLEL to each other.

triangle A triangle is a plane (flat) figure with three straight sides. *See also* EQUILATERAL TRIANGLE; RIGHT TRIANGLE; SCALENE TRIANGLE.

variable A variable is a symbol whose value can change in a FORMULA or EQUATION. It is usually represented by a letter. For instance, the AREA of a SQUARE is the square of the LENGTH of one side. The formula is $a = s^2$ where a is a variable that stands for area and s is a variable that stands for the length of a side.

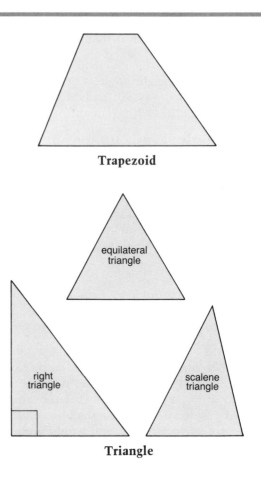

Trapezoid

equilateral triangle

right triangle

scalene triangle

Triangle

vertical A vertical line is straight up and down and is PERPENDICULAR to a HORIZONTAL line.

whole number A whole number is an INTEGER.

zero Zero (0) is the number that, when added to another number, does not change it. Thus, 3 + 0 = 3. If any number is multiplied by 0, the answer is 0: 3 × 0 = 0.

Physical Sciences

The basic ideas of chemistry, physics, and astronomy are presented here. In the next section, "Earth Sciences and Weather," important concepts from other physical sciences are introduced.

In modern science, the borderline between chemistry and physics has become fuzzy. *Chemistry* is basically the science of what things are made of, what identifies them, and how they change. *Physics* is basically the study of matter and motion. *Astronomy* uses both physics and chemistry to investigate the sun, moon, stars, and planets.

The physical sciences encompass the most enormous things that exist — stars and planets in space — but they also are concerned with the tiniest things — molecules, atoms, and parts of atoms, which are all too small to be seen with the naked eye. These sciences help us understand our place in the universe and how everything around us works.

Apollo Program. Liftoff of Apollo 16 on April 16, 1972.

acid   In CHEMISTRY, an acid is the opposite of a BASE or ALKALI. When an acid and base come together, they counteract each other and make a salt plus water. An acid tastes sour. Strong acids can be dangerous. Vinegar is a weak acid.

alkali   In CHEMISTRY, an alkali is a strong BASE, the opposite of an ACID. Strong alkalis can be dangerous.

Apollo Program   The Apollo Program was a project of NASA's designed to put a person on the moon. In 1969, during the eleventh Apollo mission, Neil Armstrong became the first person to walk on the moon.

asteroid   An asteroid is a very small PLANET.

197

astronomy   Astronomy is the science of heavenly bodies, such as the SUN, the MOON, the STARS, and the PLANETS.

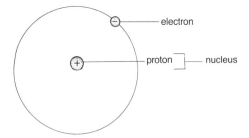

Atom. Diagram of a hydrogen atom.

atom   An atom is the smallest particle of any element that can still be recognized as that element. Atoms combine to form MOLECULES.

base   In CHEMISTRY, a base is the opposite of an ACID. When an acid and a base come together, they react to produce a salt plus water. If you mix vinegar (an acid) with bicarbonate of soda (a base), you will get a salt that is different from table salt. *See also* ALKALI.

"**F**ollow the Drinking Gourd," a well-known American folk song from the time of the Underground Railroad, refers to the route north taken by runaway slaves, who got their bearings from the Big Dipper (the Drinking Gourd). ❧

Big Dipper   The Big Dipper is a CONSTELLATION (group of STARS) that people have observed since ancient times. Its stars make a pattern in the sky that resembles a cup with a long handle for dipping. The direction north can be determined almost exactly by the NORTH STAR, which can be found by following the pointer stars of the Big Dipper — the two stars that form the outer base and lip of the cup.

boiling point   The boiling point is the temperature at which something boils, or begins to change from a LIQUID to a GAS. Every liquid has a definite boiling point. *See also* CONDENSATION POINT.

buoyancy   Buoyancy is the tendency of something to float on a FLUID because of its power to exert an upward force on objects. A balloon floats on air, which is a fluid. A cork has buoyancy when it is resting on water. A buoy is a float, attached by a long line to the bottom of a lake or ocean, that helps sailors know where they are.

carbon   Carbon is a chemical element used by all living things to make their CELLS.

centrifugal force   Centrifugal force causes an object going around in a circle to move away from the center. If you whirl a bucket of water in a circle, centrifugal force will tend to keep the water in the bucket.

change of phase   MATTER can exist as a SOLID, a LIQUID, or a GAS. When something changes from one of these forms (or phases) to another, it goes through a change of phase. For instance, when water freezes, it goes through a change of phase from a liquid to a solid.

chemical energy   Chemical energy is the energy stored in a chemical substance. Sometimes this energy is released in a chemical reaction, which occurs when one substance is changed into another. Fire is one kind of chemical reaction.

chemistry   Chemistry is the study of MATTER, especially at the level of ATOMS and MOLECULES .

combustion   Combustion means burning. In CHEMISTRY, things that combust take on OXYGEN.

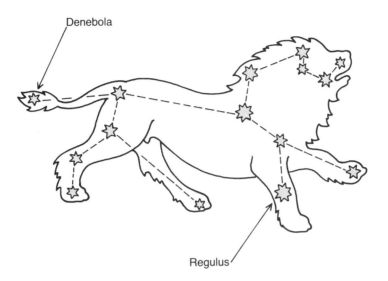

Denebola

Regulus

Constellation. The constellation Leo.

Comet. Halley's Comet in 1986.

comet   A comet is an object that circles the SUN in an extremely long ORBIT. It can be seen from EARTH only when its orbit takes it close to the sun.

compound   A compound is a substance whose MOLECULES have two or more ELEMENTS.

condensation point   The condensation point is the temperature at which a GAS condenses to a LIQUID. Every substance has a definite condensation point. *See also* BOILING POINT.

constellation   A constellation is a pattern made by a group of STARS in the sky. These patterns have been observed since ancient times and have been named for mythical figures and objects they resemble. For instance, the constellation Leo (Latin for "lion") looks somewhat like a lion.

crystal   A crystal is a SOLID in which the ATOMS or MOLECULES are arranged in a tight, orderly pattern. Snowflakes and grains of salt are crystals.

distillation   Distillation is the process of boiling a LIQUID and condensing the vapor. Drinking water and salt can be produced from sea water by distillation.

Earth   Earth is the planet on which we live. It orbits the SUN, making one revolution (complete turn) per year. It also rotates (turns on its own axis), making one rotation per day. Earth is one of nine PLANETS in our SOLAR SYSTEM. *See also* EARTH *under "Earth Sciences and Weather."*

Albert Einstein. Writing out the equation for the density of the Milky Way in 1931.

eclipse   An eclipse occurs when one heavenly body blocks light traveling from the SUN to another heavenly body. An eclipse of the sun occurs when the MOON passes directly between the sun and the EARTH (so that the sun cannot be seen or can be seen only in part). An eclipse of the moon occurs when the earth passes directly between the sun and the moon (so that a shadow moves across the surface of the moon).

Einstein, Albert   Albert Einstein was a brilliant scientist of the early 1900s who won the Nobel Prize in physics. His ideas about converting mass to ENERGY proved correct when ATOMS were first split. The explosive ENERGY of splitting atoms is the power in the atomic bomb.

electron   An electron is a very small, light particle that revolves around the NUCLEUS of an ATOM. Electrons have a negative electric charge. When free electrons flow through a wire or other CONDUCTOR, ELECTRICITY results.

element   An element is a substance that cannot be broken down into simpler substances. The ATOMS of each element have a unique structure.

> Some elements are aluminum, hydrogen, iodine, iron, mercury, nitrogen, oxygen, sodium, and zinc. ❧

energy   Energy is the ability to do WORK . To a scientist, work is done when a FORCE is used to move an object. For example, gasoline is a source of energy. When it is burned in a car engine and the car moves, the energy has been turned into work.

equilibrium   Equilibrium means balance. In chemical reactions, an equilibrium is reached when no further measurable change occurs.

evaporation   Evaporation occurs when a LIQUID turns into a GAS , or evaporates.

experiment   In science, an experiment is a strict, highly controlled test of an idea. Experiments are often carried out in laboratories.

extraterrestrial   An extraterrestrial object is one that comes from outer space.

> Meteorites are extraterrestrial objects. ❧

fluid   A fluid is something that flows and includes both LIQUIDS and GASES.

Galaxy. The Whirlpool Galaxy.

freezing point The freezing point is the temperature at which something freezes, or changes from a liquid to a solid. Every substance has a definite freezing point. *Compare* MELTING POINT.

galaxy A galaxy is an enormous group of STARS. The galaxy that contains our SUN is called the Milky Way.

> **A**fter being forced to state in public that the earth stands still, Galileo is said to have muttered under his breath, "But it does move." ✌

Galileo (gal-uh-LEE-oh, gal-uh-LAY-oh) Galileo Galilei was an Italian scientist of the 1600s. He improved the original TELESCOPES and was the first to use them for ASTRONOMY.

gas Matter can exist as a SOLID, a LIQUID, or a gas. A gas has no particular shape and can expand indefinitely, and its molecules are farther apart than those of a liquid or a solid. Air and steam are both gases.

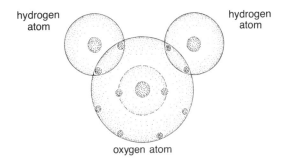

H₂O. Diagram of a water molecule.

gravity Gravity is the force that pulls objects toward each other. The EARTH's gravity pulls everything on earth toward the center of the earth. Thus, objects fall toward the ground. The SUN 's gravity keeps the PLANETS in their ORBITS. Gravity was first explained by ISAAC NEWTON.

H₂O H_2O is the scientific symbol for a water MOLECULE. Two ATOMS of hydrogen (H) and one atom of oxygen (O) join to form a molecule of water.

hydrogen Hydrogen is the lightest element. Each molecule of water is composed of two atoms of hydrogen and one atom of OXYGEN. The symbol for the water molecule is H_2O. There are many more hydrogen atoms than any other kind in the universe.

inertia Inertia is a resistance to change in motion; that is, the tendency of an object to keep moving in the same path or to stay still if it is not moving.

> **T**he heat we feel from a glowing coal or a light bulb is caused by infrared rays. ✌

infrared radiation Infrared radiation is invisible light at the opposite end of the SPEC-

Mars. Photograph of the surface of the planet.

trum from ULTRAVIOLET light. It is felt as heat, and much of the heat from the SUN comes from its infrared light.

Jupiter Jupiter is the largest PLANET in the SOLAR SYSTEM.

light year A light year is the distance traveled by light in a year, about six trillion miles. Distances between objects in outer space are often measured in light years. *See also* SPEED OF LIGHT.

liquid MATTER can exist as a SOLID, a GAS, or a liquid. In a liquid, the molecules are close together but loosely connected, so that they move around. A liquid takes the shape of its container. Water and milk are both liquids.

magnet A magnet is an object that attracts (pulls in) certain substances, especially iron.

Mars Mars is one of the PLANETS in the SOLAR SYSTEM. Because it appears to be red, it is sometimes called the red planet.

matter Matter is "stuff" — anything taking up space that you can see, hear, feel, touch, or taste. Air, stone, water, wood, skin, and the EARTH itself are all examples of matter.

melting point The melting point is the temperature at which something melts, or changes from a SOLID to a LIQUID. Every substance has a definite melting point. *Compare* FREEZING POINT.

Mercury Mercury is the PLANET in our SOLAR SYSTEM closest to the sun. Mercury is also a silvery metal that is LIQUID at room temperature; it is used in thermometers to measure the body temperature of a person.

meteor A meteor is a chunk of stone or metal that enters the EARTH'S ATMOSPHERE from outer space. When a meteor plows through the atmosphere, it burns up, making a streak of light across the sky.

Meteors that come near the earth's surface and are heated through collision with air molecules are seen as "falling stars" or "shooting stars." 🖎

meteorite A METEOR that falls to earth is called a meteorite.

Milky Way The Milky Way is the GALAXY that contains our SOLAR SYSTEM.

molecule A molecule is a tiny structure that is made up of two or more ATOMS.

moon The moon is the EARTH'S natural SATELLITE. It is much smaller than the earth. The moon revolves (turns) around the earth as the earth revolves around the SUN. It takes one month for the moon to revolve around the earth. Once a month the whole moon is visible as a round ball. At other times, only part of the moon is visible. It is described as a "half moon" when it looks like a disk sliced in half. It is described as a "crescent moon" when only its curved edge is visible. The dark patches on the moon's surface are craters, or large pits. In 1969, Neil Armstrong became the first person to walk on the moon.

Neptune   Neptune is one of the PLANETS in the SOLAR SYSTEM.

Newton, Isaac   Sir Isaac Newton was a great English scientist and mathematician of the 1600s and 1700s. He is said to have discovered GRAVITY when he saw an apple fall from a tree.

North Star (Polaris)   The North Star is found in the pattern of stars called the Little Dipper. You can find it by following the pointer stars in the BIG DIPPER. The North Star shines almost directly above the NORTH POLE and therefore always seems to stand very close to true north in the NORTHERN HEMISPHERE. The other stars seem to turn around the North Star because the EARTH spins on an axis that runs through the North and South poles.

nucleus   The nucleus of an ATOM is the part in the center that contains most of its mass. The ELECTRONS of the atom revolve around this nucleus.

orbit   To orbit something means to go around it. The earth orbits the sun and the moon orbits the earth. The force of GRAVITY keeps the earth and the moon in their orbits.

> **W**hen foods such as apples or potatoes turn brown on exposure to the air, they have undergone oxidation. ❧

oxidation   Oxidation occurs when a substance combines with oxygen. The most familiar form of oxidation is rust, which is a COMPOUND of oxygen and iron.

oxygen   Oxygen is an ELEMENT that makes up an important part of the air we breathe. Plants, animals, and most other organisms depend on oxygen to live.

phases of matter   MATTER can exist as a SOLID, a LIQUID, or a GAS at different temperatures and under different pressures. For example, water can be a liquid, a solid (ice), or a gas (steam or water vapor). The different forms of matter are called phases. See also CHANGE OF PHASE.

physics   Physics is the science that studies MATTER and ENERGY and the way they interact.

planet   A planet is a heavenly body that orbits a STAR. The planets in our SOLAR SYSTEM orbit the star we call the SUN. Unlike stars, planets do not give off light. EARTH is a planet.

Pluto   Pluto is the PLANET in our SOLAR SYSTEM whose orbit takes it farthest from the sun.

Polaris   *See* NORTH STAR.

radiation   Radiation is the general name for various kinds of light, including kinds that cannot be seen, such as INFRARED, ULTRAVIOLET, and X-RAYS.

radioactivity   Radioactivity is a property of certain substances that causes them to decay naturally, or change, over time. As they decay, they release ENERGY. Uranium and plutonium are radioactive substances.

reflection   Reflection occurs when light bounces off a surface. A mirror is a good reflector of light.

refraction   Refraction occurs when light bends as it passes through a clear substance like air or water. The denser the substance, the more the light bends.

salt   In CHEMISTRY, a salt is a COMPOUND that is produced by the reaction between an ACID and a BASE. The chemical name of table salt is sodium chloride.

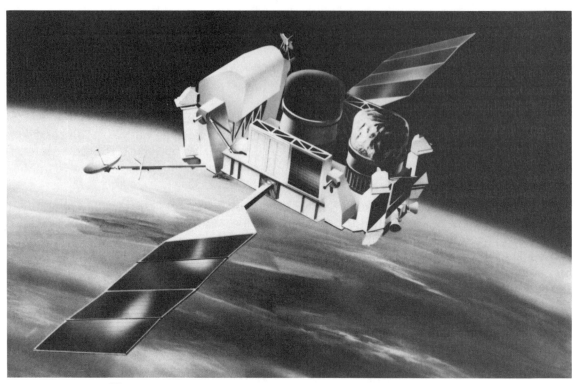

Satellite. Known as the Gamma Ray Observatory, this satellite is scheduled for launch from the Space Shuttle.

satellite   In ASTRONOMY, a body that orbits a larger body is called a satellite. The EARTH's natural satellite is the MOON. There are also many artificial satellites orbiting the earth. They transmit television signals, gather information about space, survey military installations, and help predict the weather.

Saturn   Saturn is one of the PLANETS in our SOLAR SYSTEM and is distinguished by the colored rings that surround it. These rings are huge bands of icy particles in orbit around the planet.

scientific method   Scientists have developed certain special research procedures. Taken together, they are called the scientific method. One important part of the scientific method is the rigorous testing of ideas by EX-

PERIMENTS. An untested idea is not considered scientifically sound.

solar system   The solar system is made up of the SUN and the nine PLANETS that revolve around it: MERCURY, VENUS, EARTH, MARS, JUPITER, SATURN, URANUS, NEPTUNE, and PLUTO. Solar means "of the sun."

solid   Matter can exist as a solid, a GAS, or a LIQUID. In a solid, molecules are locked together. Unlike a gas or a liquid, a solid has a fixed size and shape. A candy bar, a rock, an ice cube, and a piece of cloth are all solids.

solution   In CHEMISTRY, a solution is a uniform mixture, usually a LIQUID. If you dissolve salt in water, you will get a salt solution.

spectrum   The visible spectrum consists of the different colors of light, from red to vio-

Solar system. The planets are shown in relative size and at relative distance from the sun.

let. A RAINBOW is a visible spectrum. The entire spectrum consists of radio waves, microwaves, infrared, visible light, ultraviolet light, x-rays, gamma rays, and cosmic rays. *See also* INFRARED RADIATION; ULTRAVIOLET RADIATION.

speed of light   Light travels at about 186,000 miles per second when there is nothing to slow it down.

> **L**ight from the sun takes about eight minutes to reach the earth; light from the moon takes about a second and a half to reach the earth. ⁊

star   A star is a heavenly body that gives off light, such as the SUN. The sun looks bigger than other stars only because it is much closer to EARTH. At night, many other stars are visible as tiny points of light. *See also* CONSTELLATIONS.

sun   The sun is the STAR at the center of the SOLAR SYSTEM. It is an enormous ball of burning gases, thousands of times the size of Earth. The nine PLANETS of the system, including Earth, revolve around the sun. All life on Earth depends on light from the sun.

telescope   The telescope is an instrument used by astronomers to study the STARS and PLANETS. It was developed by GALILEO.

ultraviolet radiation   Ultraviolet radiation is the invisible light beyond violet in the light SPECTRUM. Ultraviolet rays from the sun can cause sunburn and eye damage.

Uranus   Uranus is one of the PLANETS in the SOLAR SYSTEM.

vacuum   A vacuum is space with no MATTER in it. You can make a vacuum by pumping the air out of an airtight container.

Venus   Venus is the PLANET in the SOLAR SYSTEM that is closest to Earth.

watt   A watt is a unit of electrical ENERGY. Light bulbs are rated in watts according to the amount of ELECTRICITY they use. A 100-watt bulb uses more electricity (and hence costs more to use) than a 40-watt bulb.

x-rays   X-rays are a penetrating kind of light with extremely short wavelengths that can pass through solid objects. X-rays are at the very far end of the SPECTRUM, beyond ultraviolet light. *See also* X-RAY *under "Medicine and the Human Body."*

Earth Sciences and Weather

Many kinds of scientists study the earth and its weather. Those who study the earth's history and structure are called *geologists*. They examine fossils, rocks, and minerals. Other scientists, called *meteorologists*, study the weather. They examine the causes of weather conditions and how weather can be predicted. Other earth sciences include *oceanography*, which is concerned with water and the oceans, and *geography*, which studies the surface of the earth.

air pollution Air pollution is caused when harmful gases and particles are released into the air, making it so dirty (polluted) that it threatens people's health. Exhaust fumes from cars and trucks and smoke from FACTORIES, power plants, and incinerators that burn trash are major causes of air pollution. *See also* POLLUTION; SMOG.

air pressure Air pressure is the weight of the air pressing against a surface. Air pressure changes slightly from day to day. It also decreases as elevation increases.

atmosphere The atmosphere is the layer of air that surrounds the earth.

barometer A barometer is a device for measuring AIR PRESSURE.

cirrus clouds Cirrus clouds are feathery, white clouds that float high in the sky.

The atmosphere of the earth is made up of about 80 percent nitrogen and 20 percent oxygen, with small amounts of other gases. ❧

climate The climate of a region is its weather pattern over a long period: its heat and cold, moisture and dryness, clearness and cloudiness, and wind and calm. Regions near the equator tend to have hot climates; those near the poles, cool ones.

clouds Clouds are masses of condensed water or ice particles floating in the air. Four types of clouds are CIRRUS, CUMULUS, STRATUS, and THUNDERHEADS.

coal Coal is a black or brown rock found in the ground consisting largely of carbon. It can

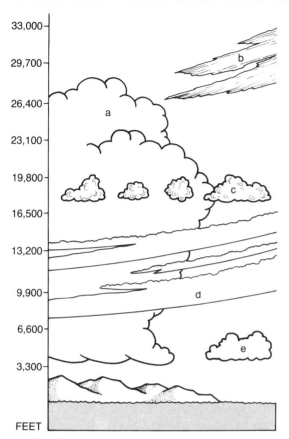

Clouds. The height at which various cloud formations occur. a. Cumulus (cumulonimbus). b. Cirrus. c. High-level cumulus. d. Stratus. e. Fair weather cumulus.

Delta. View of the Colorado River delta in Mexico, as seen from Apollo 9.

be dug up, or mined, and used as FUEL. Coal is formed when layers of earth build up for millions of years over the remains of plants and animals. *See also* FOSSIL FUELS.

cold front A front is a place in the air where two very large bodies of air meet. A cold front is the place where cold air pushes out warm air. *Compare* WARM FRONT.

conservationist A conservationist is a person who works to conserve, or protect, the earth's NATURAL RESOURCES.

continent A continent is a huge land mass. The earth has seven continents: Africa, Ant-arctica, Asia, Australia, Europe, North America, and South America.

core The core is the center of the earth and consists of hot metals.

crust The crust is the outer layer of the earth and is made chiefly of rock.

cumulonimbus clouds *See* THUNDER-HEADS.

cumulus clouds Cumulus clouds are large, white, fluffy clouds that begin low in the sky and rise up very high.

delta A delta is an area of fertile land that forms at the mouth of a river from soil that has been washed away from other regions and deposited at the mouth. It is called a delta because it resembles the triangular shape of the Greek letter delta.

earth The earth is the planet on which we live. It is a large ball made up of several layers of rock and minerals. The outer layer is called the CRUST. Beneath it is the mantle, which is

207

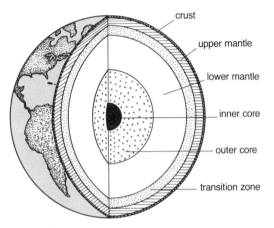

Earth. Cutaway view of the earth's layers.

crust
upper mantle
lower mantle
inner core
outer core
transition zone

Fossils. Fossil of a young dinosaur.

a thick layer of rock. Below it is the CORE, or center of the earth, which is made of hot metal. Almost three-fourths of the earth's surface is covered by water. Rock and soil cover the rest. A layer of air called the ATMOSPHERE surrounds the earth.

earthquake   An earthquake makes the ground move or shake. It is caused by the movement of PLATES, which are vast, rigid masses of rock underneath the EARTH's surface. *See also* FAULT.

E‌arthquakes can be measured according to the Richter scale, which describes the amount of energy released by the earthquake. ❧

environment   The environment is the set of external conditions that affect the internal growth and development of organisms. Weather and living space, other organisms, and food, along with their complex interactions, make up the environment. People who work to preserve clean and healthy conditions

in the environment are called environmentalists. *See also* CONSERVATIONIST; POLLUTION.

erosion   Erosion occurs when soil and rocks are worn down and moved around by water, wind, or GLACIERS. Gullies created by heavy rain are a common example of erosion.

fault   A fault is a crack in the EARTH's surface, usually just below the CRUST. Faults occur where two PLATES (vast masses of rigid rock) meet and grind against each other. EARTHQUAKES occur along fault lines when the plates move, causing the soil and rocks above the fault to shift.

fossil fuels   The fossil fuels — coal, oil, and natural gas — are created over millions of years from the remains of animals and plants.

fossils   Fossils are formed from the remains of prehistoric animals and plants and are preserved in rock or other materials. Many prehistoric animals and plants are now extinct; that is, their species no longer exist on earth. Fossils are the only traces of these species of animals and plants.

geology   Geology is the study of how the EARTH is put together and what it is made of. Geologists study surface rocks and minerals as well as the layers underneath the earth's surface. Geologists learn, among other things, how mountains are formed and what causes EARTHQUAKES.

glacier Glaciers are large sheets of ice that do not melt. They move like very slow rivers pulled by their own weight. Many valleys on our continent were carved out by glaciers long ago, when the climate was colder.

Gulf Stream The Gulf Stream is a warm current in the Atlantic Ocean that is driven north along the coast of North America by winds from the TROPICS. (A current is a flow of water in the ocean that moves in a definite direction in relation to the water around it.)

hail Hail is frozen rain in the form of small balls called hailstones. Sometimes hailstones become quite large and cause damage.

hard water Water that has MINERALS dissolved in it is called hard water. Soft water has few minerals in it. In the mountains, the water is soft because it has not run very far across the EARTH. Lower down, near sea level, the water tends to be hard because it has had a chance to dissolve minerals. Hard water does not make soapsuds easily.

humidity *See* RELATIVE HUMIDITY.

hurricane A hurricane is a large and powerful storm originating in the TROPICS, with fast, circular winds and heavy rains. A hurri-

Lightning

cane that occurs in the western part of the Pacific Ocean is called a typhoon.

ice age An ice age is a period far back in the earth's history when most of the land was covered by GLACIERS. There have been several ice ages.

iceberg An iceberg is a large mass of ice in the ocean, a piece of a GLACIER that has broken off and floated out to sea.

igneous rock Igneous rocks are made from very hot liquid matter that has cooled and hardened. Granite is an igneous rock.

isthmus An isthmus is a narrow strip of land that connects two larger land masses.

lava Lava is the red-hot melted rock that flows from a VOLCANO.

lightning Lightning is electricity that is released from CLOUDS when a large amount of static ELECTRICITY has built up in them.

> **M**ost of the ice in an iceberg is under water, leaving only the "tip of the iceberg" visible. Sometimes we use this expression to mean that the most important part of something is hidden or not obvious. ❧

209

It shoots from the clouds in bright, jagged streaks or in large flashes of light. Lightning causes THUNDER. *See also* THUNDERHEADS.

magma Magma is red-hot rock under the EARTH'S CRUST. When it erupts through the surface of the earth, it becomes more fluid and is called LAVA.

mantle The mantle is the thick layer of rock below the EARTH'S surface that surrounds the CORE, or center, of the earth.

> The earth's mantle is over two thousand miles thick. ❧

Marianas Trench (mair-ee-AN-uhs) The Marianas Trench is a deep valley in the floor of the Pacific Ocean. It is the deepest place on the earth's surface.

metamorphic rock Metamorphic rock is made when one kind of rock is changed into another by heat and pressure. For example, marble is a metamorphic rock that comes from limestone.

meteorology Meteorology is the science of weather. A meteorologist is someone who studies meteorology and attempts to predict the weather.

mineral Minerals are the various chemical compounds that make up ROCKS. A mineral is pure and uniform, made of only one kind of material. Most rocks are made of several kinds of minerals.

natural gas Natural gas is a FUEL found under the ground. It can be burned to provide heat and energy. *See also* FOSSIL FUELS.

natural resources A natural resource is any material that can be taken from the EARTH and used. Trees, oil, and water are natural resources. Some kinds of resources are non-renewable; that is, they cannot be replaced once they are used up. Coal and oil are non-renewable because they take millions of years to form. Water and cotton are renewable resources, since water can be collected or cleaned and used again and cotton can be planted and harvested each year.

nimbostratus clouds Nimbostratus clouds are the dark gray clouds that produce rain or snow. They are often called rain clouds.

oil Oil is a liquid FUEL that forms beneath the EARTH'S surface. It is used to make a number of products, including gasoline and asphalt. *See also* FOSSIL FUELS.

paleontologist A paleontologist is a scientist who studies FOSSILS in order to learn about ancient forms of life.

peninsula A peninsula is a long section of land that extends into the water. In Latin it means "almost island."

plate A plate is a vast area of rigid rock just below the EARTH'S surface. The continents and some of the ocean's floor rest on plates, which are as large or larger than continents.

plateau A plateau is a flat area high above the surrounding land.

polar regions The polar regions are the areas around the North and South poles. It stays cold all year in the these areas.

pollution Pollution is caused when substances that are harmful to life are released into the air or water or onto the land. Pollution often hurts or kills fish and animals and can endanger people's health as well. *See also* AIR POLLUTION.

precipitation Precipitation is water that falls from the air as rain, sleet, or snow.

prevailing winds Prevailing winds are those that blow consistently in a certain direction.

rain forest   *See* TROPICAL RAIN FOREST.

rainbow   A rainbow is a curve of colored light in the sky caused by sunlight shining through droplets of water in the air. The droplets break up the sunlight into colored bands.

> The colors of the rainbow are violet, indigo, blue, green, yellow, orange, and red. 🐾

relative humidity   Relative humidity is the amount of water in the air compared to the amount of water the air can hold. If the air is holding all the water it possibly can, the relative humidity is 100%. If the air is holding only half the amount of water possible, the relative humidity is 50%.

rock   A rock is a mass of MINERAL matter. The EARTH'S CRUST is composed of rock. *See also* IGNEOUS ROCK; METAMORPHIC ROCK; SEDIMENTARY ROCK.

San Andreas Fault   (SAN an-DRAY-uhs) The San Andreas Fault is a long crack in the EARTH'S CRUST along the west coast of California. Many EARTHQUAKES occur along this fault.

> Sedimentary rocks are used to make cement, glass, fertilizer, baking soda, laundry bleach, and aspirin. 🐾

sedimentary rock   Sedimentary rock is formed when layers of material from SEDIMENTATION are pressed together and hardened. Shale and limestone are examples of sedimentary rock.

sedimentation   Sedimentation occurs when particles of rock and other materials fall to the bottom of rivers, lakes, or oceans. The particles form layers of mud and debris called sediment.

seismograph   A seismograph is an instrument that detects EARTHQUAKES and measures their strength.

smog   Smog (a combination of the words *smoke* and *fog*) is the dirty fog or haze that forms when AIR POLLUTION combines with moisture in the air.

soil   Soil consists of small particles of MINERALS and organic debris mixed with water on the surface of the EARTH. It is formed by wind, water, freezing, thawing, and the actions of plants and small animals, creating a material in which plants can grow.

> The term "solar energy" can be used to mean the process of taking energy from the sun to generate heat or electricity for human use. 🐾

solar energy   Solar energy is energy from the sun that comes to EARTH in the form of light.

stratus clouds   Stratus clouds hang low in the sky and look like a smooth layer of fog.

temperate zone   A temperate zone is an area of the EARTH where the weather changes from season to season. The temperate zones are between the POLAR REGIONS, where it stays cold all year, and the TROPICS, where it stays hot. Most of the United States is in a temperate zone.

thunder   Thunder is the sound caused when LIGHTNING heats the air. The heated air expands so rapidly that it pushes the air out in a shock wave, which we hear as thunder. *See also* LIGHTNING; THUNDERHEADS.

Tornado. Tornado near Iron Ridge, Wisconsin.

Tornadoes are common in the midwestern United States. 🍃

thunderheads   Thunderheads are dense clouds that rise high into the sky in huge columns. They often produce thunderstorms, hailstorms, rain, or snow. They are sometimes called thunderstorm clouds, but their technical name is cumulonimbus clouds.

tidal wave   A tidal wave is an unusually large, high movement of water onto a seashore. It is often caused by a large storm and can be very destructive.

tides   Tides are regular changes in the height of the ocean: two high tides and two low tides occur each day. They are caused primarily by the force of the moon's gravity on the water, but the sun and other factors also affect them.

topsoil   Topsoil is the thin layer of SOIL containing organic matter and nutrients where plants get most of their food. EROSION can

destroy valuable farmland when topsoil is washed away.

tornado   A tornado is a violent storm in which the wind moves upward in a narrow, circular funnel. The winds in a tornado move fast enough to destroy buildings and uproot trees.

tropical rain forest   A tropical rain forest is a region where the weather is hot and wet all year. This climate supports many kinds of plants and trees as well as a large variety of animals and insects.

tropics   The tropics are the areas north and south of the equator where the weather stays hot all year.

Tundra is found in Lapland and in the northern regions of Alaska, Canada, and the Soviet Union. 🍃

tundra   The tundra is the vast, flat, cold area in the northern regions of the EARTH where no trees grow.

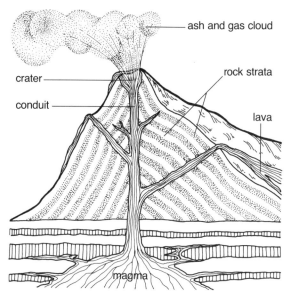

Volcano. Cross section of an erupting volcano.

volcano   A volcano is a mountain created by the flow of melted rock through an opening in the EARTH's surface. It is active when it can still erupt and release LAVA, hot gases, and dust. It is extinct when it has not erupted for millions of years.

warm front   A front is a place in the air where two very large bodies of air meet. A warm front is the place where warm air pushes out cold air. *Compare* COLD FRONT.

water cycle   The water cycle is the process in which water from the ocean evaporates into the air and then falls back to the EARTH as rain, hail, or snow. The water then flows into rivers, which return it to the ocean, and the cycle begins again.

water vapor   Water vapor is water in the air that has changed into a gas.

weather satellite   A weather satellite is a device that orbits the EARTH. It carries instruments that detect the different kinds of weather on the earth's surface and transmits the information back to meteorologists (people who study the weather).

weather service   A weather service is a group of meteorologists who study the weather and predict how it will change. Farmers and airline pilots, in particular, depend on weather services.

weathering   Weathering occurs when ROCKS are broken down to form soil. It is caused by rain, ice, and plant roots that break apart the rocks.

Life Sciences

Many important and useful terms are employed in the scientific study of living things. The life sciences include *zoology*, which is the study of animals, and *botany*, which is the study of plants. *Biology* is another name for the life sciences. In the next section of this dictionary, we explain terms that relate to medicine and the human body.

amphibians Amphibians are animals that live both in water and on land. When they are young, most amphibians breathe water by means of gills; as they grow older, they lose their gills and develop lungs for breathing air. Frogs and toads are amphibians.

> **T**he word *amphibian* is sometimes used to describe a piece of equipment, such as a vehicle that can move on both land and water. ❧

anatomy The anatomy of a plant or animal is its structure.

animals Like PLANTS, animals are organisms (living things). Animals differ from plants because they can move by themselves and do not perform PHOTOSYNTHESIS. Animals are divided into two groups: VERTEBRATES and INVERTEBRATES. Vertebrates are animals with backbones, such as mammals, reptiles, amphibians, birds, and fish. Invertebrates are animals without backbones, such as insects and mollusks.

balance of nature The balance of nature is a term for the way all parts of nature rely on one another. If one kind of animal becomes extinct, the lives of other animals and plants are changed, and the balance of nature is upset.

biology Biology is the science that studies living things. Botany (the study of plants) and zoology (the study of animals) are branches of biology.

birds Birds are animals with wings and feathers. They are warm-blooded and lay eggs. Eagles, pigeons, chickens, ducks, sparrows, and parakeets are all birds.

botany Botany is the branch of biology that studies plants.

carnivore A carnivore is an animal that eats meat. *Compare* HERBIVORE *and* OMNIVORE.

> **S**ome plants, such as the Venus's-flytrap, are carnivores. ❧

Birds. From left to right: Bald eagle, Pekin duck, and parakeet.

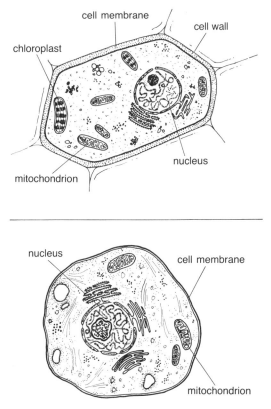

Cell. Plant cell (top) and human cell (bottom) as they appear under an electron microscope.

cell   A cell is the smallest part of any living thing that is able to function by itself. Plants and animals are made up of tiny units called cells.

chlorophyll   Chlorophyll is the substance in green plants that gives them their color and helps in the process of PHOTOSYNTHESIS.

chromosome   A chromosome is a part of the nucleus of a CELL. *See also* GENE; HEREDITY.

cold-blooded animal   A cold-blooded animal's temperature changes according to the temperature of its surroundings. Thus, if a cold-blooded animal lives in a cold place, its body will be cold; if it lives in a warm place, its body will be warm. Fish and reptiles are cold-blooded animals. *Compare* WARMBLOODED ANIMAL.

> Cold-blooded animals often sun themselves to warm their bodies. ❧

Darwin, Charles   Charles Darwin, a great English scientist of the 1800s, is known for his theory of EVOLUTION.

deciduous   Trees and shrubs that lose their leaves in the autumn are deciduous. Oaks, elms, and maples are deciduous trees. *Compare* EVERGREEN.

dinosaur   Dinosaurs were reptiles that lived millions of years ago and are now extinct.

215

Dinosaur. From left to right: Triceratops (30 feet long); Tyrannosaurus (50 feet long); Stegosaurus (29 feet long).

Some types of dinosaurs were small, but others were larger than elephants.

DNA   DNA is a large molecule that is different for each species of living thing. It is an important part of a GENE and helps determine the particular traits of each living thing.

ecology   Ecology is the science that studies the relationship between living things and their ENVIRONMENT, or surroundings.

egg   An egg is a female reproductive cell in a plant or an animal. *See also* FERTILIZATION; REPRODUCTION; SPERM.

embryo   An embryo is a very young plant or animal. The embryos of many plants are contained in their SEEDS. The embryo of a human being is carried inside the mother before birth.

evergreen   Trees and shrubs that stay green in the winter are evergreens. Pines, cedars, and spruces are evergreen trees.

evolution   Evolution is the process by which living things evolve, or change form, from one generation to the next. According to CHARLES DARWIN's theory of evolution, all existing forms of life evolved from earlier forms.

Fish. From left to right: Atlantic salmon, hammerhead shark, and seahorse.

216

fertilization Fertilization is part of the process of sexual REPRODUCTION in plants and animals. During fertilization, an egg and a sperm join to form a new cell. Over time, this cell develops into a new plant or animal.

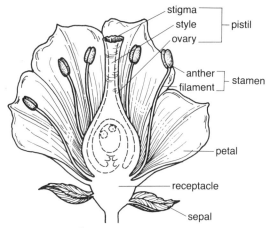

Flower. Cross section.

fish Fish are cold-blooded animals that live in water. They move by using their fins, and they breathe with organs called gills. Trout, salmon, sharks, minnows, goldfish, eels, and sea horses are all fish.

flower A flower is a plant part that produces SEEDS and sometimes FRUIT. It is often colorful to attract insects to cover the PISTIL with POLLEN from the STAMEN. The fertilized egg in the pistil makes the SEED. In most plants, both stamen and pistil are in the same flower. *See also* FERTILIZATION.

food chain A food chain is a series of plants and animals that are linked together because they feed on each other. For instance, if the sap of a plant is eaten by an insect, and the insect is eaten by a bird, and the bird is eaten by a cat, then the plant, the insect, the bird, and the cat are parts of the same food chain.

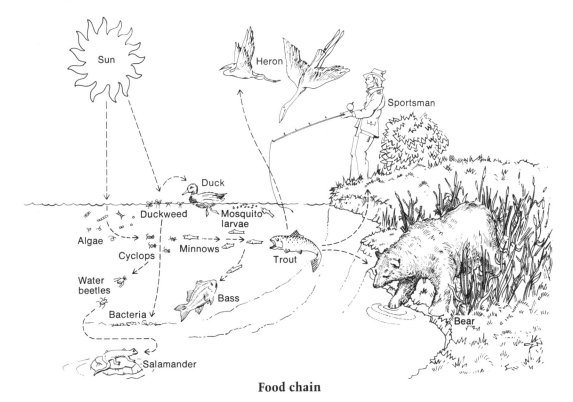

Food chain

217

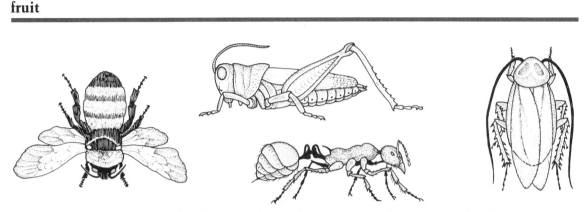

Insect. Bumblebee (left), grasshopper (top center), ant (bottom center), and cockroach (right).

fruit   In some plants, the fruit is the part of the plant that comes from the FLOWER after it is fertilized. The fruit usually contains SEEDS.

> **S**ome foods that we commonly think of as vegetables, like tomatoes, eggplants, and squash, are really fruits. 🐝

fungus   A fungus is a plant that lacks CHLOROPHYLL and lives by feeding off other plants or animals, alive or dead. The plural of fungus is FUNGI.

> **M**ushrooms, molds, yeasts, and mildew are all types of fungus. 🐝

gene   A gene is part of a CHROMOSOME in a CELL. It determines which traits will be passed on from parents to children. For instance, your parents' genes determined the color of your eyes.

habitat   The place where an animal or plant normally lives is called its habitat.

herbivore   A herbivore is an animal that eats plants. *See also* CARNIVORE; OMNIVORE.

heredity   The passing of traits from parents to children is called heredity in both plants and animals. If you have received a trait through heredity, you are said to have "inherited" it. For instance, you might have inherited the color of your hair from your mother.

hibernation   Some animals, like woodchucks, spend the entire winter sleeping. While they are sleeping they are said to be hibernating or in hibernation.

> **H**ibernating animals store up fat before the cold season in order to nourish their bodies during hibernation. 🐝

Homo sapiens   *Homo sapiens* is the scientific, Latin name for humans as a species of animal.

insect   Insects are small invertebrate animals. They have six legs and long feelers called antennae. Ants, bees, grasshoppers, and cockroaches are all insects.

instinct   Instinct is a way of behaving that is inherited (passed on through HEREDITY) rather than learned or taught. For instance, birds do not teach each other how to build nests; their instinct serves as a guide.

Metamorphosis. The metamorphosis of a butterfly from egg to larva (caterpillar) to pupa to butterfly.

invertebrates   Animals without backbones, like insects and mollusks, are invertebrates. *Compare* VERTEBRATES.

mammals   Mammals are warm-blooded animals with hair who make milk to feed their young. Cows, dogs, elephants, giraffes, horses, mice, and human beings are all mammals. Although porpoises and whales live in the sea, they are also mammals.

Mendel, Gregor   Gregor Mendel, a biologist and monk in Austria, discovered the laws of HEREDITY by experimenting with pea plants.

metamorphosis   When an animal completely changes its form, it is said to undergo metamorphosis. Metamorphosis occurs when a caterpillar changes into a butterfly.

mollusk   Mollusks are INVERTEBRATE animals with soft bodies that are often covered by hard shells. Clams, snails, scallops, and squid are all mollusks.

nucleus   Inside each CELL of an ORGANISM is a tiny round body called the nucleus. It controls the activities of the cell and contains the CHROMOSOMES.

omnivore   An animal that eats both meat and plants is called an omnivore. *Compare* CARNIVORE; HERBIVORE.

organism   An organism is a living thing. All plants and animals are organisms.

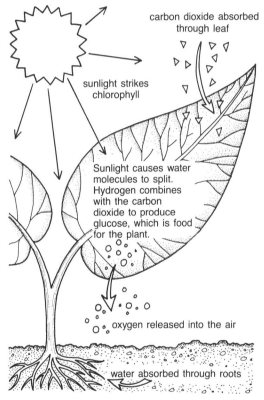

Photosynthesis

photosynthesis   Photosynthesis is a process that takes place in green plants when the plant uses the energy in sunlight to make food for itself. During photosynthesis, carbon dioxide is taken from the air and oxygen is released

219

into it. CHLOROPHYLL plays an important part in photosynthesis.

pistil   The pistil is the part of a flower that contains the egg cells. In order for the flower to reproduce, these cells must be fertilized by POLLEN. *See also* FERTILIZATION; STAMEN.

plants   Like animals, plants are organisms (living things). Plants are different from animals, however, because they cannot move by themselves and because they can usually make their own food. (Green plants use PHOTOSYNTHESIS to make their food.) Trees, bushes, grass, and flowers are plants; so are moss and seaweed. Some plants — like corn, wheat, and rice — provide human beings with food.

pollen   Pollen is a powder produced by the STAMEN of flowering plants. It fertilizes the egg cells in the PISTIL so that the plant can make SEEDS and reproduce. *See also* FERTILIZATION.

reproduction   When plants or animals produce offspring, the process is called reproduction. There are two types of reproduction: asexual and sexual. Asexual reproduction requires only one parent. For example, a tiny animal called an amoeba reproduces by dividing in two. Sexual reproduction requires the union of a SPERM and an EGG to form a new cell. This new cell eventually becomes an animal or plant. *See also* FERTILIZATION.

reptiles   Reptiles are a group of animals whose bodies are covered with scales. Snakes, lizards, turtles, and alligators are all reptiles. Like AMPHIBIANS, reptiles are COLD-BLOODED ANIMALS, but, unlike amphibians, reptiles always have lungs.

> The dinosaurs were reptiles. Sometimes the period when there were many dinosaurs on earth is called the Age of Reptiles. ❧

seed   A seed is the small EMBRYO of a plant. It usually contains some food that can be used when it starts to grow. The seed is usually protected by a covering that must be wet before it will grow. *See also* FRUIT.

species   Individual plants and animals that belong to exactly the same biological classification are said to belong to the same species. All human beings belong to the species *Homo sapiens*.

sperm   A sperm is a male reproductive cell in a plant or an animal. *See also* EGG; FERTILIZATION; REPRODUCTION.

stamen   The stamen is the part of a flower that produces POLLEN. *See also* FERTILIZATION; PISTIL.

vertebrate   Animals with backbones, like mammals and reptiles, are vertebrates. *Compare* INVERTEBRATE.

warm-blooded animal   A warm-blooded animal's body temperature does not change when the surrounding temperature changes. Thus, whether the air is hot or cold, the temperature of a warm-blooded animal stays the same. Mammals and birds are warm-blooded animals. *Compare* COLD-BLOODED ANIMAL.

zoology   Zoology is the science that studies animals.

Medicine and the Human Body

The human body is one of nature's most complicated creations. It is easier to enjoy your life if you are healthy, and it is easier to stay healthy if you know something about how your body is put together and how it works. You can learn to eat the right foods, to exercise, and to recognize the kinds of things in the body that sometimes go wrong. You can also learn how your physical condition affects your mental health. The following terms will be useful as you learn more about your health and well-being.

adolescence   Adolescence is the time of life between childhood and adulthood when the body grows and changes physically, emotionally, and mentally. *See also* PUBERTY.

AIDS   AIDS stands for "acquired immune deficiency syndrome," a condition in which the AIDS VIRUS, known as HIV-1, destroys a person's immune system. Because their immune systems are weakened, people with AIDS may contract and die from many diseases. *See also* IMMUNITY.

alcoholism   Alcoholism is a disease in which people cannot control their desire to drink alcoholic beverages.

allergy   An allergy results when the body reacts badly to outside substances such as pollen, dust, animals, or certain foods. People with allergies develop symptoms such as sneezing and rashes.

antibiotics   Antibiotics are drugs that control diseases by killing the BACTERIA that cause them.

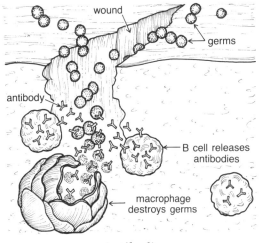

Antibodies

antibodies   Antibodies are substances made by the body that fight disease-causing germs

221

(such as VIRUSES) by attaching themselves to the germs and making them harmless until they can be removed from the body.

aorta   The aorta is the largest ARTERY. Blood leaves the heart through the aorta and circulates throughout the body.

appendix   The appendix is a tube attached to the large INTESTINE. It has no known function. If the appendix becomes infected, it causes an illness called appendicitis. When this happens, the appendix must be removed by surgery.

artery   An artery is a type of BLOOD VESSEL that carries blood from the heart to other parts of the body. *See also* CIRCULATORY SYSTEM.

baby teeth   The baby teeth are the first set of teeth to appear in a child. They fall out one by one as the permanent teeth grow in.

bacteria   Bacteria are tiny, one-celled organisms (or living things). You can see them by using a MICROSCOPE. Most bacteria are harmless. Some bacteria live in your intestines and help to digest food. Others cause INFECTIONS, such as tetanus and tuberculosis, when they enter the body.

balanced diet   A balanced diet contains all the kinds of food that a person needs to stay healthy. It includes PROTEINS, CARBOHYDRATES, fats, VITAMINS, and MINERALS. Proteins build tissues such as MUSCLE. Carbohydrates and fats provide energy. Vitamins and minerals help the body to function normally.

bicuspids   Bicuspids are the smaller, flat teeth in the inner part of the mouth. They are used to grind food.

blood   Blood is the red fluid that carries oxygen and food to the various parts of the body. Blood also removes waste products that build up after CELLS use the oxygen and food. *See also* CIRCULATORY SYSTEM.

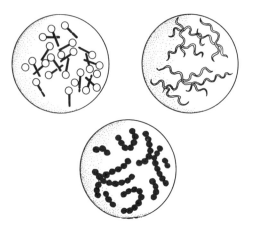

Bacteria. Magnified images of three types of bacteria.

Balanced diet. The four basic food groups.

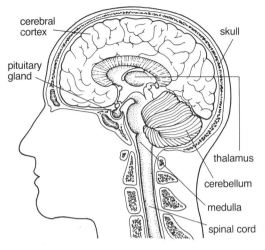

cerebral cortex

skull

pituitary gland

thalamus

cerebellum

medulla

spinal cord

Brain. Cutaway view.

blood pressure Blood pressure is the measure of how hard the blood presses against the walls of the ARTERIES. If a person's blood pressure gets too high, it can cause damage to the heart or other parts of the body.

blood vessels Blood vessels are the tubes that carry BLOOD through the body. They are made of TISSUE and MUSCLE. *See also* ARTERY; CAPILLARY; VEIN.

bone A bone is one of the pieces of hard and dense material supporting the rest of the body. For example, your arm has three main bones, one in the upper arm and two in the lower arm. The system of bones in the body is called the SKELETAL SYSTEM.

brain The brain is the very complex ORGAN inside the head that controls the rest of the body. It receives information from the SENSES and controls movement. It is also the center of thought and feeling. *See also* NERVOUS SYSTEM.

caffeine Caffeine is a DRUG found in many soft drinks, chocolate, coffee, and tea that increases the activity of the BRAIN and NERVOUS SYSTEM. Too much caffeine can make you nervous or irritable.

In general, the right side of the brain controls the left side of the body and activities such as perception of space. The left side of the brain controls the right side of the body and activities such as speech. 🐝

cancer Cancer is a disease in which CELLS in the body grow without stopping and destroy other parts of the body. Some kinds of cancer can be controlled if they are discovered early enough.

canine teeth The canine teeth are the sharp, pointed teeth near the front of the mouth on either side of the INCISORS. Canine teeth are used to bite and tear food.

capillary Capillaries are tiny blood vessels that connect ARTERIES and VEINS. They are important because they let food MOLECULES and oxygen pass from the blood to the body's cells through their thin walls. They also pick up waste products that build up when oxygen and food are used by the cells. *See also* CIRCULATORY SYSTEM.

carbohydrates Carbohydrates are foods that supply energy. Sugars and starches are carbohydrates. Common carbohydrates are bread, noodles, potatoes, and corn. *See also* BALANCED DIET.

Because cartilage can stand up to pressure, it helps to protect parts of the body from shock. 🐝

cartilage Cartilage is soft, flexible TISSUE in the JOINTS. Parts of the nose and ears are also made of cartilage.

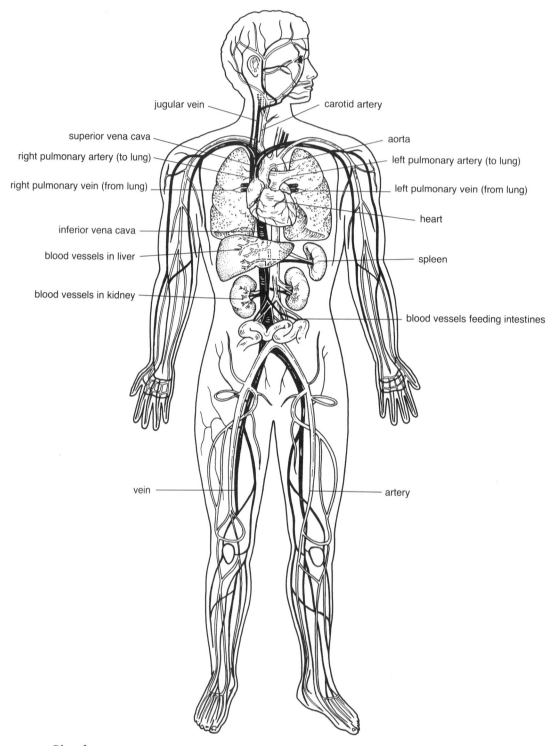

jugular vein — — carotid artery

superior vena cava — — aorta

right pulmonary artery (to lung) — — left pulmonary artery (to lung)

right pulmonary vein (from lung) — — left pulmonary vein (from lung)

— heart

inferior vena cava —

blood vessels in liver — — spleen

blood vessels in kidney —

— blood vessels feeding intestines

vein — — artery

Circulatory system. In this illustration, veins are black and arteries are white.

cavity A cavity is a hole in the surface of a tooth.

cerebrum The cerebrum is the largest part of the BRAIN and is the center of thought, feeling, and remembering. It also controls the body's movements.

chicken pox Chicken pox is a COMMUNICABLE DISEASE that is caused by a VIRUS. It often causes fever and blisters.

circulatory system The circulatory system is made up of BLOOD, BLOOD VESSELS, and the HEART. The heart pumps the blood through the body. Blood moves from the heart through the ARTERIES. The arteries get smaller as the blood gets farther from the heart. The blood then moves into tiny CAPILLARIES. The thin walls of the capillaries allow food molecules and oxygen to pass into the cells and allow waste products to move from the cells into the blood. The blood then travels through VEINS that get larger as the blood is carried back to the heart.

communicable disease A communicable disease is a disease that one person can catch from another. These diseases are caused by tiny germs, such as BACTERIA and VIRUSES. Germs spread from person to person through the air or physical contact. Colds and the flu are common communicable diseases. *Compare* NONCOMMUNICABLE DISEASE.

cornea The cornea is the clear piece of TISSUE that protects the front of the eye.

cranium The cranium is the set of bone plates in the head that protect the BRAIN. It is also called the skull.

digestion Digestion is the process of breaking down food so that it can be used by the body.

digestive system The digestive system is the group of ORGANS that take in food and break it down so that it can be used by the

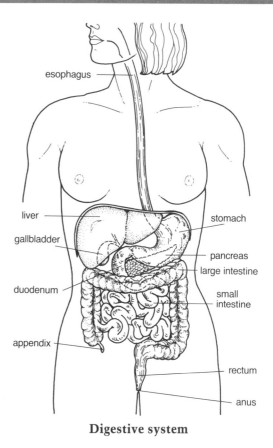

Digestive system

body. It includes the digestive tract (the mouth, throat, STOMACH, and small and large INTESTINES) and GLANDS (such as the LIVER and KIDNEYS). When food is swallowed, it enters the stomach. The stomach mixes food and digestive juices together. The juices break down the food, which then passes into the small intestine, where more digestion takes place. Waste products then pass through the large intestine and finally leave the body through the anus. *See also* SALIVA.

drug A drug is a chemical that causes changes in the way the body works. Some drugs are medicines prescribed by doctors to help people get well. Other drugs are found in foods or drinks. CAFFEINE is a drug that is found in some soft drinks and in chocolate, tea, and coffee; alcohol is a drug found in beer, wine, and other liquors. Still other drugs, like marijuana and heroin, are illegal substances; it is against the law to sell or use them. They also can cause permanent damage to the body.

Many drugs, including caffeine, alcohol, and nicotine (a chemical found in cigarettes), are habit-forming; that is, people may begin to feel that they need to take them. Such drugs can be very harmful to the body. 🙢

eardrum   The eardrum is a round piece of TISSUE at the end of the ear canal (which leads from the opening to the inner part of the ear). The eardrum is like the tightly stretched skin of a drum. Sound causes it to vibrate. The eardrum passes along the vibrations to the inner ear, which passes them to the BRAIN as nerve impulses. The brain then makes sense of these impulses, causing us to hear.

epidemic   An epidemic is an outbreak of a disease that spreads quickly and infects many people at the same time.

eye   *See* CORNEA; IRIS; LENS; OPTIC NERVE; PUPIL; RETINA.

farsightedness   Farsightedness is an eye problem that causes distant objects to appear distinct while nearby objects look fuzzy.

gland   A gland is an ORGAN in the body that makes a substance that the body uses. Saliva, sweat, and tears are made by glands.

heart   The heart is the MUSCLE in the middle of the chest that pumps BLOOD through the body. The sound made by the repeated, rhythmic action of the heart as it pumps blood is called the heartbeat.

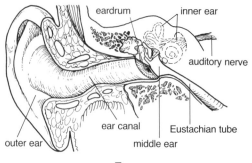

Ear

heart attack   A heart attack occurs when the heart muscle does not get enough blood. Heart attacks damage the heart and are sometimes fatal.

hormone   A hormone is a chemical produced by certain GLANDS. Hormones travel through the blood and control bodily processes such as growth and DIGESTION.

immunity   Immunity is the ability to resist disease. When your body produces enough ANTIBODIES to kill the germs that cause a particular disease, you are said to be immune to that disease.

incisors   Incisors are the flat-edged teeth at the front of the mouth that are used for biting food.

infection   An infection happens when BACTERIA, VIRUSES, or other harmful germs grow and reproduce in the body. Cuts in the skin can become infected if they are not kept clean. Colds, the flu, pneumonia, and other diseases are also caused by infections.

infectious disease   *See* COMMUNICABLE DISEASE.

intestine   The intestines are long tubes in the body below the stomach. After food is mixed with digestive juices in the stomach, it goes into the small intestine, where it is digested further. Waste products then pass into the large intestine and finally leave the body.

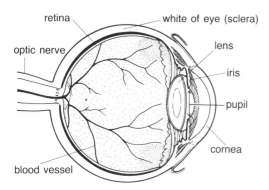

Iris. A cross section showing the right eye and optic nerve.

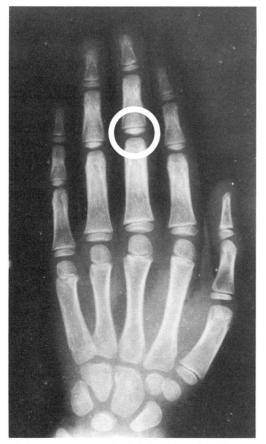

Joint. An x-ray of a left hand with a finger joint highlighted.

iris   The iris is the colored part of the eye. It controls the amount of light that is let into the eye by making the PUPIL (the dark opening of the eye) larger or smaller. If a room is dark, the eye needs more light to see, so the iris makes the pupil larger to let in more light. If it is bright, the iris makes the pupil smaller to let in less light.

joint   A joint is a place in the body where two BONES meet. Movable joints such as the knee and the elbow allow body parts to move.

kidneys   The kidneys are the ORGANS that filter liquid waste products out of the blood. They are near the lower part of the back.

lens   The lens is the part of the eye that focuses light rays onto the RETINA. It is just behind the dark opening of the eye called the PUPIL.

ligament   A ligament is a band of TISSUE that fastens BONES together at the JOINTS.

liver   The liver is a large ORGAN near the stomach that removes waste from the blood and produces digestive juices.

lungs   The lungs are the ORGANS that allow us to breathe. They are in the chest on either side of the heart. *See also* RESPIRATORY SYSTEM.

In the lungs, oxygen inhaled from the air is transferred to the blood while carbon dioxide is removed from the blood and exhaled. ❧

malnutrition   Malnutrition occurs when the body is weakened because it does not get enough of the foods it needs. Malnutrition can also be caused by diseases that keep the body from properly using the food that it does get. *See also* BALANCED DIET.

227

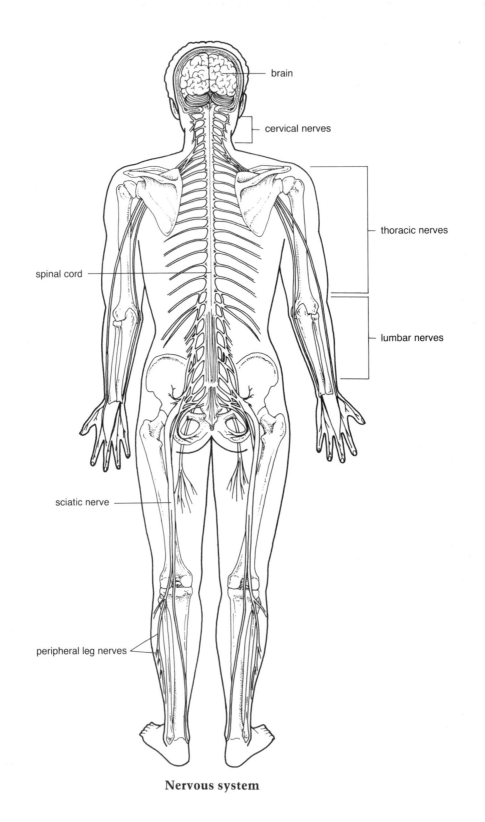

brain

cervical nerves

thoracic nerves

spinal cord

lumbar nerves

sciatic nerve

peripheral leg nerves

Nervous system

marrow Marrow is the soft TISSUE inside BONE. RED BLOOD CELLS form in bone marrow.

measles Measles is a disease caused by a virus that makes a rash of pink or red spots break out all over the skin. It is contagious, which means that a person who has it can easily give it to another person.

R ubella, a contagious disease that causes a rash, is sometimes called German measles.

minerals Minerals are substances in food that keep the body working correctly. They help keep teeth and BONES strong and also maintain MUSCLES and blood cells. Calcium is an example of a mineral.

molars Molars are the large, flat teeth at the back of the mouth that are used to grind food.

mucus Mucus is a dense, sticky liquid in the mouth, nose, throat, and lungs. It keeps dust and germs from getting far inside the body.

muscles Muscles are the TISSUES that make the body parts move. Voluntary muscles are muscles that you control, like the ones in your arms and legs. Involuntary muscles, like the heart and the muscles in the stomach, work whether or not you are aware of them.

nearsightedness Nearsightedness is an eye problem that affects the way a person sees. A nearsighted person can see nearby objects clearly, but distant objects appear fuzzy.

nerves Nerves are fibers that connect the rest of the body to the BRAIN. They make actions possible by carrying messages, called electrical impulses, from the brain and the spinal cord to the rest of the body. *See also* NERVOUS SYSTEM.

nervous system The nervous system is made up of the BRAIN, the SPINAL CORD, and the NERVES and controls the body's ORGANS, movements, and SENSES. Messages from one part of the body to another are sent by way of the nervous system, from the brain along the spinal cord to the nerves. The nerves send the messages to the MUSCLES or the organs. Messages are also sent from the body back to the brain along the same path.

noncommunicable disease A noncommunicable disease is one that is not caused by germs and cannot be caught from another person. Some noncommunicable diseases are caused by substances in the environment. For example, cancer may be caused by smoking cigarettes. Other noncommunicable diseases are inherited, or passed down to children in their genes. Still others are present in the body when a person is born (these are called congenital diseases). *Compare* COMMUNICABLE DISEASE.

nutrients Nutrients are the substances in food that provide energy and help the body to grow and stay healthy. *See also* BALANCED DIET.

nutrition Nutrition is the study of the foods people need to stay healthy. *See also* BALANCED DIET.

olfactory nerves The olfactory nerves are high inside the nose and sense the various odors and flavors we can detect. *See also* TASTE BUDS.

optic nerve The optic nerve connects the eye to the BRAIN. It carries messages from the eye to the brain, which the brain interprets, enabling us to see.

organ An organ is a part of the body that does a specific job. The HEART, STOMACH, and eyes are organs.

Pasteur, Louis (pas-TUR, pah-STEUR)   In the nineteenth century, Louis Pasteur helped to prove that many diseases are caused by small organisms such as BACTERIA. His name was given to the process known as *pasteurization*, in which fluids such as milk are heated in order to kill harmful bacteria.

pediatrician   A pediatrician is a doctor who takes care of babies, children, and teenagers.

penicillin   Penicillin was the most important early ANTIBIOTIC to be discovered that did not harm the body. Penicillin is produced by molds such as the ones that grow on bread.

permanent teeth   The permanent teeth are those that grow in after children lose their baby teeth. When permanent teeth remain healthy, they will last a lifetime. The body cannot replace them if they fall out or are damaged. *See also* BICUSPIDS; INCISORS; MOLARS.

pharmacist   A pharmacist is a person who has been trained to give out drugs prescribed by a doctor. *See also* PRESCRIPTION DRUG.

plasma   Plasma is the part of the blood that carries BLOOD CELLS. It is often used to replace the blood a person loses in an accident or during an operation.

pneumonia (noo-MOHN-yuh)   Pneumonia is a COMMUNICABLE DISEASE that causes inflammation of the LUNGS.

> **O**nce a very dangerous disease, pneumonia can now often be cured with antibiotics such as penicillin. 🐾

prescription drug   Prescription drugs are medicines prescribed by a doctor. When you are sick, the doctor examines you and decides which drugs will help you get well. A note

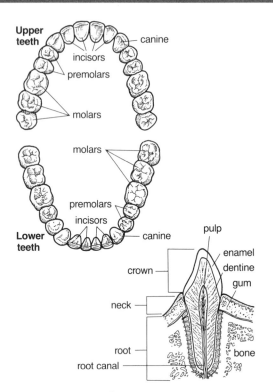

Permanent teeth. Teeth of an adult human (left) and cross section of an incisor (right).

from your doctor, called a prescription, tells the PHARMACIST what kind of drug to sell you and how much of it you should take.

proteins   Proteins are the parts of food that help the body repair itself and grow. Eggs, meat, fish, and cheese have proteins in them. *See also* BALANCED DIET.

psychiatrist   A psychiatrist is a doctor who helps people with mental or emotional problems. A psychiatrist is permitted to prescribe drugs.

psychologist   A psychologist is a person who helps people with mental or emotional problems. Unlike psychiatrists, psychologists are not doctors and cannot prescribe drugs.

puberty   Puberty is the time in life when children's bodies start to become like adults'.

During puberty, children begin to mature sexually; that is, they develop the ability to have children. *See also* ADOLESCENCE; REPRODUCTIVE SYSTEM.

pupil   The pupil is the dark opening in the eye through which light enters the eye.

rabies   Rabies is a very dangerous infectious disease. People catch it if they are bitten by an animal that is infected with the disease.

A vaccine to prevent rabies was developed by the French scientist Louis Pasteur. 🐾

---

red blood cells   Red blood cells are the cells in the blood that carry oxygen from the LUNGS to the body's cells and remove carbon dioxide.

reproductive system   The reproductive system is the group of GLANDS and ORGANS that allow people to reproduce, that is, to have children. The female reproductive glands are called the ovaries; they produce egg cells. The male reproductive glands are called the testes; they produce sperm cells.

respiration   Respiration is the action of breathing. When you inhale, or breathe in, oxygen is taken into the body and used by the cells. Cells produce carbon dioxide as a waste product, which is released from the body when you exhale, or breathe out. *See also* RESPIRATORY SYSTEM.

respiratory system   The respiratory system is the mechanism that allows you to breathe. It is made up of the LUNGS and the tubes that connect your nose and mouth to the lungs. The lungs pull air into the body to get oxygen. They transfer the oxygen to the bloodstream and remove carbon dioxide from the BLOOD. The lungs then push the carbon dioxide out of the body and pull in fresh oxygen. They also act as filters to prevent germs and dust in the air from getting into the bloodstream.

retina   The retina is a layer of TISSUE at the back of the eye. Light rays are focused onto the retina, where they form an image. The retina then transmits the image along the OPTIC NERVE to the BRAIN.

ribs   The ribs are the series of curved BONES in the chest that are attached to the SPINAL COLUMN. Ribs protect the ORGANS in the chest, such as the LUNGS and HEART.

saliva   Saliva is the fluid produced by the GLANDS in the mouth. It keeps the mouth moist and softens food so that it can be chewed and swallowed.

senses   The five senses tell the BRAIN what is happening in the outside world: sight, hearing, touch, taste, and smell. The body also learns what is going on inside through a sense of hunger, thirst, or fatigue (feeling tired). The senses send messages to the brain so that it can tell the body how to react. For example, if you touch something that is too hot, your brain "tells" your hand to pull away before it is badly burned. If you have not eaten for a long time, your sense of hunger "tells" you that your body needs food.

Sometimes we talk about a "sixth sense," meaning a way of guessing something without being told by one of the five senses. 🐾

---

shock   Shock occurs when a person's ORGANS do not get enough blood because the blood's circulation is too slow. It is sometimes caused by an accident or a serious illness. A person in shock must be kept warm until medical help arrives.

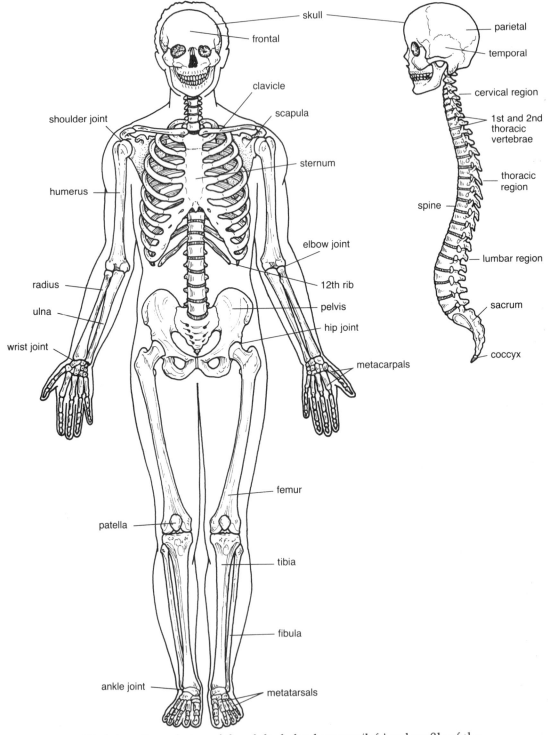

Skeleton. Frontal view of the adult skeletal system (left) and profile of the adult skull and spine (right).

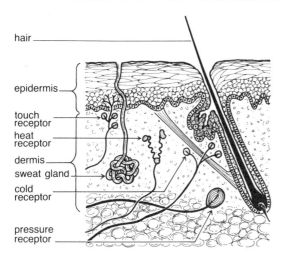

hair

epidermis

touch receptor

heat receptor

dermis

sweat gland

cold receptor

pressure receptor

Skin. Cutaway view of the layers of human skin.

skeletal system   The skeletal system, or skeleton, is the system of BONES that supports the body and holds it together. Some parts of the skeletal system protect internal ORGANS. The CRANIUM protects the BRAIN; the SPINAL COLUMN protects the SPINAL CORD; the rib cage protects many of the organs in the chest.

skin   The skin is the outer layer of the human body. It helps to protect the inside of the body and keep the body's temperature at the proper level. Skin also keeps the body in touch with the outside world by sensing heat and cold and by allowing us to feel things.

spinal column   The spinal column, also called the backbone, or spine, is a series of linked BONES that protect the SPINAL CORD.

spinal cord   The spinal cord is a long piece of nerve TISSUE that runs from the BRAIN down through the backbone and connects the brain to the NERVES. The backbone, or SPINAL COLUMN, protects the spinal cord from injury.

stomach   The stomach is the place where food goes when it is swallowed. The stomach mixes food and digestive juices together. The

juices break down the food so that it can be used by the body. The food then moves into the small intestine, where further digestion takes place. *See also* DIGESTIVE SYSTEM.

> The taste buds can detect four basic tastes: sweet, sour, salty, and bitter. ❧

taste buds   The taste buds are groups of cells in the tongue. They sense the chemicals in food and send information about them to the BRAIN, allowing us to notice tastes that are bitter, salty, sweet, or sour. *See also* OLFACTORY NERVES.

teeth   *See* BABY TEETH; PERMANENT TEETH.

tendons   Tendons are the strong pieces of TISSUE that connect the MUSCLES to the BONES.

tissues   Tissues are groups of cells that act together to perform a specific job.

vaccination   Vaccination is a method that doctors use to protect the body against disease. They inject a small amount of a weakened or dead VIRUS, called a VACCINE, into the body, which then produces ANTIBODIES to fight the virus. The antibodies stay in the body and protect it against the disease caused by that particular virus.

vaccine   A vaccine is a substance that causes the body to make ANTIBODIES. Vaccines are usually weak or dead VIRUSES or BACTERIA. *See also* VACCINATION.

vein   A vein is a BLOOD VESSEL that carries blood back to the HEART. *See also* CIRCULATORY SYSTEM.

virus   A virus is an extremely small organism that causes disease. Viruses cannot be seen without using a very powerful MICROSCOPE.

> **F**oods that are rich in vitamins include green, yellow, and red vegetables as well as fruits, meats, and some grains (bread and cereals). 🍂

vitamins Vitamins are the substances in foods that help the body to use other food groups, such as carbohydrates and proteins. Although the body needs only small amounts of vitamins each day, they do many things to keep the body healthy. *See also* BALANCED DIET.

white blood cells White blood cells are the cells in the blood that help the body fight disease. They surround and kill germs or other harmful substances that enter the body.

x-ray An x-ray is a form of energy like light. X-rays can go through many surfaces that stop light. Doctors use x-rays to take pictures of the inside of the body so that they can see things that may be wrong.

Technology

Technology concerns inventions and techniques that affect every part of your life. You already know many examples of modern technology. Cars and airplanes allow us to travel faster and farther than used to be possible; furnaces and air conditioners keep us comfortable in any weather; movies and television entertain us; computers make many kinds of work faster and easier. Examples of modern technology such as ovens and heaters are in almost every home in the industrial nations of the world.

Technology is not just another word for machine, however. A book is an example of technology; so are a pen and paper. The invention of writing was a major advance in technology. For thousands of years the wheel has been used to move things, the plow has been used to till fields, and axes and knives have been used to break things apart.

This section does not attempt to mention every important invention and technological discovery. Instead, it notes some terms, ideas, and machines that will help you understand the modern technology that affects your life each day. It also names a few people who have helped create the technology of the modern age.

alloy   An alloy is a material made by mixing metals together. It is designed to be stronger or last longer than the individual metals. Bronze is an alloy usually made of copper and tin.

alternating current   An alternating current, also called AC, is an ELECTRIC CURRENT that regularly changes direction. AC is created by GENERATORS. Most homes in the United States use alternating current. *Compare* DIRECT CURRENT.

aluminum   Aluminum is a lightweight silver metal that does not rust easily, like iron. Airplanes are often made of aluminum because it is both light and strong. Drinking cans, aluminum foil, and other household products are also made of aluminum.

ampere   An ampere measures the rate of ELECTRON flow in an electric circuit. *See also* VOLTAGE; WATT.

amplifier   An amplifier is a device that takes a weak electric signal and makes it stronger without changing its pattern.

> **A**mplifiers are used in stereo systems, electric guitars, and some loudspeakers. ❧

Assembly line. In an automobile plant.

Automation. In an automobile plant.

assembly line An assembly line is a way of putting products together by a series of individual tasks. A car, for example, moves through a number of work stations. At each station, workers do something, such as bolt a door onto the car or put in the engine. Each person on an assembly line has one special job and repeats it over and over again.

automation Automation is the use of machines rather than people to do a job. For example, a THERMOSTAT automatically keeps a room's TEMPERATURE the same, so you do not have to adjust the heat yourself. Automation is also used to do jobs more quickly or accurately than people can do them.

axle *See* WHEEL AND AXLE.

battery A battery is a device that makes ELECTRICITY through chemical action.

Bell, Alexander Graham Alexander Graham Bell invented the telephone in the late 1800s.

capacity *See* VOLUME.

Celsius scale (SEL-see-uhs) The Celsius scale is used to measure TEMPERATURE in scientific work and in most countries except the United States. On the Celsius scale, water freezes at 0 degrees (0°C) and boils at 100 degrees (100°C). An example of a temperature below the freezing point is −8°C. *See also* CENTIGRADE. *Compare* FAHRENHEIT.

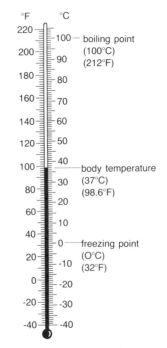

Celsius scale. Celsius readings are on the right; Fahrenheit, on the left.

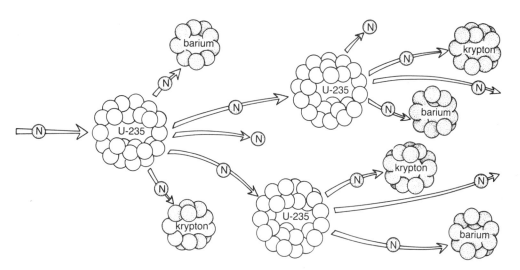

Chain reaction. Nuclear chain reaction. A low-energy neutron hits the nucleus of a uranium-235 atom, causing it to split into two smaller atoms (in this case, barium and krypton). At the same time, at least two additional low-energy neutrons are released that repeat the process, thus creating a chain reaction.

centigrade   The centigrade TEMPERATURE scale is the CELSIUS SCALE. Centigrade, from the Latin word for one hundred (*centum*), means "divided into one hundred parts." The Celsius scale divides the range of temperature between water's freezing and boiling points into 100 degrees.

chain reaction   A chain reaction is a process that keeps going by itself once it is started. A bad forest fire is a chain reaction. After the fire starts, the flames from one tree set the next tree on fire, and so on, until something stops it. The term also refers to a nuclear chain reaction, when the NUCLEUS (or center) of an ATOM splits and releases high-energy particles. These particles split the centers of other atoms, which then split others as the reaction keeps going. Nuclear chain reactions release tremendous amounts of energy.

circuit   A circuit is the path that an ELECTRIC CURRENT travels. Computers contain very complicated circuits.

Compass

compass   A compass is a device with a magnetic needle that points to the north. The needle is directed by the earth's magnetic field toward a spot near the North Pole.

computer   A computer is a device that stores information and follows instructions very rapidly. *See also* FLOPPY DISK; HARDWARE; SOFTWARE.

conductor A conductor is a substance that can carry an ELECTRIC CURRENT or other forms of ENERGY such as heat. Metals such as copper and silver are good conductors of heat and electricity. *Compare* INSULATOR.

direct current A direct current, also called DC, is an ELECTRIC CURRENT that flows in one direction. BATTERIES produce a direct current. *Compare* ALTERNATING CURRENT.

Edison, Thomas A. Thomas A. Edison was an inventor of the late 1800s and early 1900s who perfected the electric light bulb and the phonograph, an early form of the record player.

Edison was called "the Wizard of Menlo Park," after his home town in New Jersey. He gave us the proverb "Genius is one percent inspiration and ninety-nine percent perspiration." 🐦

electric current An electric current is the flow of ELECTRONS along a material (such as a wire) that can carry them. *See also* ALTERNATING CURRENT; CONDUCTOR; DIRECT CURRENT.

electricity Electricity is a form of ENERGY caused by the movement of tiny particles called ELECTRONS. Electricity is used to create light, heat, and power. It also occurs in nature, for example, as LIGHTNING.

electron microscope An electron microscope is a MICROSCOPE that uses a beam of ELECTRONS to detect extremely tiny particles and ORGANISMS. It has greater magnification than an ordinary microscope.

electronics Electronics is a use of ELECTRICITY that employs special control devices, such

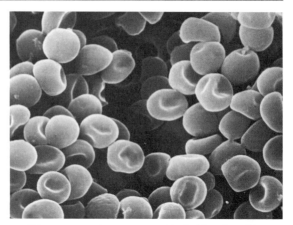

Electron microscope. Red blood cells, magnified 6000 times, as seen through an electron microscope.

as TRANSISTORS, small SWITCHES, and AMPLIFIERS, which make electricity perform complex tasks. Some electronic devices are COMPUTERS and tape recorders.

engineering Engineering is the use of scientific knowledge for practical purposes. Engineers design and build all kinds of useful items, from tiny calculators to huge dams and bridges.

factory A factory is any place where products are made in large quantities. Factories replaced small shops and home crafts in the INDUSTRIAL REVOLUTION. *See also* MASS PRODUCTION.

Fahrenheit scale (FAIR-uhn-heyet) Fahrenheit is the TEMPERATURE scale most commonly used in the United States. In the Fahrenheit scale, water freezes at 32 degrees (32°F) and boils at 212 degrees (212°F). The normal temperature of the human body is 98.6°F. *Compare* CELSIUS SCALE; CENTIGRADE.

floppy disk A floppy disk is a disk with magnetic material on it that can store information for a PERSONAL COMPUTER. It is called floppy because it is made of a flexible material.

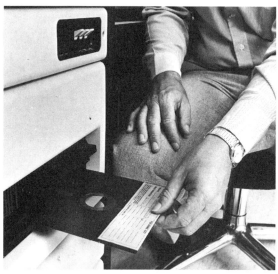

Floppy disk

force   A force is a push or a pull on something. *See also* ENERGY; WORK.

> **O**ne kind of force is gravity. ❧

friction   Friction is the FORCE that slows down a moving object when it rubs against a surface. If you shove a pencil or a shoe across the floor, friction will keep it from going very far. Carpeting produces more friction than a bare floor.

fuel   Fuel is anything that can be burned to make ENERGY. Wood, gasoline, and OIL are fuels.

fulcrum   A fulcrum is the point on which a LEVER rests.

Fulton, Robert   Robert Fulton invented the steamboat in the early 1800s.

gear   A gear is a simple machine — a wheel with teeth cut in it — that makes it easier to move another object. Many turns of a small gear make one turn of a large gear. The relative

Gear. A spur gear.

size of the gears determines how hard it is to turn the wheel. Most hand drills and can openers use gears.

generator   A generator is a machine that, when turned rapidly, produces ELECTRICITY. Small generators make power for a single machine or house. Large generators the size of buildings provide electricity for cities and states.

hardware   In COMPUTER terminology, hardware is the wiring that is built into a computer. *See also* SOFTWARE.

hydroelectric power   Hydroelectric power is created when ENERGY from running water is turned into ELECTRICITY in a GENERATOR in a hydroelectric plant. Hydroelectric power plants can use natural waterfalls, artificial waterfalls created by dams, running water in rivers, or waves to turn the TURBINES of generators.

> **W**ell-known hydroelectric power plants are at Niagara Falls, New York; at the Nile River in Egypt; and at the Yangtze River in China. ❧

inclined plane   An inclined plane is a slanted surface, or ramp, that makes it easier to move objects to a higher place or let them

239

Inclined plane

roll down again. People use inclined planes to load things into trucks because it is easier to roll or carry an object up an inclined plane than to lift it off the ground.

insecticides   Insecticides are chemicals used by farmers and gardeners to kill insects. On large farms, airplanes are used to spray insecticides on crops.

insulator   An insulator is a substance that does not easily carry ELECTRICITY or heat. Wood and rubber are good insulators. *Compare* CONDUCTOR.

internal combustion engine   An internal combustion engine burns fuel inside the engine itself, as in a car engine. In other engines, such as STEAM ENGINES, the burning occurs outside the engine.

Internal combustion engines usually burn fossil fuels and are often a major cause of air pollution. ⁊⬩

---

irrigation   Irrigation is the process of bringing water to land that would otherwise be too dry to grow crops.

jet engine   A jet engine creates a high-speed rush of gases by burning fuel and air. The enormous thrust of the gases pushing out behind the engine moves it forward. *See also* ROCKET ENGINE.

laser   A laser is a device that makes a highly concentrated beam of light. The beam is so powerful that it can be used to cut metal. It is also so narrowly focused that it can be used to perform delicate surgery.

length   *See* LENGTH *under "Mathematics."*

lens   A lens is a piece of curved glass or plastic that can bend light rays. Lenses are used in cameras, projectors, eyeglasses, TELESCOPES, and MICROSCOPES.

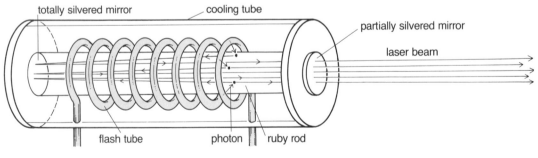

Laser

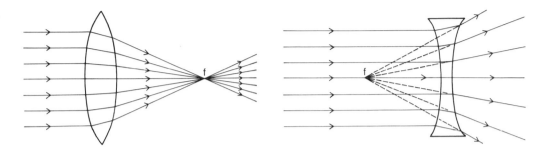

Lens. Light passing through a double-convex lens (left), and light passing through a double-concave lens (right). The "f" indicates the focus (or focal point).

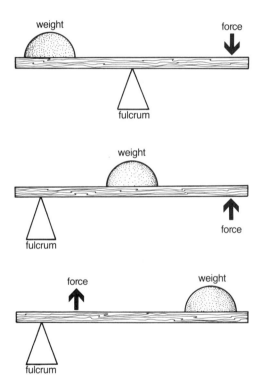

Lever. From top to bottom: First-class lever, with the fulcrum between the weight and the force (for example, removing a nail with a claw hammer); second-class lever, with the weight between the fulcrum and the force (for example, lifting the handles of a wheelbarrow); third-class lever, with the force between the fulcrum and the weight (for example, bending one's elbow).

lever   A lever is a bar or pole that rests on a point called a FULCRUM. It is a simple machine that makes it easier to move objects. For example, you can raise a person of your own size who is sitting on a seesaw (which is a lever) much more easily than you could by yourself.

magnet   A magnet is a device, usually made of iron, that creates a magnetic field. When a wire moves through a magnetic field, it makes ELECTRICITY. When electricity passes through a wire, it makes a magnetic field. These facts are the basis of GENERATORS. Magnets have positive and negative poles. Opposite poles attract each other; like poles repel each other.

mass media   The mass media are the methods of communication used in modern society to reach large numbers of people at the same time. They are television, newspapers, movies, radio, books, and magazines.

mass production   Mass production is the fastest and least expensive way of making many identical things. For example, a cookie FACTORY can make and pack thousands of cookies in the time it would take you to make and pack a small batch.

mechanical energy   Mechanical energy is the ENERGY possessed by something that is moving.

241

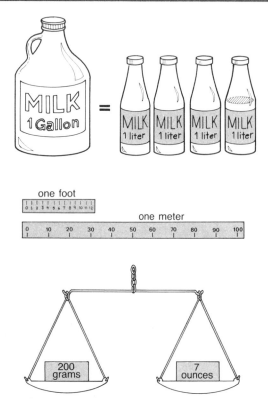

Metric system. One gallon is approximately 3.75 liters; one foot is just under one third of a meter; 200 grams equals 7 ounces.

metric system The metric system is used to weigh and measure things by scientists and by people in most of the countries in the world. Everything in the metric system is based on the meter, which is about three feet long. Weight is defined by the gram, which is the weight of one cubic centimeter of water. (A centimeter is one-hundredth of a meter.) Area is defined by square meters. A unit of VOLUME is the liter, which is 1000 cubic centimeters, about one quart.

microscope A microscope is an instrument that uses LENSES to make small, very close objects appear larger. It can be used to see objects too small to be seen with the eye alone. *Compare* TELESCOPE.

> **C**ommon microscopes use lenses; other types of microscope use electrons, x-rays, or other kinds of radiation. 🙠

microwave A microwave is a kind of ENERGY. It is commonly used in microwave ovens, which can cook food much faster than ovens that use heat. Microwaves are a kind of light wave that are longer than infrared waves and shorter than radio waves.

Morse, Samuel F. B. Samuel F. B. Morse invented the TELEGRAPH in the 1800s. He also devised the MORSE CODE.

Morse code The Morse code is a set of short and long signals ("dots" and "dashes") that stand for letters and numbers. For instance, SOS, the signal for emergencies, is [. . .——— . . .]. Morse code was invented to send messages over a TELEGRAPH but can also be transmitted by radio and with flashes of light. *See also* MORSE, SAMUEL F. B.

nuclear energy Nuclear energy is ENERGY that comes from the NUCLEUS, or center, of an ATOM when part of its matter is converted to energy. It is the most powerful energy source known. A nucleus changes matter to energy when it splits apart or when it fuses with another nucleus. *See also* CHAIN REACTION.

nuclear reactor A nuclear reactor is a device that produces NUCLEAR ENERGY in a gradual, controlled way to make ELECTRICITY.

nuclear weapons Nuclear weapons create powerful explosions by producing NUCLEAR ENERGY suddenly in a CHAIN REACTION. They also release deadly radioactive particles into the air. Some nuclear weapons, such as atomic and hydrogen bombs, can destroy a city with a single blast. *See also* RADIOACTIVITY.

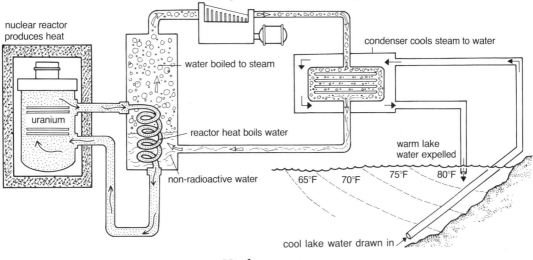

steam spins generator that makes electricity

nuclear reactor produces heat

water boiled to steam

condenser cools steam to water

uranium

reactor heat boils water

warm lake water expelled

non-radioactive water

65°F 70°F 75°F 80°F

cool lake water drawn in

Nuclear reactor

patent A patent is a legal document that says that no one may use, make, or sell a person's invention without permission. The government issues a patent when a person applies for it and the invention is accepted as a new product.

T he words *Patent Pending* or *Pat. Pend.* printed on an object mean that the inventor or manufacturer has applied for a patent. 🐋

personal computer A personal computer is a small COMPUTER that is used by one person at a time, unlike a larger computer, which is used by many.

pipeline A pipeline is a chain of connected pipes designed to carry water, natural gas, oil, or other fluids over long distances.

piston A piston is a solid CYLINDER set inside a hollow tube that is slightly bigger than the cylinder, allowing it to move back

and forth. The pressure from expanding GASES or from LIQUIDS under pressure moves the cylinder forward. Then the pressure is released and the piston moves back. The piston is attached to a rod that transfers the back-and-forth movement where it is needed. Most car engines use pistons.

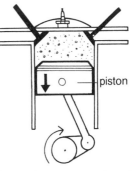

piston

Piston. The power stroke of an internal combustion engine.

pollution Pollution is caused when substances that are harmful to life are released into the ENVIRONMENT. Many technological and industrial activities cause pollution. Ex-

243

haust fumes from cars, trucks, airplanes, and other forms of transportation are the major causes of AIR POLLUTION. Smoke from factories, power plants, and incinerators that burn trash also pollute the air. Sewage, trash dumped in the oceans, and oil spills pollute WATER. Other kinds of pollution are not so obvious but are still harmful. For example, when water used to cool NUCLEAR REACTORS is warmed and released into oceans, lakes, or streams, it raises the TEMPERATURE of the water. This increase is called thermal pollution, and it harms the plants, fish, and animals that live in or near the water.

program   In COMPUTER terminology, a program is a set of instructions that directs a computer. A general term for computer programs is SOFTWARE.

pulley   A pulley is a simple machine made of a wheel with a rope moving around it. Several pulleys working together make it easier to raise and lower heavy objects.

radar   Radar is an ELECTRONIC device that uses radio waves to find objects too far away to be seen. It works by bouncing the radio waves off the objects and receiving the waves that are reflected back. Radar equipment tracks the movement of objects and can determine their speed, as used by highway police. Airplanes and airports use radar to find objects in the sky.

refinery   A refinery is a factory where natural materials are purified and made into useful products. An oil refinery takes crude oil and turns it into FUEL.

resistance   In an electric CIRCUIT, resistance slows down or stops the movement of ELECTRONS, converting their flow into WORK or heat. Resistance is measured in ohms.

rocket engine   A rocket engine moves by creating a fast rush of GASES. The force of the gases pushing out behind the engine moves it

forward. A rocket engine is different from a JET ENGINE because it needs no air to burn its FUEL. All the chemicals it burns are inside the rocket. Because rockets do not need to mix fuel with air, they can be used in outer space, where there is no air.

The first people to make rockets are thought to have been the Chinese, who propelled bamboo tubes with gunpowder 1900 years ago. ❧

screw   A screw is a simple machine that works like an INCLINED PLANE twisted into a spiral. Wood screws and drills use the screw's action to move into or through a surface. The propellers that move planes and boats are called screws because they use the same spiral action to move through the air and WATER.

short circuit   A short circuit occurs when wires in a CIRCUIT that are not supposed to touch are brought into contact. Because there is little RESISTANCE, the amount of ELECTRIC CURRENT in the circuit increases and becomes high enough to generate a dangerous amount of heat. Short circuits can cause fires.

software   In COMPUTER terminology, software refers to the PROGRAMS that a computer can run. *See also* HARDWARE.

solar cell   A solar cell is a device that converts solar ENERGY (energy from the sun) into electrical energy.

solar power   Solar power is ENERGY that comes from the sun. Solar energy comes to earth in the form of light. Special materials can change solar energy into usable heat or electricity. *See also* SOLAR CELL.

sonic boom   A sonic boom is the loud sound made when an airplane travels faster than the speed of sound.

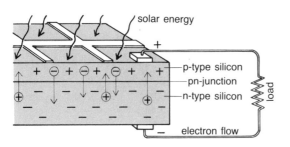

Solar cell

Space Shuttle. The Space Shuttle lifting off from its launch pad at the Kennedy Space Center.

Space Shuttle The Space Shuttle is a vehicle that can fly into space with passengers and cargo and return to the earth. Unlike earlier space vehicles, the Space Shuttle can be used again and again.

space station A space station is an artificial SATELLITE that orbits the EARTH. Eventually, space stations will be big enough for many people to live and work in. They could serve as laboratories for scientific EXPERIMENTS and as bases for further explorations of outer space.

static electricity Static electricity is the name for electrical charges that are not moving in a CIRCUIT. (Static means "not moving.") The shock you get when you walk across a thick carpet on a dry day and then touch a doorknob is caused by static electricity. It also makes some kinds of clothes cling together after they come out of a dryer.

steam engine A steam engine uses steam — the GAS given off when WATER boils — to make MECHANICAL ENERGY. The steam engine was the first engine powerful enough to run FACTORY machines and to propel large boats and trains, and it made modern industry possible. *See also* INDUSTRIAL REVOLUTION; WATT, JAMES.

> **M**ost steam engines have been replaced today by electric motors, turbines, and internal combustion engines. 🐚

steel Steel is a strong and durable metal made by purifying iron and mixing it with other materials. It is used to make machines and large buildings. *See also* ALLOY.

supersonic Supersonic means "faster than the speed of sound." Airplanes that travel faster than the speed of sound are called supersonic planes.

switch A switch is a device that can open or close an electric CIRCUIT.

technology Technology refers to any machine or process that makes work easier or that helps people to get something they need or want. The wheel and the plow are examples of early technology. When people use the word now, they usually mean the advanced technology of modern society, such as television, rockets, automobiles, lasers, and computers.

The term *high technology* or *high tech* is sometimes used to refer to the latest, most advanced technology. ❧

telegraph The telegraph was the first device that used ELECTRICITY to send messages over long distances. It was invented by Samuel F. B. Morse in the early 1800s. The first telegraphs used a key that sent electrical impulses along a wire. The impulses could be heard on the other end of the wire as a series of clicking sounds. Telegraph operators used the MORSE CODE, to spell out messages using the clicks. Now, telegraphs are attached to typewriter keyboards and can be used to send printed messages.

telescope A telescope is an instrument that can be used to see objects that are very far away because it makes them appear larger. (In Greek, *tele* means "far away," as in telephone and television.) Telescopes are used to study the STARS and the PLANETS. *Compare* MICROSCOPE.

temperature Temperature is the measure of how hot or cold a substance is. Its temperature is related to how fast its MOLECULES are moving. (Molecules are the smallest parts of a substance.) For example, when WATER molecules are heated, they move faster and faster until they become steam. When the water

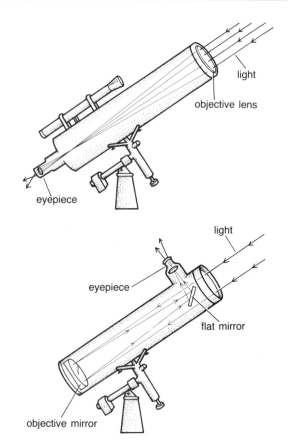

Telescope. Refracting telescope (top) and reflecting telescope (bottom).

molecules get colder, they slow down until they become ICE. *See also* THERMOMETER.

thermometer A thermometer is a device used to measure TEMPERATURE.

thermostat A thermostat is an automatic device that senses and controls TEMPERATURE. In a room, it keeps the temperature the same by sending signals to the furnace. The thermostat will turn on the furnace when the temperature gets too low and turn it off when the temperature gets high enough.

transformer A transformer is a device that increases or decreases the VOLTAGE of an ALTERNATING CURRENT.

transistor   A transistor is a tiny device that is operated by one ELECTRIC CURRENT to influence another one. It can act as a small AMPLIFIER.

Transistors are used in small electronic devices (for example, portable radios) and in computers. ❧

turbine   A turbine is a wheel with fins. A fan, for example, is a turbine. The wheel can be moved by water, heated air, or steam. Many GENERATORS use turbines.

utility   A utility is a company that provides a necessary service to the people of a given area. The phone company, the electric power company, and the water company are all utilities. Utilities are often regulated in some way by the local, state, or national government.

vacuum   A vacuum is a space in which there is no MATTER or air.

The saying "Nature abhors [hates] a vacuum" refers to the fact that in the natural world, air will flow into regions where there is a vacuum. ❧

volt   *See* VOLTAGE.

voltage   Voltage signifies the force that moves ELECTRONS in a CIRCUIT. *Compare* AMPERE; RESISTANCE; WATT.

volume   Volume is the measure of the space inside an object or container. It is measured in units such as the cubic inch, which is the amount of space inside a CUBE with edges 1 inch long. Some common units of volume are:

cubic inch (cu in or in³)
1 cubic foot (cu ft or ft³) = 1728 cubic inches
1 cubic yard (cu yd or yd³) = 27 cubic feet

Some metric units of volume are:

cubic centimeter (cu cm or cm³)
1 cubic meter (cu m or m³) = 1 x 10⁶ cubic centimeters or 1.3 cubic yards

The volume of a liquid is often measured in ounces:

1 fluid ounce (fl oz) = 1.8 cubic inches
1 pint (pt) = 16 fluid ounces
1 quart (qt) = 2 pints
1 gallon (gal) = 4 quarts

The most common metric liquid measurement is the liter (l); 1 liter is a little less than 1 quart. *See also* METRIC SYSTEM.

water power   Water power is provided by moving water, such as a waterfall. *See also* HYDROELECTRIC POWER.

watt   A watt is a unit of electrical power that combines VOLTS and AMPERES.

Watt, James   James Watt improved the steam engine in the 1700s. His engine was the first one that was efficient enough to be used widely in industry.

wedge   A wedge is a simple machine made of two planes that meet to form a sharp edge. Wedges such as axes and knives make it easier to break things apart.

weight   Weight is the measure of how heavy something is. Some common units of weight are:

ounce (oz) (the weight of one ounce of water by volume)
1 pound (lb) = 16 ounces
1 ton = 2000 pounds

Some common metric units of weight are:

1 milligram (mg) = 0.001 gram
1 centigram (cg) = 0.01 gram (the weight of one cubic centimeter of water)
1 gram (g) = 100 centigrams or 0.035 ounces
1 kilogram (kg) = 1000 grams or 2.2 pounds

T o reinvent the wheel means to do something very basic all over again. ❧

Eli Whitney. Whitney's cotton gin.

wheel and axle   A wheel and axle is a simple machine made of a wheel turning around a rod. The wheels on a car or a wagon use the wheel and axle to make it easier to move things.

Whitney, Eli   Eli Whitney invented the cotton gin in the late 1700s. The cotton gin was a machine that removed the seeds from cotton plants much faster than people could do it by hand.

work   In science, work is what happens when a FORCE is used to move an object through a distance.

Guide to Further Reading

The following is a selection of books appropriate for ages six through twelve. We have included reference works and anthologies as well as a few descriptive lists of books. A fuller compilation, containing 362 titles, can be found in a publication of the New York Public Library entitled *Reference Books for Children's Collections* (1988), which is cited here under General Reference. The editor wishes to thank the New York Public Library for permission to use its guide as the basis for the following selection and for permission to quote from the descriptions found in this work. The prices cited below may differ slightly from current prices. Works that were out of print when the guide was produced are indicated by "o.p." The guide itself can be ordered, for $5 per copy plus shipping, from the Office of Children's Services, The New York Public Library, 455 Fifth Avenue, New York, New York 10016.

General Reference

The American Heritage Student's Dictionary, Rev. ed. Houghton Mifflin, 1986. $11.95. Detailed, clear definitions in basic dictionary format; illustrated. Marginal notes contain word histories, grammar and usage, and supplementary materials such as Roman numerals, Morse code, and the metric system.

Information Please Almanac, Atlas and Yearbook, 1947–. Houghton Mifflin, 1947–. Annual. $12.95; $6.95 pap. Basic almanac format; geared to statistical, factual information.

Macmillan Dictionary for Children, 1st rev. ed. Collier–Macmillan, 1982. $13.95. Bright, colorful design with simple, clear definitions make this an inviting choice for beginning readers through the middle grades. Current, one of the finest.

The New Book of Knowledge Encyclopedia. 21 vols. Grolier, 1987. $449. Curriculum-oriented, highly reliable, and current, it is designed and organized to be especially useful in meeting children's needs for information both in and out of the classroom. Its broad coverage of general information is presented in language easily comprehended by elementary school children. Superbly illustrated. Dictionary index with encapsulated fact entries.

Scott, Foresman Beginning Dictionary. Doubleday, 1983. $19.95. Authoritative, appealing, up-to-date vocabulary. Profusely illustrated.

Scott, Foresman Intermediate Dictionary. Doubleday, 1983. $22.50. Contains the most entries and the clearest format of all comparable books examined; basic dictionary format. Includes scientific terms and word histories.

Vogliano, Dolores. *Reference Books for Children's Collections*. The New York Public Library, 1988. $5 pap. Annotated bibliography of 362 reference books arranged by subject for ages six through twelve. Includes resources for adults concerned with literature for children.

World Almanac and Book of Facts, 1868–. Doubleday, 1868–. Annual. $14.95; $6.95 pap. Basic almanac format. Concentrates on year covered, giving statistical information, chronological survey. Information is in brief form. Excellent index.

The World Book Dictionary. 2 vols. World Book–Childcraft, 1986. $59. Supplements *World Book Encyclopedia*. Carefully edited, unabridged dictionary. Definitions, usage notes, and word histories; accurate, accessible to young readers, and up-to-date.

World Book Encyclopedia. 22 vols. World Book Childcraft International, 1987. $455. Curriculum-oriented, this superior encyclopedia is well edited and produced to meet the reference and informational needs of students from grade four through high school. Continues a long-standing tradition of excellence for readability, accuracy, authoritativeness, objectivity, judicious and extensive use of graphics and time lines.

Literature

Chute, Marchette G. *Stories from Shakespeare*. New American Library, 1976. $3.95 pap. Retelling of the 36 plays in the First Folio.

Cohn, Amy L. *Children's Classics: With Lists of Recommended Editions*. Horn Book, 1985. $3 pap. Lists current editions of titles historically considered classics for children. Approximately 58 titles listed, mostly historical rather than contemporary.

Ferris, Helen J. *Favorite Poems, Old and New*. Doubleday, 1957. $15.95. Comprehensive collection; longtime favorites and modern verse.

Gillespie, John Thomas. *Introducing Books: A Guide for the Middle Grades*. Bowker, 1970. $13.95. Children's room "masterplots." Summaries, book talk suggestions, and related material for more than 80 titles suitable for children age eight to fourteen.

Hadlow, Ruth. *Children's Books Too Good to Miss*, rev. and enl. 8th ed. Lucas Communications Group, n.d. N.p. Highly selective list with critical appraisals of books of "outstanding merit." Excellent recommendations for reading aloud.

A Multimedia Approach to Children's Literature: A Selective List of Films (and Videocassettes), Filmstrips, and Recordings Based on Children's Books, 3rd ed. American Library Association, 1983. $15 pap. Buying guide for book-related nonprint materials for preschool through sixth grade. Useful for building children's literature collections in a variety of formats.

Opie, Iona A. *The Oxford Dictionary of Nursery Rhymes*. Oxford University Press, 1952. $47.50. The origin and history of more than 500 traditional rhymes, songs, and riddles arranged alphabetically by key word. Index of notable figures associated with rhymes.

Rollock, Barbara. *The Black Experience in Children's Books*. The New York Public Library, 1984. $3 pap. Annotated list of folklore, fiction, and nonfiction portraying black life for children from preschool to age twelve. Arranged geographically; appendix lists black authors and illustrators whose works appear in this list.

Stevenson, Burton E. *The Home Book of Verse for Young Folks*, rev. ed. Holt, Rinehart & Winston, 1957 (o.p.). Poems arranged by theme; emphasis on nineteenth and twentieth centuries. Indexed by author, first line, and title.

Stott, Jon C. *Children's Literature from A to Z: A Guide for Parents and Teachers*. McGraw-Hill, 1984. $12.95 pap. Short essays on notable authors and illustrators. Information includes a brief biography of the author and the major themes and characters found in the author's works. Includes essays on typical genres of children's literature, such as folk tales and fantasy. Popular folk tales such as "Cinderella" and "Hansel and Gretel" are discussed. After each entry there is a brief section — Tips for Parents and Teachers — that suggests the best way to present the author's works to children. Particularly good for those who are new to children's literature.

Trelease, Jim. *The Read-Aloud Handbook*, rev. ed. Penguin Books, 1985. $6.95 pap. A resourceful guide that discusses why, how, and when to read aloud and offers an annotated list of more than 300 recommended books. The list is divided into categories ranging from wordless books to anthologies. Within each group books are alphabetized by title, with suggested grade level for each. Author/illustrator index is included.

Mythology

Barber, Richard. *A Companion to World Mythology*. Delacorte, 1979 (o.p.). Prepared for juvenile readers. Dictionary of figures, places, and stories of major mythologies. Includes information on heroes and legends.

Burland, Cottie Arthur. *Mythology of the Americas*. Hamyln, 1970 (o.p.). Information on North, Central, and South American Indian beliefs and mythological figures.

Funk & Wagnalls Standard Dictionary of Folklore, Mythology, and Legend. Crowell, 1972. $23. Comprehensive coverage of customs, beliefs, songs, tales, and heroes of world cultures. Explains allusions to legendary characters and gods and the significance of plants and animals in folklore. Survey articles, bibliographies, and biographies.

Stapleton, Michael. *The Concise Dictionary of Greek and Roman Mythology.* Peter Bedrick Books, 1986 (1982). $4.95 pap. Originally published in 1978 under the title *A Dictionary of Greek and Roman Mythology*, it presents the themes, characters, and legends of Greek and Roman mythology. All the great epics and the principal Greek tragedies are outlined; places of particular importance, such as Troy and Mycenae, are described, and the special nature of Roman mythology is stated. The only thing concise about this book is its size and the size of the type. Definitions are factual and detailed. Includes extensive bibliography and index of minor characters and place names.

Music

Browne, C. A. *The Story of Our National Ballads*, rev. ed. Crowell, 1960. $13.70. Patriotic songs and war ballads from the Revolutionary War to World War II, with biographies of many of their authors.

Ewen, David. *Great Composers: 1300–1900.* Wilson, 1966. $33. Complete and detailed biographical, historical, and critical information on about 200 composers of the past plus listings of their principal works and bibliographies. Most have portraits.

Folk Song U.S.A. New American Library, 1975 (o.p.). Collection of 111 best-known American ballads.

Gombrich, E. H. *Story of Art.* 14th ed. Enl. & rev. Prentice-Hall, 1985. $22.95 pap. Informative and readable introduction to the history of art; a supplementary source suitable for elementary and junior high school students.

Minton, Lynn. *Movie Guide for Puzzled Parents: TV, Cable, Videocassettes.* Delacorte Press, 1984. $12.95 pap. 1500 reviews from 1973 to 1983. Evaluates each film with reference to sexual content, violence, raw language, and societal, political, and moral values. Includes lists of films on particular themes — family, black heroes, strong female, homosexuality, inspirational, those not recommended for specific ages, et al.

National Anthems of the World. Edited by W. L. Reed. 6th rev. and enl. ed. Blanford Press, 1985. $34.95. Music and lyrics for over 150 countries in the original language and in English, including brief historical notes.

Sleeman, Phillip J. *200 Selected Film Classics for Children of All Ages: Where to Obtain Them and How to Use Them.* C. C. Thomas, 1984. $19.95 pap. Emphasizes quality of films and quality of the books on which the films are based. Alphabetical by title; annotation gives production data, theme indicators, program ideas, age group. Author index, but no subject index.

The Bible and Religion

Ben-Asher, Naomi. *The Junior Jewish Encyclopedia,* 10th rev. ed. Shengold, 1984. $19.95. Guide to the history, customs, literature, and other aspects of Jewish life. Includes biographies; profusely illustrated.

Bible. *The Holy Bible.* Contains the Old and New Testaments and Apocrypha. Authorized King James version. Nelson, n.d. $8.95. New American Library, 1974. $7.95 pap. Protestant.

Bible. *The Holy Scriptures According to the Masoretic Text.* 2 vols. Authoritative English translation of the Hebrew Bible. Jewish Publication Society, 1917. $35. English and Hebrew text. Jewish.

Bible. *The New American Bible.* Catholic Biblical Association of America. Roman Catholic; replaces Douay edition; modern English translation. A new edition is in process.

Bible. *The New Oxford Annotated Bible with the Apocrypha.* Expanded ed. Revised standard version, containing the second edition of the New Testament and an expanded edition of the Apocrypha. Oxford University Press, 1977. $29.95. Ecumenical study edition; modern translation with notes for all faiths.

Eerdman's Family Encyclopedia of the Bible. Eerdmans, 1978. $18.95. All-purpose reference on biblical topics in ten sections. Contains biographical dictionary, gazetteer, dictionary of terms, atlas. Colorful illustrations and limited vocabulary make this more appealing to young readers.

Gaer, Joseph. *Holidays Around the World.* Little, Brown, 1953 (o.p.). Simply written information on Chinese, Hindu, Christian, Jewish, and Moslem holidays. Each section approved by an authority of the respective faith.

———. *How the Great Religions Began,* new & rev. ed. Dodd, Mead, 1956. $6.95 pap. Origins of the religions of the world, including Buddhism, Jainism, Hinduism, Confucianism, Taoism, Shinto, Zoroastrianism, Judaism, Christianity, and Islam. Includes biographies and discussion of the Reformation. For the middle grades.

United States History and Culture

Brown, Francis James. *One America: The History, Contributions, and Present Problems of Our Racial and National Minorities*, 3rd ed. Greenwood, 1970 (1952). $34. Historical information on older immigrant groups for the middle grades.

Concise Dictionary of American History, rev. ed. Scribner, 1983. $70.00. Covers facts, events, movements, treaties, court cases, historical theories, et al. Excellent for ready reference and obscure information.

DeGregorio, William. *The Complete Book of U.S. Presidents*. Dembner/Norton, 1984. $25. From Washington to Reagan. Informally written with detailed information on each president, including physical description, life story, significant events during presidency, role in history, and bibliography.

Ebony Pictorial History of Black America. 4 vols. Johnson Publishing Company, 1971–1973. $38.90. Traces the history of American blacks from the golden age of Africa through 1972. The many pictures and a readable text make this a useful reference tool.

Findlay, Bruce A. *Your Rugged Constitution: How America's House of Freedom Is Planned and Built*, 2nd rev. ed. Stanford University Press, 1974 (1969). $17.50; $5.95 pap. A clear presentation of the organization and meaning of the various sections of the Constitution. Includes the 26th Amendment (1974).

Grant, Bruce. *American Indians, Yesterday and Today*, rev. ed. Dutton, 1960 (o.p.). A profusely illustrated encyclopedia of the American Indian. Dictionary format; useful for ready reference.

Ross, Frank X. *Stories of the States: A Reference Guide to the Fifty States and the U.S. Territories*. Harper & Row, 1969 (o.p.). Concise descriptions of states, territories, and trusts. Information on history, state song, state motto, and state flag for young readers.

Urdang, Laurence. *The Timetables of American History*. Simon & Schuster, 1983. $13.95 pap. Current through 1980. What happened and who did what in America at the same time in history plus major concurrent events elsewhere. Events are listed under the following categories: history and politics, the arts, science and technology, and miscellaneous. Illustrated with photos and engravings.

World History and Culture

Adams, Russell L. *Great Negroes, Past and Present*, 3rd ed., rev. Afro-American Publishing Company, 1984 (1969). $15.95; $10.95 pap. Over 180 personalities from ancient times to the present and from many professions, including science, business, education, literature, and the arts, discussed briefly in an accessible style. Includes portraits and bibliographies.

Ancient Civilizations. Warwick/Watts, 1978. $10.90. Concise information on the ancient world, including Mesopotamia, Egypt, Greece, Persia, Phoenicia, Rome, India, and China.

Davis, Williams Stearns. *A Day in Old Athens*. Biblio and Tannen, 1960. $12. Everyday life and customs in 360 B.C.

———. *A Day in Old Rome*. Biblio and Tannen, 1972. $12. Everyday life and customs in A.D. 134.

Flags of the World. Edited by E. M. C. Barraclough and W. G. Crampton. 2nd ed. (of 1978 ed.) with revisions and supplement. Warner, 1981. $30. History and description of the flags of the United States, Latin America, Asia, Africa, and Europe, with special emphasis on British flags. Also international and signal flags, etc. Color plates and drawings. Standard reference.

Hartman, Gertrude. *Medieval Days and Ways*. Macmillan, 1965. $14.95. Description of medieval life in clear and simple language and covering all phases of medieval life in Europe — trade, customs, religion, medieval society, etc. Illustrated with reproductions of manuscripts, prints, and woodcuts. For the middle grades.

Hornburger, Jane M. *African Countries and Cultures: A Concise Illustrated Dictionary*. McKay, 1981. $13.95. Brief descriptions of individual countries and general information on the language, traditions, and lifestyles of various cultures and people; also biographical data.

Mills, Dorothy. *The Book of the Ancient World for Younger Readers: An Account of Our Common Heritage from the Dawn of Civilization to the Coming of the Greeks*, 2nd ed. Putnam, 1951 (o.p.). In-depth coverage of the Egyptians, Hebrews, Hittites, Persians, and Phoenicians.

Schon, Isabel. *A Hispanic Heritage, Series I: A Guide to Juvenile Books about Hispanic People and Cultures*. Scarecrow, 1980. $16.50. A critical annotated list of books written in English and published in the United States through the late 1970s. Divided by country and alphabetical by author. Indexed by author, subject, and title, with bibliography.

———. *A Hispanic Heritage, Series II: A Guide to Ju-*

venile Books about Hispanic People and Cultures. Scarecrow, 1985. $15. Continues Series I, concentrating on books published in the late 1970s and early 1980s.

Siegel, Mary-Ellen. *Her Way: A Guide to Biographies of Women for Young People,* 2nd ed. American Library Association, 1984. $20 pap. Greatly expanded second edition of a source book of biographies about women: more than 1000 short profiles of notable women throughout history followed by a list of annotated biographies suitable for students from elementary through high school. Also an annotated list of collective bibliographies. Appended are lists of "Nationality other than American," "Americans Classified by Ethnic Groups," and "Vocations and Avocations." Includes an author-title index and subject index.

The South American Handbook, 1924–. Rand McNally, 1924–. Annual. $29.95. Essentially a travel guide, it includes useful historical, economic, political, and social information on the countries in South America, Central America, Mexico, and the West Indies.

Tappan, Eve M. *When Knights Were Bold.* Houghton Mifflin, 1939 (o.p.). Excellent source on life in the Middle Ages.

United States Geography

Gilbert, Martin. *Atlas of American History.* Reprint. Dorset Press, 1984, 1968. $17.95. 112 maps tracing the history of the United States from earliest exploration and settlements to 1968; useful for younger children. Originally published under the title *American History Atlas.*

National Geographic Society. Washington, D.C., Book Service. *National Geographic Picture Atlas of Our Fifty States.* National Geographic Society, 1980 (o.p.). Supplementary reference for the middle grades arranged by geographical area, with excellent resource and product maps for each state.

World Geography

Goode, John Paul. *Goode's World Atlas,* 17th ed. Rand McNally, 1986. $22.95. Physical, political, and economic atlas arranged by continent and region. Includes metropolitan area maps and much statistical data. Number of thematic maps has been increased. Standard atlas for elementary school children.

The Times Concise Atlas of World History. Edited by Geoffrey Barraclough. Hammond, 1982, 1978. $40. Over 300 color maps and charts arranged chronologically from prehistoric times to 1980. Includes historical information on each period, bibliography, and index.

Webster's New Geographical Dictionary. Merriam-Webster, 1984. $19.95. Concise gazetteer, listing both ancient and modern place names. Most entries include pronunciation, brief description, population, and brief history. Includes numerous charts and lists, some maps, and a list of geographical terms from other languages.

Mathematics

Bendick, Jeanne. *Mathematics Illustrated Dictionary: Facts, Figures, and People Including the New Math.* McGraw-Hill, 1972 (1965). $10.95. Alphabetical listing of historical and current mathematical terminology geared for elementary school children; charts, tables, and biographical sketches of mathematicians.

Physical Sciences and General Science

Lewis, Richard S. *The Illustrated Encyclopedia of the Universe: Exploring and Understanding the Cosmos.* Harmony Books, 1983. $24.95. A comprehensive work providing scientifically accurate information on the universe, the solar system, and the space program. Examines the origin and evolution of the universe, galaxies, and stars; covers planets (with basic data charts), sun, moon, meteorites, and comets; presents future possibilities of space exploration and colonization, sources of energy, extraterrestrial resources; details space exploration from the Sputniks of 1956 to the end of 1983. Profusely illustrated with color photographs, drawings, and diagrams. Glossary and index.

Wilma, Denise Mureko. *Science Books for Children: Selections from Booklist, 1976–1983.* American Library Association, 1985. $15 pap. Approximately 500 best books from picture books for preschoolers to adult titles for junior high school use. Lengthy annotations include grade level; author-title and subject indexes included.

Wolff, Kathryn. *The Best Science Books for Children.* American Association for the Advancement of Science, 1983. $15.95. Briefly annotates more than 1000 books for children age five through twelve. Many of the titles were published in the 1970s; none after 1981. Updated in the periodical *Science Books & Films.*

Earth Sciences

Pough, Frederick H. *A Field Guide to Rocks and Minerals*. 4th ed. Houghton Mifflin, 1976. $17.95; $12.95 pap. Each entry includes a detailed description of physical attributes, chemical composition, and localities of occurrence. Photographs in color and black and white of crystal formation.

Life Sciences

Chinery, Michael. *Concise Color Encyclopedia of Nature*. Crowell, 1972 (o.p.). Guide to the plant and animal kingdoms arranged topically, with more than 1000 color and black and white illustrations; information on ecology, evolution, and prehistoric life.

Edlin, Herbert L. *Atlas of Plant Life*. Crowell, 1973. $14.37. Survey, region by region, of the various wild and cultivated plants of the world; detailed distribution maps and listing of the scientific names of principal plants.

Macmillan Illustrated Animal Encyclopedia. Edited by Philip Whitfield. Macmillan, 1984. $35. A comprehensive catalogue of the animal kingdom divided into five categories of vertebrates arranged by order and family. Each entry includes scientific and common name, habitat, physical and physiological characteristics, and conservation status. Illustration in color of almost 2000 species.

National Geographic Book of Mammals. 2 vols. National Geographic Society, 1981. $25.95 set. Each concise entry includes physical characteristics, habitat, food, life span, and behavior. Over 1000 color photographs of the animals in their natural setting.

Sattler, Helen R. *The Illustrated Dinosaur Dictionary*. Lothrop, Lee & Shepherd, 1983. $17.50. Excellent resource; complete compendium of information on this subject in alphabetical order; pronunciation, etymology of name, and brief information usually accompanied by line drawings; short articles under subject headings.

Technology

Bragonier, Reginald. *What's What: A Visual Glossary of the Physical World*. Hammond, 1981. $30. Ballantine, 1982. $9.95 pap. Picture dictionary; clear, detailed, full-page black and white illustrations (drawings and photographs) of everyday objects in which all visible parts are identified and labeled.

Macaulay, David. *The Way Things Work*. Houghton Mifflin, 1988. $29.95. Profusely illustrated and entertaining guide to the principles and workings of machines.

Yenne, Bill. *The Encyclopedia of US Spacecraft, Produced in Cooperation with NASA*. Exeter Books, 1985. $12.88. This catalogue of the spacecraft developed in the United States for commercial, military, and NASA programs describes in detail the physical characteristics of the various spacecraft and gives a brief description of the mission it was used for. Numerous photographs, maps, and charts. Difficult to use because there are few cross-references and no index.

Zehavi, A. M. *The Complete Junior Encyclopedia of Transportation*. Watts, 1972 (o.p.). Comprehensive encyclopedia of all methods of transportation. Signed articles arranged in alphabetical order in varying lengths. Dated, but best source for historical material.

Illustration Credits

LITERATURE

Alice in Wonderland From *Alice's Adventures in Wonderland*, by Lewis Carroll **Brer Rabbit** From *Uncle Remus and his Friends*, by Joel Chandler Harris **Cheshire Cat** From *Alice's Adventures in Wonderland*, by Lewis Carroll **Cinderella, Emily Dickinson, Don Quixote** Historical Pictures Service, Chicago **Fox and the Grapes** Bettmann Archive **Gulliver's Travels** Historical Pictures Service, Chicago **Hare and Tortoise** Bettmann Archive **Homer** Courtesy, Museum of Fine Arts, Boston **Humpty Dumpty** Bettmann Archive **King Arthur** From *Stories of Legendary Heroes*, selected and arranged by E. M. Tappan. Drawing by Daniel Maclise. **Legend of Sleepy Hollow, Little Red Riding Hood** Bettmann Archive **Mother Goose** From *St. Nicholas*, vol. 40, pt. 1, November 1912–April 1913. Courtesy of the Boston Public Library, Jordan Collection. **Rapunzel** From *Household Stories from the Bros. Grimm*. Courtesy of the Boston Public Library, Jordan Collection. **Mark Twain** Library of Congress **Tweedledum and Tweedledee** From *Through the Looking Glass*, by Lewis Carroll **Wizard of Oz** Copyright 1939 Loew's Inc. Ren. 1966 Metro-Goldwyn-Mayer Inc.

MYTHOLOGY

Adonis *Venus and Adonis*, Titian. National Gallery of Art, Washington; Widener Collection. **Athena** Bettmann Archive **Cupid** Historical Pictures Service, Chicago **Diana** Library of Congress **Hercules** Courtesy, Museum of Fine Arts, Boston **Juno** Bettmann Archive **Mars** Courtesy, Museum of Fine Arts, Boston **Odysseus, Pegasus** Bettmann Archive **Romulus and Remus** Library of Congress **Trojan Horse** Bettmann Archive

MUSIC, ART, AND ARCHITECTURE

Acropolis Photograph © by Russell A. Thompson/Taurus Photos **Arch** Photograph © by Stanley Rowin/Picture Cube, Inc. **Ballet** Photograph © by Jack Mitchell/Boston Ballet **Beethoven** AKG/Photo Researchers, Inc. **Big Ben** British Tourist Authority **Brass Instruments** Laurel Cook **Colosseum** Photograph © by David M. Grossman/Photo Researchers, Inc. **Conductor** AP/Wide World Photos **Eiffel Tower** Photograph © by Pierre Berger/Photo Researchers, Inc. **Golden Gate Bridge** Photograph © by Russell A. Thompson/Taurus Photos **Leaning Tower** Photograph © by Peter Menzel/Stock, Boston *Mona Lisa* Photo Researchers, Inc. **Musical Notation** From *The Return Quick Step*, composed by Zetzsche. Courtesy of the Boston Public Library, Print Department. **Orchestra, Percussion Instruments** Laurel Cook **Pyramids** Photograph © by George Holton/Photo Researchers, Inc. **String Instruments** Laurel Cook **Taj Mahal** Photograph © by Nat Norman/Photo Researchers, Inc. *Venus de*

Milo Alinari/Art Resource, N.Y. **Woodwind Instruments** Laurel Cook

THE BIBLE

Books of the Bible Copyright © 1985 by Houghton Mifflin Company. Adapted and reprinted by permission from *The American Heritage Dictionary, Second College Edition.* **Adam and Eve** Courtesy, Museum of Fine Arts, Boston **Crown of thorns** Historical Pictures Service, Chicago **Daniel in the lion's den** Bettmann Archive **Jerusalem** Historical Pictures Service, Chicago **Jonah** Bettmann Archive **The Last Supper** Historical Pictures Service, Chicago **Mary** *The Small Cowper Madonna*, Raphael. National Gallery of Art, Washington; Widener Collection. **Moses** Library of Congress **Noah and the Flood, Plagues of Egypt, Satan** Bettmann Archive

RELIGION AND PHILOSOPHY

Buddha Photograph © by David S. Strickler/Picture Cube, Inc. **Confucius** *1989 Information Please Almanac.* Copyright © 1988 by Houghton Mifflin Company. Reprinted by permission of Houghton Mifflin Company. **Jesus** Photograph © by Omikron/Photo Researchers, Inc. **Martin Luther** H. Armstrong Roberts **Mecca** Photo Researchers, Inc. **Pope** Photograph © 1980 by Ulrike Welsch/Photo Researchers, Inc. **Socrates** The Metropolitan Museum of Art, Wolfe Fund, 1931. Catharine Lorillard Wolfe Collection (31.45). **Torah** Photograph © by Peter Southwick/Stock, Boston **Western Wall** Photograph © by Jan Lukas/Photo Researchers, Inc.

AMERICAN HISTORY TO 1865

Boston Tea Party Bettmann Archive **The Constitution** The National Archives, Washington, D.C. **Declaration of Independence** Left: AP/Wide World Photos; Right: Historical Pictures Service, Chicago **Benjamin Franklin** Historical Pictures Service, Chicago **Liberty Bell** Photograph © by Rick Smolan/Stock, Boston **Abraham Lincoln** Historical Pictures Service, Chicago *Mayflower* Library of Congress **Pony Express** The Thomas Gilcrease Institute of American History and Art, Tulsa, Oklahoma **Paul Revere** Bettmann Archive **Totem pole** Bettmann Archive **George Washington** The Metropolitan Museum of Art, Gift of John Stewart Kennedy, 1897 (97.34). All rights reserved. The Metropolitan Museum of Art.

AMERICAN HISTORY SINCE 1865

Susan B. Anthony Schlesinger Library, Radcliffe College **Alexander Bell** Historical Pictures Service, Chicago **Thomas Edison** Collections of Greenfield Village and the Henry Ford Museum, Dearborn, Michigan. Neg. no. B34599. **John F. Kennedy** Photo no. AR7595B, John F. Kennedy Library **Martin Luther King, Jr.** UPI/ Bettmann Newsphotos **Pearl Harbor** National Archives and Records Service **Franklin D. Roosevelt** AP/Wide World Photos **Babe Ruth** Historical Pictures Service, Chicago **Sitting Bull** Bettmann Archive **Wright Brothers** Bettmann Archive

POLITICS AND ECONOMICS

The Capitol Library of Congress *E pluribus unum* The Great Seal of the United States of America, as it appears on the back of an American dollar bill. Dept. of the Treasury, Bureau of Engraving and Printing. **NASA** NASA **Pentagon** AP/Wide World Photos **Statue of Liberty** Photograph © by Peter Menzel/Stock, Boston **Supreme Court** Architect of the Capitol **Uncle Sam** Historical Pictures Service, Chicago **Washington Monument** H. Armstrong Roberts **White House** White House Photo Office

WORLD HISTORY TO 1600

Alexander the Great Historical Pictures Service, Chicago **Aztecs** Photograph © by George Holton/Photo Researchers, Inc. **Christopher Columbus** Library of Congress **Hieroglyphics** Marburg/Art Resource, N.Y. **Incas** Photograph © by Ira Kirschenbaum/Stock, Boston **Knight** Bettmann Archive **Roman Empire** Jacques Chazaud **Sphinx** Bettmann Archive **Stonehenge** Gatewood/Art Resource, N.Y.

WORLD HISTORY SINCE 1600

Winston Churchill Bettmann Archive **Anne Frank** AP/Wide World Photos **French Revolution** Historical Pictures Service, Chicago **Mohandas Gandhi** AP/Wide World Photos **Adolf Hitler** Copyright © Mary Evans Picture Library/Photo Researchers, Inc. **Mao Zedong** AP/Wide World Photos **Napoleon** Bettmann Archive **Florence Nightingale, Stalin** AP/Wide World Photos *Titanic* Historical Pictures Service, Chicago **United Nations** United Nations Photo **Queen Victoria** Bettmann Archive

UNITED STATES GEOGRAPHY

United States Copyright © 1986 by Houghton Mifflin Company. Adapted and reprinted by permission from the complete volume of *A People and a Nation: A History of the United States*, 2nd edition. **Grand Canyon** Grant Heilman Photography, Inc. **Middle Atlantic States, The Midwest** Jacques Chazaud **Mount Rushmore** Photograph © by Leonard Lee Rue III/Photo Researchers, Inc. **New England** Jacques Chazaud **Niagara Falls** New York State Dept. of Economic Development **Pacific Coast States, Rocky Mountain States, The South, The Southwest** Jacques Chazaud

WORLD GEOGRAPHY

The World, Africa, Asia, Australia and Oceania, Europe, North America and the West Indies, South America Jacques Chazaud

MATHEMATICS

Angle, Area, Bar Graph, Circle, Cone, Cylinder, Diagonal, Ellipse, Hexagon, Intersect, Line Graph, Octagon, Parallel, Pentagon, Pie Chart, Pyramid, Quadrilateral, Sphere, Trapezoid, Triangle Laurel Cook

PHYSICAL SCIENCES

Apollo Program NASA **Atom** Laurel Cook **Comet** AP/Wide World Photos **Constellation** Laurel Cook **Albert Einstein** AP/Wide World Photos **Galaxy** Ewing Galloway **H_2O** Laurel Cook **Mars, Satellite** NASA **Solar System** Laurel Cook

EARTH SCIENCES AND WEATHER

Clouds Laurel Cook. *Investigating the Earth,* © 1987, adapted with permission, Houghton Mifflin Company. **Delta** Grant Heilman Photography, Inc. **Earth** Laurel Cook **Fossils** Photograph © by Bucky Reeves/Photo Researchers, Inc. **Lightning** Photograph © by Ed Carlin/Picture Cube, Inc. **Tornado** UPI/Bettmann Newsphotos **Volcano** Laurel Cook

LIFE SCIENCES

Birds, Cell, Dinosaur, Fish, Flower Laurel Cook **Food Chain** Copyright © 1984 by Houghton Mifflin Company. Adapted and reprinted by permission from *Spaceship Earth: Earth Science*, rev. ed. **Insect, Metamorphosis, Photosynthesis** Laurel Cook

MEDICINE AND THE HUMAN BODY

Antibodies, Bacteria, Balanced Diet, Brain, Circulatory System, Digestive System, Eardrum, Iris Laurel Cook **Joint** Photograph © by Martin M. Rotker/Taurus Photos **Nervous System, Permanent Teeth, Skeleton, Skin** Laurel Cook

TECHNOLOGY

Assembly Line Photograph © by Michael Hayman/Stock, Boston **Automation** Photograph © by Tom McHugh/Photo Researchers, Inc. **Celsius Scale, Chain Reaction** Laurel Cook **Compass** Photograph © by Barry L. Runk/Grant Heilman Photography, Inc. **Electron Microscope** Grant Heilman Photography, Inc. **Floppy Disk** Photograph © by Bob Daemmrich/Stock, Boston **Gear** Laurel Cook **Inclined Plane** Photograph © by Barbara Rios/Photo Researchers, Inc. **Laser, Lens, Lever, Metric System, Nuclear Reactor, Piston, Solar Cell** Laurel Cook **Space Shuttle** NASA **Telescope** Laurel Cook **Eli Whitney** Historical Pictures Service, Chicago

Index

All numbers in italics refer to illustrations

Index

Index

Index

Index